NEW TALES
OF
OLD ROME

But I will sing above all moniments
Seven Romane hils, the world's seven Wonderments.

SPENSER.

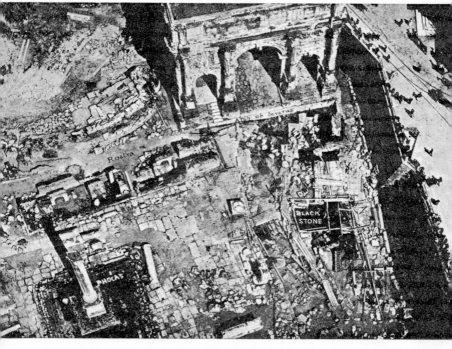

POSITIONS OF THE BLACK STONE, THE ARCH OF SEVERUS, AND THE
COLUMN OF PHOCAS

(From an aerial photograph taken by Captain Moris, R. E., June, 1899)

NEW TALES
OF
OLD ROME

RODOLFO LANCIANI

Benjamin Blom / *Publisher*

First Published 1901
Reissued 1967 by Benjamin Blom, Inc., New York 10452
Library of Congress Catalog Card No. 67-29707

Manufactured in the United States of America

DEDICATION

DEAR PRINCIPAL DONALDSON:

I TAKE the liberty of inscribing your name to this volume in grateful remembrance of the hospitality I have enjoyed in the University of St. Andrews, as Gifford lecturer for 1899–1900. The volume contains those parts only of my lectures which refer to recent archæological and historical research in Rome, and which have not appeared in my previous publications.

RODOLFO LANCIANI.

ROME, July 1, 1901.

To JAMES DONALDSON, M. A., LL. D.,
  Vice-Chancellor and Principal of the University of St. Andrews.

CONTENTS.

LIST OF ILLUSTRATIONS.

FULL–PAGE PLATES.

ILLUSTRATIONS IN THE TEXT

NEW TALES OF OLD ROME.

CHAPTER I.

THE NEW DISCOVERIES IN THE FORUM.

A DISCOVERY made on the borderline between the Comitium and the Forum, on June 15, 1899, has set the
archæological world astir, and given rise to a much debated
controversy. To make the matter clear to the reader, I
must go back to the very beginning of the present campaign
of exploration, which will remain memorable forever in the
archæological records of Rome.

The reason why the exploration has proved so successful
must be found in the fact that former excavations — those
included in which I have had a personal share, since 1871 —
have seldom reached the deepest levels.   As soon as a
paving-stone, or a brick or marble floor was found, whether
imperial, or Byzantine, or mediæval, it did not matter, we
were made to stop, without trying to ascertain whether older
and more important relics were concealed in the lower strata.
I do not mean to say that the surface ruins ought to be
sacrificed to the requirements of a deeper exploration, because no archæologist in the world, however great his fame
and his independence, has the right to break one single link
in the chain of chronology of superposed structures, every
one of which has an equal claim to existence : but there
are gaps and free spaces enough between the surface ruins
to allow occasionally the search to be carried down to the
virgin soil.

When the space between the temples of Julius Cæsar and of Castor and Pollux was cleared away in 1882, we gave up the search at the level of the street pavements, dating from the sixth or the seventh century after Christ. Six years later Professor Otto Richter was enabled to discover the remains of the triumphal arch of Augustus, only nine inches below the line at which we had stopped in 1882.[1]

In 1879, when the new boulevard Principe Eugenio was laid open across the old Licinian Gardens, between the so-called Minerva Medica and the Porta Maggiore, we came across a section of the palace of Gallienus, which had been excavated by Piranesi, about a century before. Piranesi, and his associate Belardi, having reached the level of the drains, considered their task finished, and turned the spade to a more promising spot; and yet far below those drains lay buried nine columbaria, rich in cinerary urns, inscriptions, paintings, statuary, and objects of value, which I have illustrated in the " Bullettino archeol. comunale " for 1880.[2]

The present exploration of the Forum and neighboring sites has been undertaken, therefore, with the view of reaching the early imperial, the republican, the kingly, or even the prehistoric strata, wherever it was possible to do so without special injury to the later and higher structures. The results have been quite satisfactory, as I shall have occasion to prove more than once in the following pages. The one which comes within the scope of the present chapter is the discovery of the cenotaph (*sepulcrum inane*) and national monument (heroon) of Romulus, the founder of

---

[1] Richter, *Mittheil. d. arch. Inst.* vol. iii. (1888), p. 99 ; *Antike Denkmäler*, 1888, p. 14 ; *Bull. arch. comunale*, 1888, p. 167; Thédenat, *Le Forum romain*, p. 180.

[2] Page 51, pl. 2, 3.   Compare *Corpus Inscr.* vol. vi. part ii. p. 976.

THE REMAINS OF THE ARCH OF AUGUSTUS

the City. It took place under the following circumstances : —

The area of the Comitium is, or rather was, separated from that of the Forum by a mediæval road leading up to the arch of Severus, so negligently paved with blocks of silex that the grooves of cart-wheels with which they are marked appear sometimes perpendicular to the line of the road. The embankment, moreover, on which they are laid is made up of loose earth and bricks and stumps of columns, and even inscribed pedestals, one of which, bearing the name of the emperor Constantius, and the date 356–359 A. D., was found September 1, 1803, "sub silicibus viæ stratæ per arcum Severi." [1] In trying to ascertain how far and how deep the area of the Comitium — which is paved, like that of the Forum, with slabs of travertine — extended under this late road, Commendatore Boni, who is in charge of the excavations, discovered on January 10, 1899, an enclosure twelve feet long, nine feet wide, screened by a marble parapet on three sides, and paved with slabs of the blackest kind of Tænarian marble.

In estimating the value of this discovery we must bear in mind two facts. The first is that the Forum, the Comitium, the Sacra Via, and the surrounding edifices were seriously injured or completely destroyed by the fire of Carinus, 283 A. D., the damages of which were made good by Diocletian, who rebuilt the Basilica Julia, the Forum Julium, the Græcostasis, and the Senate House; by Maxentius, who rebuilt the temple of Cæsar, the Regia, the Porticus Margaritaria, and the temple of Venus and Rome, and by the S. P. Q. R., which "(templum Saturni) incendio consumptum restituit," as the inscription on the pronaos asserts. We therefore see the

[1] *Corpus Inscr.* vol. vi. n. 1161: "under the paving-stones of the road which passes through the arch of Severus."

Forum and the Comitium not as they were seen and described by the classic writers of the Republic and of the early Empire, but as they were manipulated and rearranged by Diocletian and Maxentius after the disaster of 283.

Now, as among the many acres of public squares, or streets, or sacred enclosures, or courts laid bare at Rome, Ostia, Tusculum, Præneste, Tibur, Cures, Veii, not an inch of black flooring has ever been found, this small corner of the Comitium, "stratum lapide nigro," unique in its kind, must have a special meaning. Considering, furthermore, that ancient writers mention the existence of a Black Stone in this identical spot, we cannot help connecting the find with their testimony, and we come to the conclusion that we actually behold one of the most famous relics of the early days of Rome. Of course we are not sure whether the black slabs are the identical ones set up in the Comitium at the time of the Kings; I believe they are not: but what we know for certain is that when Diocletian repaved the Comitium in 284, slightly raising its level, he thought it necessary to perpetuate the memory of the place by paving with Tænarian marble a small enclosure in front of the Senate House, making use probably of the same slabs which had marked the spot since the time of Augustus or Domitian.

So far so good. The difficulties begin when we endeavor to find out why the " lapis niger " was set up in the Comitium, and what its meaning was. Ancient writers agree on one point, that it was an enclosure sacred to the memory of the dead, but they vary as to its significance. Sextus Pompeius Festus, a Roman grammarian of the second century, whose treatise " De verborum significatione " is abridged from a greater work on the same subject by M. Verrius Flaccus, another celebrated etymologist of the

time of Augustus, says: " The Black Stone in the Comitium marks a place of ill omen, destined as a grave to
Romulus, although the hero was not actually buried there:
others say that either Faustulus, the Palatine shepherd, or
Hostilius, the grandfather of King Tullius," lies buried
there instead of Romulus. The text of M. Terentius Varro,
whose vast and varied erudition in almost every department

The Lapis Niger or Black Stone.

of literature earned for him the title of prince of the
Roman men of letters, is lost, but what he thought about
the Black Stone is told us by three commentators of Horace.[1] Varro thought it marked the tomb of Romulus, the
founder of the City, because, he says, " two stone lions have
been erected to guard it, like that of a hero ; and because
funeral orations in honor of great men are still delivered

[1] Porphyrion in Horace, *Epod.* xvi. 13 ; the Scholiast of Cruyg, *ibid.*, and the
anonym of Cod. Parisin. 7975.

from the Rostra close by." Dionysius speaks of one lion
as being still visible in his days. Lastly, we hear that those
stones of ill omen marked the spot where Romulus had been
cut to pieces (*discerptus*) by the mob. Speaking of this
conflicting evidence, in the sitting of the Reale Accademia
dei Lincei of January 22, 1899, I remarked that the fact
of the enclosure and of the black floor having been re-
constructed at so late an age, by Diocletian or Maxentius,
in preference to many other landmarks of this famous district, shows how essential it was in the mind of the Romans
to perpetuate the tradition. Considering, therefore, that
the place has not been disturbed since the fall of the Empire, it was easy to ascertain, by tunnelling the ground at
the proper level, whether anything remarkable was buried
under that floor, like an earthen jar, a stone coffin, or
some other relic from the prehistoric age.

Nearly five months elapsed before the exploration could
be carried through : but we did not lose much by waiting.
First to appear was a grave (*fossa*) once guarded by two
great stone lions : the lions have disappeared, but their
oblong pedestals are almost intact. A sacrificial stone is
laid over the grave or cenotaph, while on the right side of
the lions stand upright in their original position a conical
pillar, and a pyramidal stone covered with Greek letters of
archaic type. Back of this monumental group, the various
parts of which are so intimately connected with one another,
a raised platform was found, 3.44 metres long, 1.60 metres
wide, so similar to the Argæan altars of the Cermalus and
of S. Martino ai Monti, that it was undoubtedly intended
for a similar use. I confess that in my long experience of
Roman excavations I was never more impressed than at the
sight of this venerable monument raised in honor of the
founder of the City not long after his death, a simple and yet

not inelegant work of an Etruscan stonecutter of the time of
Servius Tullius.   The various parts of the group, the lions,
the pillar, the stele, and the altar have all been purposely
injured and mutilated by the violence of man.   The pillar

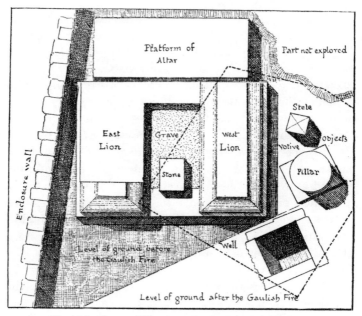

Plan of the Heroon of Romulus under the floor of black stones.

and the stele are broken off at about one third of their
original height ; the plinth of the left lion is half destroyed,
half moved out of place.   The whole group was found im-
bedded in a layer of sacrificial remains, from fifteen to
twenty inches thick, such as charred bones of victims (young
bulls, sheep, goats, swine), small vases, clay disks representing cakes, figurines cast in metal or cut in bone, pieces of
" æs rude," and so forth.   It has been said, but we have as

yet no official confirmation of the fact, that the layer contained also two or three small chips of the black flooring itself, which must have been broken and split by the same hands by which the Comitium was reduced to a heap of smouldering ruins.

Whose hands were they? There seems to be but one answer to the query. We behold the palpable, the speaking evidence of the storming and sacking of Rome by the Gauls in 390 B. C. Whether the senators and the patricians, who had deemed it inconsistent with their dignity to abandon the City and their duties by an ignoble flight, were actually murdered here, as stated by Plutarch (Camill. 21), or in the vestibules of their houses, as stated by Livy (v. 40), or whether they were murdered at all, is still a matter of discussion ; but the incident of the centurion, related by the same historian (v. 50), certainly refers to the place now excavated. While the senators were assembled on the site of the Curia Hostilia to discuss the proposal of emigrating to Veii, and the people crowded around to learn the result of their deliberations, a company of soldiers happened to cross the Comitium, and the centurion, whether by chance or by design, gave the command, "Ensign, fix the standard here: *hic manebimus optime!*" Senators and plebeians accepted the omen, and the emigration to Veii was unanimously negatived. Now one of their first thoughts in undertaking the reconstruction and the reorganization of the City was to purify it from the profanation it had suffered at the hands of the barbarians. "Senatus consultum factum," Livy says, "fana omnia, quod ea hostis possedisset, restituerentur, terminarentur, expiarenturque: expiatio eorum per duumviros quæreretur."[1] The purification was

---

[1] "It was decreed by the Senate that all sacred places which had been occupied [and profaned] by the enemy should be rebuilt, purified, and their

the more necessary for the Curia and the Comitium, as they were both consecrated places.

It was suggested at first that the layer of votive offerings by which the Heroon is enveloped is not the result of sacrifices performed here for a certain number of years or of centuries, but the outcome of the purification made after the retreat of the Gauls. The analysis of the single objects,

The Heroon of Romulus; a view taken under the floor of black stones, showing the relative position of lions, pillar, and stele.

however, has proved that they are not contemporary, not even approximately so; but that the formation of the heap must have required several centuries.

In studying the group constituting, as it were, the national monument to the founder of the City, we must take into consideration its various parts, viz., the cenotaph guarded by the lions, the sacrificial stone, the pillar, the inscribed

limits marked out ; and that special magistrates should be selected to carry out the decree."

pyramid, the altar, and the wells or receptacles for votive offerings which are to be found by scores in the neighboring district.

First as to the tomb. In the early days of Rome, when the population was still dwelling within the limits of the Palatine hill, the *mundus* or round pit that marked the centre of the consecrated space was obviously in the centre of the hill itself, at the intersecting point of the two meridian lines, the *cardo* and the *decumanus*. Its location was indicated by a heap of stones, which in course of time took the shape of a square altar, named the Roma Quadrata, a venerable relic preserved through the lapse of centuries to the end of the Empire. Had the Latin element of the population determined to raise a memorial to its leader, apart from their neighbors, the Sabines and the Etruscans, they would no doubt have located it at their own *mundus*, viz., at the Roma Quadrata. The monument we have found, however, has a much higher signification : it is the joint offering of all the elements of the Roman population dwelling on the Septimontium, after their amalgamation into one body by Numa and Servius. Its site, therefore, was selected outside the boundaries of the Sabine, the Aboriginal, the Etruscan, and the Latin sections, occupying respectively the Quirinal, the Capitoline, the Cælian, and the Palatine hills ; and the monument rose, as it were, on neutral or common ground, in the hollow space between those heights, where the bartering trade between the various tribes had already given rise to a rudimentary Forum.

According to the Roman legend, Romulus and Tatius, after the mediation of the Sabine women, met on the spot where the battle had been fought, and made peace and an alliance. The spot, a low, damp, grassy field, bordering on the marshes of the lesser Velabrum, and exposed to the floods of a local stream, named (probably) Spinon, took the name of *Comitium*, from the verb *coire*, to assemble. Other reasons justified the selection of the site. Here was the Volkanal, where business of state between the two kings, Romulus and Tatius, and their councillors had been transacted for a while ; and here was the stone hall, or Curia, where the meetings of the Senate of the federal or amalgamated city were henceforth to take place. Here ran a stream of living water, with which, on the commemorative feast of the hero, the flamen could purify himself before offering the sacrifice. For this reason, and also because of the thought that life is like the water of a river that flows into the sea of eternity and disappears, memorials to heroes were raised in preference along the banks of rivers. Thus Æneas was buried on the river Numicius, at the foot of the hills of Lavinium. Romulus, on his part, had his memorial both on the river which ran through the heart of the Etrusco-Sabino-Latin Rome, and in the Agora or market-place, which, according to a tradition dating as far back as Theseus, was the place of honor in Argæan and Pelasgic cities. The location, in fact, was so happily selected that the centre, the ὀμφαλὸς, the *umbilicus Romæ*, was never shifted from this spot, even when the population rose to one million, and the great city expanded miles away from the original nucleus on the Palatine.

The Heroon sacred to Romulus, the protecting genius of the City, became an object of popular worship, and propitiations were offered and sacrifices performed at its altar, especially in troubled or dangerous times. For this purpose a *fossa* or receptacle was always attached to the Heroon, to which the victim was brought, and where it was slain so that its blood might flow inside, and give joy and satisfaction to the spirit of the hero and appease his wrath.   The mysterious and irresistible power of the same spirit was symbolized by one or two lions, — an Oriental conception which, from immemorial times, had been popular in the Ægean islands, in Greece, and in Italy.   I need hardly quote the well known instance of Leonidas, in whose memory a lion was raised on the hillock in the pass of Thermopylæ, where he and his gallant followers had made their last stand.   Varro, speaking of the lions of Romulus, uses the expression, "sicut in sepulchris videmus" (as we see in other [heroic] tombs).

I am not sure whether the sacrificial stone which we see still lying over the *fossa*, between the pedestals of the lions, is the original one, or whether it is a restoration after the invasion of the Gauls.   In either case, it must certainly have witnessed some extraordinary and blood-curdling scenes. There is no doubt that the small figurines of clay, bone, bronze, and amber found in the layer of votive offerings are real νεκρῶν ἀγάλματα — images of the dead — indicative of human sacrifices.   They represent a stiff, naked human figure with the arms stretched close to the body, without any sign of life, very different, therefore, from the figurines found in or near the temples of the gods, which appear full of life and brightness.

It is true that only bones of young animals have been found in the sacrificial strata ; but it is not improbable that — under exceptionally anxious circumstances — human victims were slain over this stone, and human blood was made to flow into the cenotaph below.   We must not forget that Numa Pompilius, or whoever first organized Roman worship and dictated the code of Roman religion, was imbued with the dark and cruel principles of the Sabine belief, which Livy (i. 13) calls " sad and awe-inspiring." If the great Æneas himself had endeavored to assuage the wrath of Pallas with human blood, the descendants of his race might equally well have resorted to the same means of pro-pitiation when the interests, nay, the very safety of the Commonwealth were at stake. Roman writers as-sert, it is true, that Druidic rites were excluded from the national religious code after the time of the Kings, but we know that on more than one occasion cruel deeds were perpetrated. A man and a woman were im-molated in the Forum Boa-rium after the battle of Cannæ; and although Livy

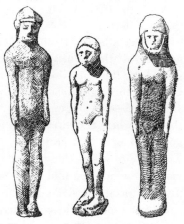

Figurines, probably representing human victims.

gives the excuse that the immolation was against the law, — *minime romano sacro,* — still we have reason to suspect that exceptions to the rule were not infrequent. A Senatus-consultum was actually passed as late as 96 B. C. forbid-ding *ne homo immolaretur.* And to what purpose? Not speaking of what continued to take place in certain savage countries, nominally subjected to the Empire, like Armorica and the Cottian Alps, human blood was shed in the Campus Martius at the time of Cæsar, and human victims were slain at the old federal temple on Monte Cavo and in Diana's grove at Nemi, under the Empire. The Christian apolo-gists, Justin, Tatian, Minucius Felix, Tertullian, Lactan-tius, and Prudentius are unanimous in attributing the deed to the pagans. Perhaps they exaggerate; perhaps their complaints have no more ground to stand upon than those which are repeated in our own days against the Russian or the Hungarian Jews ; but I am not speaking of the third or fourth century after Christ. I am speaking of the early days of the City, when the people had not yet developed the wonderful practical sense of a later age, when little value was attached to human life, and when religion had not yet lost the ferocity common to uncivilized races. Why should we find in Rome so many substitutions for a regularly recurring human sacrifice if it had not been actually practised in bygone times ? We find them in the *ver sacrum* when the firstborn of a tribe was devoted to a god, and sent out from the City ; we find them in the *Lupercalia* when the young men were smeared with the victim's blood ; we find them in the spilling of the blood of a gladiator at the *feriæ Latinæ* on the Alban hills. These rites were meant to perpetuate the cruel tradition in a mysterious and attenuated form. Every year, in the month of June, when the fishermen of the Tiber celebrated their gathering, live fishes were offered to Vulcan as substitutes for human souls (*pro animis humanis*). The Vulcanal was the scene of another strange performance on the feast day of Maia, the wife of Vulcan, when heads of garlic and of poppies were offered to her in substitution for infants, whose sacrifice, tolerated by the Kings, was only abolished by Brutus after the expulsion of the Tarquins. In the month of May rush-puppets resembling men, tied hand and foot, were cast into the Tiber from the Sublician bridge. As a last instance I quote the fate of Mettus Curtius, and his leaping into the chasm, the edges of which closed over him like the lid of a grave ; because, considering the fact that the plague was raging in Rome at the time, his action must be interpreted as a human sacrifice, as a self-immolation.

Considering all these things, we cannot behold these figurines of men stiff in the rigidity of death, or wound up in bands like mummies, without a certain emotion, connected as they are with the severe and melancholy practices of early Sabino-Roman worship. The sacrificial layer of which they form part contains other objects of interest, which are now exhibited in a room on the Sacra Via, near the remains of the arch of Fabius.[1] Numerous above all are the fragments of black ware which was never used for the necessities of life, but made expressly for funeral purposes. The goblets and cups are never whole, being represented, as a rule, by one single fragment, in accordance with another ritual practice significant of the end of the funeral banquet.

A votive terracotta panel.

These vases are either of buccaro (black clay) or of local imitation of buccaro; a few other fragments belong to Greek pottery which must have been imported into Rome by the way of Etruria. The cut on page 19 represents a piece of a Chalcidian amphora, with the figure of Dionysos riding a donkey, and holding the drinking cup with the right hand, in a style which is peculiar and characteristic of the end of the seventh and of the beginning of the sixth century B. C. This piece was found nearer to the bottom than to the sur-

---

[1] A special museum for the antiquities of the Forum will shortly be established in the ex-convent of S. Francesca Romana, by the Temple of Venus and Rome.

face of the votive layer. Taking, therefore, the end of the seventh century as the beginning of the formation of the layer, we are sure that the hero-worship, in this rude primitive form, lasted for a long time, because other fragments of Attic pottery have been picked up near the surface which date from about 550 B. C. I do not mean to say that the practice of offering ex-votos was given up at that date ; on the contrary, we have reason to believe that it was continued as late as the burning of Rome by the Gauls in 390 B. C., and even later, but the upper strata have disappeared in the general wreck of the Comitium, together with the lions and the upper portions of the pillar and the pyramid. When the damages of the wreck were made good, the Senate House rebuilt, the Comitium restored to its original design, its level raised by about three feet, and the Heroon concealed for the first time under a flooring of black stones, regular wells were provided all round, so that the votive offerings would no longer be cast loose and spread all over the place, but put down in regular and duly consecrated receptacles. The number of these votive wells known to us is constantly increasing : probably there were as many as there were tribes in Rome, viz., thirty-five. Some are diamond shaped, some trapezoid ; but the majority are square and about four feet deep. Unfortunately they have been found empty, or, to speak more exactly, filled only with mud and fine earth, that had filtered through the interstices of the lid with which their openings were sealed when the Forum and the Comitium were raised to a still higher level. One of these sacred wells appears in the plan of the Heroon given above (p. 9).

The sacrificial layer contains a great variety of objects : some of personal wear, like fibulæ and clay beads ; some connected with the pleasures of life, such as dice and astra-

galoi. No trace of coined metal has been found, but only
bits of copper or bronze, the analysis of which has not been
published yet. I believe that when the Forum was raised
to its highest level, about the time of Sulla or of Cæsar,
the contents of the wells were spread over and around the
Heroon. No wonder, therefore, that the layer should contain objects pertaining to the last century of the Republic.

Pillars, according to Servius, are another characteristic
mark of the graves of heroes. The one discovered near the
pedestal of the west lion — overthrown by the Gauls so that
only its lowest section is left standing to tell the tale — is
slightly tapering in shape. Without borrowing from Greece
and Sicily instances of this architectural device to honor and
perpetuate the memory of great men, we find in the Forum
itself parallel cases in the Columna Mænia, in the Columna
Julia, in the grave of the Charioteer, and in the naval pillar
of Duilius. The fate of the Charioteer is told by Dionysius.
He was struck by lightning while racing in the Circus, and
his remains were interred at the foot of the Janiculum ;

but mysterious events began to
spread such terror in the neighborhood that the Senate ordered
the body to be removed to the
Vulcanal, where a column with
the effigy of the deceased was
raised over the grave.

When the partisans of Cæsar,
the first deified Roman of historical times, determined to con-
secrate the spot where his body
had been cremated, at the east

Fragment of a Chalcidian amphora.

end of the Forum (just as the opposite or west end was
sacred to the memory of the founder of the City), they

saw no better means of carrying out their design than the raising of a column of Numidian marble, twenty feet high, inscribed PARENTI PATRIÆ (to the Father of the country).

The pedestal of this column is still to be seen in a semi-circular recess in front of the temple of Cæsar, as shown in the illustration below.

The interest of this beautiful chain of discoveries culminates in the inscribed stele or pyramid, still standing, after

The newly found base of the Julian pillar.

twenty-five centuries, on the identical site where one of the Kings had set it up, near the place of assembly of the Elders. The inscription was engraved by the stonecutter while the block lay horizontal, running first from the right to the left, and going on backwards and forwards like the plough in the wheatfield (βουστροφηδόν). This very early style of palæography, not uncommon in Greece, was unknown to the Etruscans, Umbrians, Oscans, and also (we believed) to the Latins. It appears in a few inscriptions from Picenum and Marsica, lands inhabited by a rough and uncultured race, which followed early traditions and habits to a very late period. Considering that the βουστρο-φηδόν was in use only during the seventh and sixth centuries B. C., and, furthermore, that the words of the inscription are separated by three vertical dots, — a mode of punctuation which dates also from the end of the seventh and the beginning of the sixth century, — we are entitled to believe that the stele must belong to the same age.

The stele or inscribed pyramid.
General view.

It seems that the primitive Romans became acquainted with the Greek (Doric-Corinthian) alphabet, not by the way of Cumæ, as was thought at first, but by the way of Cære. From Cære, likewise, came the alphabet in use at Veii, a splendid specimen of which was discovered in my presence at Formello in 1878, engraved on a buccaro vase[1] now in the collection of Prince Chigi. In fact, the Romans borrowed from Cære not only the fifteen or sixteen letters of their early alphabet,[2] but also their religious

---

[1] Moulded in black clay, dull, not shiny.

[2] According to Iginus, Carmenta transferred to Latium only fifteen letters, while Plutarch asserts that sixteen were in use at the earliest epoch. Compare

institutions (*Cære*moniæ, ceremonies).   The stele of the
Comitium leaves no doubt on this subject : it proves, moreover, how exact are early Roman annalists and historians —
whose authority it has been the fashion to deny, and whose
word it has been the fashion to disbelieve — when they
speak of the laws of the Kings and of public treaties
engraved on wood or stone in a language that could be
understood no more.   Polybius (iii. 22) mentions this fact
apropos of the convention, signed Anno Urbis 245, between
the Romans and the Carthaginians.

Dionysius (iv. 26) describes a bronze stele of the time of
King Servius Tullius upon which archaic Greek letters were
engraved.   Livy (xl. 29) says that the volumes found in
Numa's coffin in the field of L. Petillius were written in
Greco-Latin characters.   Pliny (xvi. 87) describes a venerable oak in the Vatican district, believed to be older than
Rome itself, to which a label written in Etruscan letters
was nailed, declaring the tree to be a sacred object.   Tacitus
himself compares the lettering of these ancient records to
the oldest Hellenic specimens of handwriting.

All these invaluable documents perished in the Gaulish
fire of 390 B. C.   " Parvæ et raræ per eadem tempora literæ
fuere," Livy says, vi. 1, " quæ in commentariis pontificum
aliisque publicis privatisque erant monumentis, incensa
urbe (a Gallis) pleræque interiere." [1]   This rough block of
stone, discovered June 15, 1899, is the only one, as far as
we know, that partially escaped destruction in that great
catastrophe.   It contains a pontifical law, which is at the

Bréal, *Sur les rapports de l'alphabet étrusque avec l'alphabet latin*, in *Mém.
Société Linguistique*, Paris, viii., 1889, pp. 129–134. Lenormant, *Mélanges
d'archéol. et d'hist.*, 1883, p. 302.

[1] " Literature was then in its infancy : the rare and simple documents of
those early days, such as the pontifical records, and public and private deeds,
were lost, save a few exceptions, in the Gaulish fire."

same time a royal law, specifying the ritual of certain public sacrifices, in the dialect spoken in Rome towards the end
of the seventh century before Christ. It appears as if Livy
must have had this stele before his eyes, or fresh in his
memory, when he wrote the well-known passage (i. 20):

The stele of the Comitium. Details of the east face.

" Numa Pompilius selected a high priest, and gave him a
sacred code, in which the ritual of sacrifices was specified,
what victims ought to be slain, on what days of the year,
at what temples," etc. The whole inscription of the stele

is summarized in Livy's words : *quibus hostiis* (FORDAS, SORDAS) *quibus diebus* (EIDIASIAS, NOUNASIAS) *ad quæ templa* (SAKROS SESED, SAKROS SED).[1] The document abounds in words — abounds, in comparison with the total — which do not appear in the Latin language : another proof of remote antiquity, because, as Horace expresses it, " words are formed and die out like the leaves of the tree," but the years in the life of words are centuries !

Professor Ceci reads the inscription and supplies the missing words as follows : —

" Quoi ho(rdas veigead, veigetod) sakros sesed. Sor(das sakros sed. Eid)iasias regei lo(iba adferad ad rem d)evam. Quos re(x per mentore)m kalatorem hap(ead endo ada)giod, ioux menta capia(d) dota v(ovead. Ini)m ite ri k(oised nounasias i)m. Quoi havelod nequ(am sied dolod malo)d, diove estod. (Qu)oi voviod (sacer diove estod)."

" Whoever wants to immolate pregnant cows [fordas], he should do it by the shrine. Pregnant sows should be immolated away from the shrine. The ritual cakes used in sacrificing should be brought to the rex sacrorum at the time of the full moon.[2] Whoever wants to immolate pregnant cows or sows, having obtained leave from the rex sacrorum through the kalator, must take the auspices, and present his votive offerings. The same rules must be followed when sacrifices are performed at the first quarter of the moon [the Nonæ of later times]. Whosoever disregards the sacred

[1] Compare Livy, v. 52, where Camillus speaks of the sacred laws, stating the days as well as the places chosen for the performing of sacrifices. Dionysius (ii. 73, 74) says that Numa's legislation on religious matters was collected in eight volumes, as many as there were priestly colleges.

[2] The Idus, in the later sense of the word, indicates the 13th day of the month, except in March, May, July, and October, when it fell on the 15th ; but originally it indicated the full moon, from the Etruscan verb " iduare," to divide, because the full moon divides the lunar months.

laws concerning the auspices and the votive offerings, let him be sacred to Jupiter" (which means that he may be killed with impunity).

Professor Ceci ends his report with this remarkable sentence: " I shall not say that the discovery of the stele marks the ' bankruptcy ' of the modern hypercritical school, especially German, but one thing is certain : the discovery will shake the faith of the many who have sworn blindly by the word of Niebuhr and Ihne and will revive the hopes of the few who trust to the authority of Livy, and believe in the historical value of early Roman traditions."

These words, the reader may well imagine, have occasioned a great outcry on either side of the Alps, for the hypercritical school counts many adepts in Italy, even more " negative " than their ultramontane teachers ; they remind us of certain adepts of the Wagnerian school, who, in their attempt to follow in the wake of the great master, have gone to extremes unknown to him, and have produced lacerating sounds instead of harmony.

A just and impartial account of the controversy over Ceci's publication has been given by Giacomo Tropea, professor of ancient history in the University of Messina ; [1] another by Raffaele de Cara, in the last two volumes of the Civiltá Cattolica. We do not know whether Professor Ceci is right or wrong ; but his interpretation of the stele has nothing to do with the main question at issue. The date of the monument does not depend exclusively upon the meaning of the words inscribed on it ; but it can be determined from other points of view, such as that of its topographical sur-

---

[1] *La stele arcaica del foro romano : Cronaca della scoperta e della discussione*, May to December, 1899. Messina, D' Amico. Compare, also, Von Duhn, *Fundumstände und Fundort der ältesten lateinischen Steininschrift am Forum Romanum*, a reprint from the *Neue Heidelberger Jahrbücher*, July, 1899.

roundings and of its depth below the level of the republican and imperial fora. The Heroon occupies the level trodden by human feet in the valley of the Forum at the time of the Kings when the greater part of the space between the Capitoline and the Palatine hills was a swamp fed by the unruly river, which drained the valley of Quirinus, the Subura, the Carinæ and the Argiletum, and by copious local springs. Now the first thought of the dwellers on the Palatine, as soon as they had joined hands with the Sabines of the Quirinal, and made one city out of the various tribal settlements of the Septimontium, was to drain the land which they had selected for their market, and where they were wont to assemble on election days. The scheme, according to tradition, was carried into execution by the elder Tarquin, who lined the banks of the stream (Spinon ?) with great square blocks of stone, leaving a channel about five feet wide so as to prevent the spreading of flood-water, and to provide the low-lying district with a permanent outlet. The increase of the population, the development of public and private constructions, the expansion of traffic soon made it necessary to cover the channel and make it run under-ground. This second step was taken under the rule of the second Tarquin, as described by Livy in chapters xxxviii. and lvi. of the first book. We need not, however, depend upon the testimony of ancient writers in ascertaining the chronology of these undertakings, so essential to the welfare, nay, to the very existence of a city, especially when the city occupied the centre of " a pestilential region." That the Cloaca Maxima was built and vaulted over at the time of the Kings, before the middle of the third century of Rome, by Etruscan masons and Etruscan engineers, is a fact absolutely unquestioned in the mind of any one acquainted with the hydrography, geology, and archæology of Rome and

Etruria. Now when the Heroon of Romulus was put up in the Comitium within a few feet of the Cloaca Maxima, this

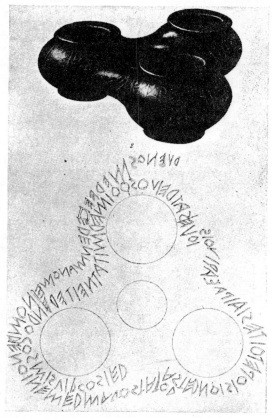

The votive vase of Dvenos.

last was still an open channel without a roof! The level of the Heroon is three or four feet lower than the vaulted ceiling of the cloaca, which must have run in its turn two or three feet below the level of the ground.

The arguments which the hypercritics bring forth, in their attempt to break this chain of evidence, are rather vague and frail.   They insist on the fact that the stele must have been inscribed and set up in the Comitium after the retreat of the Gauls, 390 B. C. ; and that it is, therefore, a much later legend than that engraved on the votive vase of Dvenos,[1] because the plinth of the lions and the sacrificial stone were cut by a workman acquainted with the value and the use of the Attic foot; and as this standard measure was unknown in Rome before the time of the Decemvirs (451–449 B. C.), the Heroon must be a work of that comparatively late period.   This argument is a favorite one with the skeptical school, as it gives them the means of denying and upsetting not only the history but the topography of Rome for the first three centuries of its existence.   In fact, the Romans being an ignorant, barbarous, wild race, the like of which, according to the skeptics, could hardly be found now in the central wilderness of New Guinea, how could they be supposed to have lived in a city built in harmony with the rules of civilization ?   Down, therefore, with the walls of the Palatine city, with those of Servius Tullius ; down with the Prison of Ancus Marcius, with the Cloaca Maxima of Tarquinius Priscus, with the temple of Jupiter Capitolinus of Tarquinius Superbus !   All these landmarks of the early days of Rome must be later than the Decemvirs, because their builders knew the existence of the Attic foot !   And when I announced in 1882 the discovery of Antemnæ, as that of a settlement contemporary

[1] The votive vase of Dvenos, with its remarkable archaic inscription, was discovered in 1880 in the foundations of the Villa Huffer, on the south slope of the Quirinal, near the church of S. Vitale.   No satisfactory interpretation of the text — edited first by Heinrich Dressel in *Annal. Instit.*, 1880, p. 158 — has been given yet.   At all events, it *was* the oldest known Latin inscription before the discovery of the stele.

with the foundation of Rome, I must have been laboring under a delusion, because the stones with which the walls of that place are built measure exactly two feet in height!

It seems hardly credible that such theories can be advanced in the presence and in the light of so many discoveries by which the fundamental truth of Roman tradition is amply justified. From the earliest days the Romans borrowed masons and stonecutters from their immediate neighbors, the Etruscans of Veii,[1] just as they had borrowed from the Etruscans of Cære their ceremonies and their alphabet, from the Etruscans of Vulci their *vulcani* or coppersmiths. If we find a similarity between the Attic, the Etruscan, and the Roman foot in those remote days, the reason is evident; the fundamental principles of their architecture and metrology descend from a common source. The prehistoric fortified villages, known by the name of Terramare, discovered

Pedestal of the east lion.

by Pigorini in the valley of the Po and of its affluents, were also designed and built by engineers familiar with the

---

[1] The connection between the two cities was so close that the bank of the Tiber, opposite the Palatine hill, was named RIPA VEIENTANA.

principles of the "agrimetatio" on the basis of the foot
(.297 metres). For all purposes let me repeat that the use
of the Attic foot, as far as the Heroon Romuli is concerned,
has been ascertained only in connection with the plinth of
the pedestals of the lions (which measures .29 metres in
height) and with the sacrificial stone (which is one foot
thick, and two and a half feet long). All the rest seems
to be cut at random.

This affair of the Attic measure finds its counterpart in
another statement of the negative school, that the laws
of the XII. Tables are also a product of the time of the
Decemvirs, because we find used in them the word *pœna*,
which must have been imported from Greece (ποινή) by the
Decemvirs themselves !

To conclude. Since the discovery of the Heroon Romuli
in the Comitium and of the archaic stele, — whatever the
meaning of its legend may be, — the history of ancient
Rome cannot longer be written in the distrustful spirit of
the hypercritical school. The future rests with our con-
servative party, of which I was a convinced member even
at a time when it required a certain amount of courage to
be recognized as such and to meet the accusation of credu-
lity, when a lecturer could not name the founder of the
City as a man who had actually existed, without blushing
before his audience. As Professor Otto Schmidt remarks in
the "Neue Jahrbucher f. Deutsch. Liter." (Leipzig, 1900,
p. 52): "Whoever is conversant with recent German literature on the history of Rome will acknowledge that the con-
servative party is gaining ground every day. The future
is in the hands of the conservatives." It seems to me rather
a good turn of fortune that while our opponents were proclaiming the Forum not older than 400 B. C., that dear
old place should reveal to us the most convincing proof
of its remote antiquity.

The tradition about the grave of Romulus never died out in Rome ; it was kept alive in the Comitium by outward signs long after the original monument had been concealed from view under a flooring of black stones. In fact, we find it confirmed by imperial authority, in the most solemn form, at the beginning of the fourth century after Christ, when Maxentius raised, in front of the Senate House, the pedestal inscribed : —

> MARTI · INVICTO · PATRI
> ET · ÆTERNÆ VRBIS SVÆ
> CONDITORIBVS !

("To Mars the invincible father, and to the founders of his eternal City ! ") This pedestal, discovered November 12, 1899, dates probably from 312 A. D. It seems that at the beginning of that eventful year, Maxentius, having declared war against Constantine under the plea that he had caused the death of his father Maximianus, not only made elaborate preparations to stop the advance of Constantine's army, but endeavored also to propitiate the gods in his favor, those especially to whom the welfare of the City was entrusted. It is necessary to remember that when Diocletian divided the Roman empire into two parts and four sections, and gave them up to his colleagues, Maximian, Galerius, and Chlorus, besides his own leading share, — and when Nicomedia was chosen as the capital of the eastern, and Milan of the western empire, Rome, the glorious City which had ruled the world for centuries, was reduced to the rank of a provincial town.

After the abdication of Diocletian and Maximian, May, 305, Galerius and Chlorus became emperors (Augusti), while Severus and Daza were raised to the rank of Cæsars. The presence of so many barbarians at the head of the state exasperated the army; revolutions and civil wars broke out in Brittany, in northern Italy, and in the East, with the result that, three years later, in 308, the number of rulers had increased to six, the last comers being Constantine son of Chlorus, and Maxentius son of Maximian. Maxentius had a true Roman heart. In spite of the anxious political situation which gave him no peace and no rest, he tried to revive in Rome the tradition of its old greatness, and to emulate the Emperors of the golden days in the magnificence of his structures. I shall describe in the next chapter his reconstruction of the Clivus Sacræ Viæ, which he transformed from a narrow irregular lane into a great avenue sixty-seven feet wide, lining it on one side with the Porticus Margaritaria, on the other with the Heroon of his son Romulus and with the Basilica Nova. In the outskirts of the city he transformed the old Triopium of Herodes Atticus, described in "Pagan and Christian Rome," p. 287, into an imperial suburban residence, adding to the accommodations of the place a circus, a palace, a basilica, and a family mausoleum. He considerably improved his own family estate at the fourteenth milestone of the Via Labicana, changing it from a farm into a villa. I visited this delightful corner of the Campagna, now called San Cesario, in the course of last winter. The villa rivals in extent that of the Quintilii on the Appian Way, while it surpasses it in natural beauty, with its well-wooded and well-watered dales, winding among vine-clad hills, with the mountains of Præneste for a background, shaded by olive groves, and crowned by the Pelasgic fortress of Castel S. Pietro. Here two pedestals were found in 1705, dedicated by Valerius Romulus, one to his father Maxentius "patri benignissimo pro amore caritatis eius," one to his mother Valeria Maximilla "matri carissimæ pro amore adfectionis eius." These terms of filial devotion and endearment were not dictated for appearance, nor intended to be read by outsiders ; therefore they speak the truth, and give us a glimpse of the intimate life of the happy trio in their peaceful retreat on the Via Labicana, which they had enriched with a magnificent collection of works of art. The many specimens of statuary, and the set of portrait-busts found by the present owners of the estate, have just been sold to a dealer, and dispersed among various collectors on either side of the Atlantic.

If we add to the list of these works the restoration of the

Marbles discovered in the villa of Maxentius at S. Cesario.

Appian Way from Rome to Brindisi, of the road to Laurentum, and of several aqueducts, we must admit that very few Emperors have done as much, in the space of four years, as Maxentius did between April 21, A. D. 308, the date of his accession to the throne, and October 27, 312, the day he was drowned in the Tiber while retreating from the battle-field of Saxa Rubra. The pedestal lately found in the Comitium testifies to the true Roman spirit of Maxentius, in his attempt to relieve the fortunes of his dear city. Another inscription found in the Forum, which begins with the words, " censuræ veteris, pietatisque singularis, domino nostro Maxentio," seems to allude to this tenacity of purpose for the preservation of its historical greatness against the attempts of Diocletian and his colleagues.[1] He raised the pedestal to Mars, to Romulus and Remus, because he knew that under the flooring of black stones, near by, there lay deep underground the cenotaph of the founder of the City, of the son of Mars and Rhea Silvia, whose name he had given to his own son. And to make the connection between the old and the new monuments more evident, he selected for the dedication of this last the anniversary day of the foundation of the City, the glorious Paliliæ, April 21 : " Dedicata die XI Kal. Maias ! "

In the legend of his coins Maxentius always addresses Rome as the " æterna urbs sua," and speaks of himself as the " conservator urbis suæ." These coins show on the reverse the figure of Rome seated on a throne in her own temple on the Summa Sacra Via, on the pediment of which we see the infant twins sucking the wolf. Even more interesting from the point of view of the last discoveries is a medal described by Eckhel,[2] in which the figure of Mars appears in company with that of the wolf and her nurslings. These facts and these considerations give weight to the conjecture that the pedestal of Maxentius did not support a statue of Mars, but the bronze wolf now in the Capitoline museum.

[1] *Corpus Inscr. Latin.* vi. 1220, 31394.
[2] *Doctrina numm.* viii. p. 56.   Cohen, *Monn. imper.* vi. 28.

The origin of this celebrated work of art is rather obscure. It seems that in the old days of Rome there was a statue of Atta Navius on the steps of the Curia on the left, marking

The Bronze Wolf.

the spot where the miracle-working augur, challenged by Tarquin, had cut the whetstone with a razor. A fig-tree close by was held in veneration, first, because it had been struck by lightning and made sacred, and again because it symbolized the Ruminal tree, under the shade of which the wolf had tendered maternal care to the twins. In fact, the people believed it to be the original one, transported from the Velabrum to the Comitium by a prodigy. It seems that two bronze images of the wolf had been placed under the fig-tree at different times : the first by Atta Navius himself, and this one probably perished in the Gaulish fire; the second in B. C. 295, by the brothers Cnæus and Quintus Ogulnii, who devoted to its casting the fines collected from the usurers. Ancient writers mention a third wolf, also cast in bronze and gilded, placed somewhere in the Capitol; and because this last was struck by lightning, under the consulship of Cotta and Torquatus, B. C. 64, many antiquarians have identified it with the one now exhibited in the Palazzo de' Conservatori, which shows the right hind leg split open as if by a stroke of some kind. However, this cannot be the case, because Cicero and Dion Cassius distinctly state that both the beast and the infants were wrenched from their stand and melted; [1] and besides, the existing replica has never been gilded.

Can we then identify it with the original placed by the brothers Ogulnii in the Comitium ? Helbig says no, and I beg leave to quote at length the statement he makes in vol. i. p. 460 of his " Guide to the Collections of Classical Antiquities in Rome," first ed., 1895. " The she-wolf of Rome was conceived of by ancient artists in two different ways. The usual mode represents her suckling the twins and turning her head to look at them. More rarely she is seen without the twins, and in a threatening attitude, as, for instance, on the denarii of Publius Satrienus [p. 37]. The Capitoline wolf reproduces the latter motive. With flashing eye and gnashing teeth she menaces an approaching foe. The terror-striking effect of the head was enhanced by the glittering enamel of the deeply incised pupils, a fragment of which still remains in the right eye. If we may assume that the development of early Roman art was parallel with that of Etruria, we may ascribe the execution of this work to the fifth century B. C. In any case, we

[1] Cicero, *Catilin.* iii. 7 ; *De divinat.* i. 13 ; ii. 20. Dion Cassius, xxxvii. 9.

must reject the hypothesis that it is identical with the she-wolf which the Ædiles Cnæus and Quintus Ogulnius erected by the Ficus Ruminalis in 295 B. C. with the money paid in fines. At that epoch the Romans were masters of Campania, and had there become familiar with both Hellenic and Hellenistic art, and hence it seems incredible that in the year 295 B. C. so archaic a work as the Capitoline wolf could have been publicly installed in Rome." Helbig's difficulty may be obviated by supposing that the artist was commissioned by the Ogulnii to reproduce the lost original of Atta Navius, rather than to model a new figure.

Again, we cannot agree with Helbig as regards the origin, or rather the discovery, of the Capitoline bronze. "The basilica of St. John Lateran," he says, "was entirely rebuilt under Pope Sergius III. (904–911) after its destruction by an earthquake in 896. It would appear quite natural that a desire should then have arisen to adorn the piazza in front of it with the emblem of Rome. As the sculptors of the time were incapable of pro- ducing a statue in any degree satisfactory, search was made for some ancient work of the

The Wolf in the coins of P. Sa- trienus.

kind. The she-wolf was then discovered, lying ruined and forgotten, perhaps in the cellars of some pagan temple, and was entrusted to a coppersmith near by, to be patched up for its position in front of the Lateran." [1] These conjectures would be acceptable if the wolf were the only work of art cast in metal collected by the Popes round their episcopal palace : but besides the wolf, there was the equestrian statue of Marcus Aurelius ; the Camillus, known in the middle ages by the name of La Zingara or the Gypsy, from the supposi-

---

[1] Helbig thinks that the wolf " has been most barbarously treated by a stupid restorer."

tion that the right hand was stretched forward for purposes of palmistry; the Boy extracting a thorn; the colossal head of Nero; the hand of another colossal statue; the bronze globe, etc., all of which were removed to the Conservatori palace at the time of Sixtus IV. (1471). All these celebrated bronzes cannot have been found " in the cellars of some pagan temple " at the time of Sergius III., viz., after Rome had been pillaged by the barbarians and by her own citizens a hundred times at least, and after even the roofs of old buildings had been stripped of the bronze tiles. The Lateran collection must have been formed long before the tenth century, when bronze works of art were still plentiful.

The wolf, at all events, is mentioned long before the time of Sergius III. Benedict of Mount Soracte speaks of the institution of a court of justice " in the Lateran palace, in the place called *the Wolf*, viz., the mother of the Romans," as an event of the beginning of the ninth century. Trials and executions at the Wolf are recorded from time to time until 1438. The illustration on p. 39 refers to the cruel punishment of Capocciolo and Garofolo, on September 12 of that year, for having stolen certain precious stones from the busts of SS. Peter and Paul, which were then kept in the ciborium or canopy of Urban V. above the high altar of the Lateran. Capocciolo and Garofolo, who were beneficiaries of the chapter, had their right hands cut and nailed at the Wolf, before they were themselves nailed to the stakes and burnt alive. The scene of their execution, and that of their accomplice, Nicola da Valmontone, who as a canon of the same chapter was only hanged on a tree, was painted on the wall of the transept by order of Cardinal Angelotto de Foschi. The original was destroyed by Clement VIII. in 1587, but a copy is preserved in the archives of the chapter, from which my illustration is taken.

I have no doubt myself that the wolf, kept from immemorial times at the Lateran, is the very one that Maxentius replaced on the newly found pedestal, after the fire of Carinus, by which the Curia and the Comitium were so seriously damaged. But whether I am right or not in my belief, whether the wolf or any other image stood on

An execution " at the Wolf," A. D. 1348: from a painting formerly in the Clementine transept, at the Lateran.

that pedestal, its connection with the Heroon of Romulus is evident ; and we cannot read without emotion this last appeal of a true and brave emperor to the founders of his dear city at the moment he was going to face Constantine on the field of battle. Really, between this unfortunate prince, Roman to the core, and his antagonist, who was going to abandon the glorious city for Constantinople, we cannot help siding with the first ; we cannot help wishing that the battle of Saxa Rubra had had a different issue.

The grave of Romulus the founder of the City, at one end of the Forum, and the memorial of Romulus the son of Maxentius, at the other, mark the beginning and the end of the history of classic Rome.

The floor of the Comitium in front of the Senate House, a perspective view of which is reproduced (page 41), may be called an historical and topographical palimpsest. We can see at a glance several pavements at various levels, each one retaining traces of the special treatment to which the Comitium was subjected at that particular period of its history. Thus, in the last floor but one we perceive signs of a line of columns (A, A') running parallel with the front of the Curia at the foot of the steps (B, B'), which were inclosed and separated from the public section of the Comitium by a bronze railing or transenna (C C'). A gutter (D D') runs along the transenna, to carry off the rain-water from the enclosure. And when all these things were finally covered by a stone floor (E, E'), a beautiful fountain was set up in front of the main door of the Curia, and the gutter was utilized to lay the lead pipe which carried the water for the jet.

Nothing is left of the fountain except the lower basin (F F'), which collected the drippings from the tazza above, and the foundations of the octagonal pedestal which supported the tazza. The history of the tazza is at all events very interesting.

First of all, the setting up of this fountain in the last days of classic Rome belongs to a cycle of works carried on in the Senate House and its neighborhood at the beginning of the fifth century, when the principal hall was restored by the prefect Næratius, and the Secretary's offices by the prefect Flavius Annius Eucharius. Both edifices must have been damaged by the Goths of Alaric in 410. The fountain was not made for use here, but was removed to the Comitium from some other place. Its mouldings are too graceful, and the cutting of the slabs too neat to be attributed to a stonecutter of the fifth century. It seems, in fact, that when the basin was lifted to its new level or moved to its new place, the workmen marked its eight marble segments with the first eight letters of the alphabet so as to avoid any difficulty in rejoining them. The B and

THE PAVEMENT OF THE COMITIUM

the F can still be seen at the joints of the second and sixth segments.

The fountain lasted for a long period, probably until the cutting of the aqueducts by Vitiges, for the surface of the basin was worn out by the dripping of the tazza, and a thick line of lime deposit was formed around the rim. At all events, this was not the only fountain of the Comitium : there was another into which the water flowed from the urn of a recumbent River-god known, since the early middle ages, by the name of Marforio (Martis forum).

This loquacious and sarcastic River-god has had the fortune, in common with the Nile and the Tiber now in the

The Marforio.

Piazza del Campidoglio, of having never been buried and removed from sight since the downfall of Rome. We can follow his career before and after the Norman pillage of 1084, which marks the first disappearance of the Forum and the Comitium under a bed of rubbish. The so-called Anonymus of Einsiedeln saw it near the church of S. Martina (the Secretarium Senatus) before the pillage ; and it is constantly

mentioned in the Guide-books for pilgrims, or Mirabilia, of
a later date. When Giovanni Ruccellai visited Rome in the
Jubilee of 1450 he was struck at the sight of the colossal
figure of Marforio, and so was Nicholas Müffel of Nurem-
berg, who followed Frederick III. in his visit to Nicholas V.
in 1452. They both speak with admiration of the " gran
simulacro a giacere," and they both mention the tazza of
granite into which he used once to pour water. This feeling of admiration lasted all through the sixteenth century. Speaking of Michelangelo's David, Vasari says : " It
stands foremost among all ancient and modern works of
statuary, and neither the Marforio, nor the Tiber and Nile
of Belvedere, nor the Horse-tamers of the Quirinal can bear
comparison with it." The same genial biographer relates
of Baccio Bandinelli, that finding himself one morning in
the workshop of Girolamo del Buda, while the adjoining
Piazza di S. Apollinare was covered with a sheet of snow,
the young artist modelled with it a Marforio, eight cubits
long, which was a marvel to behold.

The original statue was removed from the site of the
Comitium at the time of Gregory XIII., and after many wan-
derings was given a resting-place in the Piazza del Campidoglio, on the side facing the Palazzo dei Conservatori, where
the Museo Capitolino now stands, and while old Marforio
was thus joining company with the Tiber and the Nile, which
Michelangelo had already located on the south side of the
same piazza against the steps of the Palazzo del Senatore,
the granite tazza was left abandoned near S. Martina until
1593. On October 22 of that year the city magistrates obtained from Cardinal Alessandro Farnese a piece of ground
near the " three columns " of Castor's temple, where the
basin was set up and furnished with three jets of the
Felice water which Pope Sixtus V. had just gathered from

THE FOUNTAIN OF CAMPO VACCINO

the springs of Pantano. It was finally removed to its present site, between the Horse-tamers in the Piazza del Quirinale, by Pius VII. in 1817. (See page 49.)

Marforio's position amongst the loquacious statues of Rome is not prominent like that of Pasquino, his duty being confined to answering his friend's sallies, not to originating them. However, " a neat repartee maketh glad the heart of the utterer." We have seen what the career of the River-god was, after the water ceased to flow, from the urn on which his elbow rests, into the fountain of the Comitium. Pasquino's origin is altogether obscure. This battered torso, this mutilated fragment of a group considered to represent Menelaus supporting the dead body of Patroclus, seems to have been discovered by Francesco Orsini while building his palace in the region of Parione; and when the palace — demolished by Pius VI. to make room for his own Palazzo Braschi — was rented by Cardinal Oliviero Caraffa, towards the end of the fifteenth century, the torso was set upon a pedestal with the inscription : " I owe my existence to Oliver Caraffa : A. D. 1501." How was it, then, that the almost shapeless fragment became the greatest object of curiosity in Rome ? According to Castelvetro's version, it derived name and notoriety from a sharp-tongued and witty tailor named Pasquino, who kept a shop opposite the Orsini palace, and whose sallies against the Pope, the Cardinals, and the Court were widely circulated and vastly appreciated in Rome. Others substitute for the tailor a barber gifted with the same satirical propensities. We owe to Count Domenico Gnoli the revelation of the truth.[1]

On April 25 of each year, being the feast day of St. Mark the Evangelist, a procession used to start from the

[1] Gnoli, Domenico, " Le origini di Maestro Pasquino " in *Nuova Antologia*, January, 1890.

church of S. Lorenzo in Damaso and pass in front of the
Pasquino and the Orsini palace, where the officiating priests
rested on a certain stone bench, decked for the occasion
with tapestries and evergreens. Cardinal Caraffa, considering that Pasquino was not fit to witness such a holy scene
in his battered condition, caused him to be restored in plaster
and dressed up for the occasion, the type and the costume

Pasquino.

changing every year.
Thus between 1501 and
1507 he became in turn
Saturn, Jupiter, Miner-
va, Apollo, Mars, Mer-
cury, and Neptune; he
became Arpokras in
1508, Janus in 1509,
Hercules in 1510,
"Mourning" in 1511,
and so on. The dis-
guises were chosen in
connection with the
greatest or latest event
of the year; for in-
stance, "Mourning"
in 1511, on account
of Cardinal Caraffa's
death; Hercules killing
the Hydra in 1510, on

account of Julius II.'s victories over the Venetians, etc.

The care of arranging Pasquino's disguises was entrusted
by Cardinal Caraffa to a certain Donato Poli, a lecturer on
geography in the university or "studio," as it was then
called; a man deformed in appearance, surnamed by his
pupils "Diciamo, diciamo" (Let us say, let us say), because

he repeated these words with every utterance; but otherwise a good and serviceable friend, with longing aspirations for the heights of Parnassus. Donato took advantage of the festival of St. Mark to promote emulation among his pupils, causing them to compose Latin or Italian elegies, epigrams, and mottoes which were pasted on Pasquino's

The Fountain of the Comitium.

pedestal. The custom met with such favor, first with the students, later on with the many poets of the court of Leo X., that the number of verses rose from a few scores in 1501 to three thousand in 1509. Jacopo Mazochio, the enterprising manager of the university press, at once saw his chance of making a profit out of this competition; but, as the show lasted only a few hours, because the papers were removed as soon as the procession had passed, and as

many fought for the privilege of reading and copying the
epigrams, Mazochio's reporters had a difficult time in ac-
complishing their task.   His pamphlets, published year by
year under the title, " Carmina quæ ad Pasquillum fuerunt
posita in anno —," have become exceedingly rare, only the
editions of 1509–1514, 1521, and 1525 having come down
to us.   The others were probably lost in the Sacco di
Roma.

A perusal of these pasquinades show them to be mostly
the work of inexperienced and silly boys ; they never deal
with politics or religion.   Those, therefore, who have spoken
of Pasquino as waging a fierce war against the Popes, as
being imbued with a spirit of rebellion and reform, and
thrusting the darts of satire against the members of the
Curia, are altogether mistaken.   The only strokes of license
to be noticed in these early pasquinades are directed against
professors of the university obnoxious to students, such as
Augusto Baldo from Padua, and his assistant Basilio Cal-
condila, who occupied the chair of Greek.   The celebrations
were interrupted in 1517 by the sad end of their founder,
Donato Poli, who was killed with a hammer by his own valet
for the sake of the few florins he had saved out of a scanty
salary of 150 florins a year.   The place of protector of
Pasquino had been taken by Cardinal Antonio del Monte
after the death of Caraffa, and the directorship of the competition was given to Decio Sillano da Spoleto after the
murder of Donato.   The institution collapsed altogether
with the Sacco di Roma.   As long as Pasquino was left free
to speak, no harm was done ; but when the reaction against
the reform broke out under Adrian VI. and Paul IV., Pasquino became in some measure the anonymous organ of
public opinion, and part of the social system of Rome.   It
is related that Adrian VI. attempted to stop his career by

ordering the statue to be burnt and thrown into the Tiber, but one of the courtiers, Ludovico Suessano, saved him by suggesting that his ashes would turn into frogs and croak more audaciously than ever.

Pasquino was not the only statue patronizing poetry in Rome. There was another one quite celebrated at the time, now almost lost in oblivion, the Sant' Anna of Jacopo Sansovino, classed by Vasari amongst the masterpieces of Italian art. The statue, which stands now in the church of S. Agostino, on the second altar at the left, had been originally set up against the third pilaster of the nave on the same side of the church, below Raphael's fresco representing the prophet Isaiah and two angels holding a tablet. Both painting and statue had been made at the expense of Johann Goritz of Luxembourg, the Coricius of contemporary humanists, whose garden, on the slope of the Capitoline hill towards Trajan's forum, planted with lemon-trees and full of antiques, was the rendezvous of the learned men of the age. Every year, on the feast day of Sant' Anna, Coricius's friends would place by the statue in S. Agostino, or hang to the lemon-trees of the garden, odes and sonnets in praise of their kind host, which he collected and brought home for remembrance. In the tenth year after the first keeping of Sant' Anna's day, the bundle of MSS. was stolen by Blosio Palladio, while Coricius was asleep, and printed as a surprise to him (1524) under the title of " Coryciana." It contains contributions from one hundred and thirty poets ; among the names ·I notice that of Ulrich von Hutten, the author of the incendiary epigrams to Rubiano on the state of Papal Rome, who afterwards became one of the leaders of the Reformation in Germany.

Poor old Coricius ! His end was nearly as cruel as that of Donato Poli. During the fearful sack of 1527 he saw his house and his dear garden wrecked by the lansquenets, and his money stolen, while he was nearly beaten to death. Fleeing from the accursed city towards his native land, he died at Mantua from grief and exhaustion.

CHAPTER II.

THE religion of the builders of Rome did not differ from that of other superior races at an early stage of civilization. They worshipped nature in its manifold manifestations, and paid homage to the beings supposed to preside over the necessities of life, to those who made the spring of Juturna flow from the rocks upon which their village was perched, who kept away the wolves from their flocks grazing on the uplands of the Velia and the Oppian, who supplied their hearthstones with fire, protected their ancestral fields from the encroachments of neighbors, and their family tombs from profanation, and who guaranteed the sanctity of agreements, oaths, matrimony, and hospitality. It was only at a later stage that the Romans borrowed new rites and superstitions from the Sabines, the Etruscans, the Greeks, the Egyptians, the Phrygians, and the Persians, — in fact, from every nation they came in contact with, or subjugated to their rule. The outcome of this process of assimilation was a complicated religious syncretism, which had no nationality or individuality of its own. Such has been the evolution of all conquering nations ; in fact, the loss of the original simplicity of faith seems to have been shared by all races which have not kept themselves strictly apart from the rest of mankind, or " walled themselves in " like the sons of Sem in the far East.

The latest excavations along the " sacred way " of primitive Rome have brought us in contact over and over again with the centre of early Roman worship, when man lived in harmony with nature, when every natural mystery was to him a sacred one. In those early days, whenever the intervention of the Deity was sought for in domestic emergencies, the duty of performing the supplication rested, naturally, with the paterfamilias; but when prayers and sacrifices had to be offered for the sake of the whole village, or tribe, or nation, the duty devolved upon a public delegate or representative. The Latin tribes called to those high and noble duties men who in their estimation ranked above others, — the " makers of roads and bridges," or, in short, the " pontifices." Many etymologies have been suggested for this word. Quintus Scævola derived it from " posse " and " facere "; Varro from " pons " or bridge, because the priests had thrown across the Tiber the first Roman bridge, the Sublician. Others have suggested that " pontifex " is a substitute for " pompifex," a leader of public processions. However, as the word " pons " originally meant " way," so the word " ponti-fex " must mean a " maker of roads and bridges." These men were certainly possessed of a great geodetical knowledge and engineering skill. The " Terramara," or prehistoric fortified station discovered by Pigorini at Castellazzo di Fontanellato, of which I have given an illustration in " Ruins and Excavations of Ancient Rome," p. 115, is a marvel and model of ingenuity, both in design and in execution.

The dignity of supreme priesthood belonged to the king, who, as the head of the state religion, performed his official duties in a hut on the Sacra Via, near the place where the public fire was kept, and watched by the Vestals. Vesta's hut was round. The " Regia," as the High Priest's offices were called, seems to have been in the shape of an oblong square or parallelogram. Its first construction is attri-

PLAN OF THE HOUSE OF THE VESTALS, TIME OF SEPTIMIUS SEVERUS

(Built over the Domus Publica of the time of Augustus. From an aerial photograph by Captain Moris, R. E.)

buted to Numa, and it probably retained its original shape and simplicity of style until its destruction by the Gauls in B. C. 390.

After the overthrow of the monarchy, and the consequent separation of the political from the religious power, the Regia was used as the office of the supreme priesthood, not as a dwelling-house for the Supreme Priest. The Regia was a " fanum," viz., the habitation of gods, not of mortals ; and we know besides, from other sources, that the Pontifex dwelt in a separate house on the same Sacra Via, called the " domus publica." We know, also, that when Augustus, after an interval of four hundred and eighty-eight years, united again in his own person the political and the religious power, as in the days of the Kings, and became Pontifex Maximus, he built a new " domus publica " on the Palatine and made a present to the Vestals of the old one. Its remains are to be seen to the present day, below the level of the house of the same virgins, with which they form an angle of about 30°. They include a small basilica with a fine mosaic pavement, a court surrounded by a peristyle of fluted stone columns coated with plaster, a " triclinium " or dining hall, and other apartments in which every style of masonry used in Rome from the Gaulish fire to the end of the Republic is represented. The plan of this pontifical residence, the witness of so many historical events, can be made out — as far as the present stage of the excavations allows it — in the aerial view here reproduced. This photograph was taken by that gallant officer of the Royal Engineers, Cavaliere Moris, whose name I shall have occasion to mention again with praise and gratitude in the following pages.

As regards the Regia, it survived the disastrous fires of 210, 148, and 36 B. C. and 65 A. D., down to the fall of the

Empire, a lovely marble building sheltering within its enclosure or under its marble and mosaic pavements many
characteristics of the time of the Kings. Its plan, here
given for the first time, is difficult to understand in some
parts, altogether incomprehensible in others; but our investigation of the place may be found easier if we recall
to mind the manifold duties devolving on the college of
the pontiffs, whose official residence it was. They were
entrusted with the care of regulating the worship of the
people, of watching over the maintenance of the public fire,
of keeping records of time, of registering great events
and prodigies, and of making seismic and meteorological
observations.

As far as the religious Code is concerned, it is enough to
say that it comprised two sections. One called the " Indi-
gitamenta " contained the authorized names of the gods
and explained the manner in which they were to be addressed in public worship; the other contained ritual regulations and the " jus pontificum." These fundamental
points of Roman religion, set down by Numa Pompilius,
were altered or more accurately defined in progress of time;
hence the origin of the official bulletin of the supreme
priesthood, called " Commentarii sacrorum," intended to
bring to the notice of the public the new regulations, with
an explanatory text.

The pontiffs, as I have said, watched over the maintenance
of the public fire, and this with the help of the six Vestal
maidens, whose life and sacred ministry I have illustrated
at length in " Ancient Rome." If I mention here again the
institution common to all tribal settlements of prehistoric
ages, it depends on the fact that the Vestals did not represent an independent sisterhood, but they simply performed
duties which originally pertained to the pontifex. In fact,

the Regia was for our primitive Latin settlements (Bovillæ, Velitræ, Lanuvium, Tusculum, etc.) what the Prytaneum was in the Greek lands, when each tribal nucleus had a

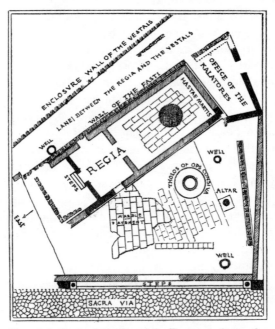

Plan of the Regia of the time of the Flavians, built over the old foundations of the time of the Kings.

common hearth in the chief's house. Any book on the folk-lore and customs of primitive nations will show the universality of this practice. The perpetual maintenance of the fire was the duty of the chief, which he delegated to his daughters or to his slaves ; in Latium, no doubt, to daughters, who reappear in history as the Vestals. Hence the connection both moral and material between the two huts raised in the early days of Rome near the market

(Forum) and the village fountain (Juturna), which were destined to become in progress of time, one the Regia, the other the temple of Vesta.

The new search made through the cloisters in the summer of 1899 has led to no important results. These cloisters — at least the wing which borders on the Nova Via and supports its embankment, twenty-two feet high — were not a healthy residence. Their position right under the shade of Caligula's palace, towering one hundred and fifty feet above the floor of the Atrium, was most unfavorable, and the rooms of the ground floor were so permeated with damp as to be unfit for human habitation. To avoid the evil, or rather to lessen its effects on the health of the sisters, two precautions were taken. Double and triple walls were set up against the embankment of the Nova Via, with a free space between them to allow the circulation of dry or hot air ; and the pavements of the cells were raised by a couple of feet. This last operation was carried on rather awkwardly, and in a way quite characteristic of the decadence of sanitary engineering in Rome, in the course of the fourth century. Thus, in the rooms on either side of the Tablinum we find the later and higher pavements resting on large earthen amphoræ, sawn across into halves ; others rest on brick supports, like those used in forming hypocausts ; others on a simple bed of rubbish. The most remarkable fact is that, when this general raising of the floors took place, the beautiful old pavements of the time of Julia Domna were not taken up and made use of again, but left, in a more or less perfect state, at the old level. Two or three have just been rediscovered, and they are most beautiful ; their pattern is geometrical, and the marbles with which they are inlaid (giallo and pavonazzetto for the brighter tones, africano and portasanta for the shady effects)

THE SHRINE OF VESTA

harmonize so perfectly in color and shape as to please the eye exceedingly.

On December 17, 1899, a " ripostiglio," or hidden treasure of gold pieces was discovered in a drain near the west corner of the edifice. It consists of 397 aurei, which must have been thrown into that strange place of concealment in a leather bag, or done up in a piece of cloth. The oldest coin dates from the time of Constantius II., 337–361 A. D.; the latest from that of Leo I., whose death took place in 474. By far the greatest number of pieces, three hundred and more, belong to the Emperor Anthemius, son of Procopius, slain by his son-in-law Ricimer in 467, while the rarest of all bear the name and effigy of Ælia Marcia Euphemia, daughter of the Emperor Marcianus and wife of Anthemius.

It is difficult to connect the burial of this considerable sum of money with any particular event in the history of the disasters which befell the city at the end of the fifth century. There is no doubt that the gold was thrown into the cesspool under the apprehension of an impending pillage. The house of the Vestals, abandoned by the sisterhood since its suppression in 393, was probably falling into ruin, and the owner of that little treasure selected the hiding-place so skilfully that not only did it escape being plundered by the barbarians, but the owner himself could not recover it after the danger was over. Perhaps he lost his life in the defence of the city ; perhaps he was carried away into slavery ; perhaps the ceilings of this suite of rooms fell to the ground, and the hiding-place was buried under heavy masses of masonry.

The 397 aurei or solidi were found to weigh 1778 grammes, an average of $4\frac{1}{2}$ grammes apiece. There is, however, considerable variation between the maximum

(4.515 gr.) and the minimum (4.250 gr.) in the fifty-six varieties of coins. Considering that, by a decree issued by Valentinian in 445 A. D., seventy-two solidi were required to make a pound, we assume, from the most careful weighing of 300 solidi of Anthemius all sharp and fresh from the mint, that the exact value of the pound in the first half of the fifth century was 322.56 grammes.

Another quite recent discovery has stirred up once more the controversy concerning the fate of the Vestal whose name was erased from the pedestal discovered November 5, 1883, at the north corner of the cloisters, on the right of the entrance door, a detailed account of which is given in "Ancient Rome," p. 170. The inscription describes how a statue and a pedestal had been raised in honor of . . . , high priestess, by the college of the pontiffs, as a testimonial to her chastity and profound knowledge of religious matters. Why was the memory of such a chaste and learned lady condemned, after the statue was set up A. D. 364, and why was her name hammered away from the pedestal? Probably because she became a Christian. An alleged confirmation of this surmise has been found in the discovery made September 17, 1899, of a mutilated statue, which seemed to have been purposely buried three feet below the mosaic floor at the west corner of the Atrium, as if the High Priests, not satisfied with the erasure of the abhorred name of the traitress, had overthrown the statue, and buried the scattered portions in various corners of the place. The statement is absolutely fanciful, I am sorry to say ; the battered torso of the Vestal was not concealed from view out of disrespect for the titular, but simply made use of by a late occupant of the Atrium to repair the roof of a local drain. The practice of using the finest productions of classic sculpture for this disreputable purpose was rather

in vogue in mediæval Rome. The exquisite panel from
the Basilica Æmilia, reproduced on page 149, was discovered by Boni walled in the ceiling of the sewer of the
street ad Janum. When Lorenzo Ghiberti visited Rome in
1420, a beautiful statue was discovered in his presence in
the drain which runs by the church of S. Celso in Banchi.
" I saw in the 440th Olympiad," Ghiberti writes in Cod.
Magliabecch. XVII. n. 33, " a simulacrum of an hermaphrodite of the stature of a girl of thirteen, modelled with wonderful grace, which had been placed across the drain of S.
Celso, to strengthen its ceiling. A sculptor who happened
to witness the find, caused the statue to be raised from its
disgraceful grave, and removed to the church of S. Cecilia,
where he was putting up the tomb of a cardinal." [1] My
own experience in this line of discoveries has been remarkably interesting. The frieze attributed by Visconti to the
temple of the Earth with scenes from the Gigantomachia ;
the trapezophoroi from the house of Numicius Pica Cæsi-
anus on the Viminal, monuments of great artistic and archæological value described in the " Bullettino Comunale,"
1874, p. 223, and 1887, p. 247, and the greater part of
the panels exhibited in the Sala delle Terre-cotte in the
Conservatori Palace, have experienced the same fate with
the statues of the Hermaphrodite of Ghiberti, and of the
Vestal Virgin lately found in the Atrium.

Prudentius, the prince of Christian poets, seems to allude
to the fate of this last priestess in his canticle to St. Lawrence, when he says, " Ædemque, Laurenti, tuam Vestalis
intrat Claudia " (Claudia the Vestal Virgin enters thy
shrine). These words are interpreted by Marucchi, not as

---

[1] Probably of Cardinal Adam of Hertford, who died 1397. The tomb, a
true gem of the early Renaissance, was pulled to pieces by Cardinal Sfrondato
in 1599.

a general and impersonal indication of the conquests made
by the gospel among the last champions of polytheism, but
as the proof of a special conquest, made in the Atrium
itself, of a distinguished priestess named Claudia ;[1] in
which case the mention of the Basilica of S. Lorenzo fuori
le Mura cannot be taken as fortuitous, but as the evidence
of a true and real event connected with the history of that
celebrated sanctuary. The tomb of the Levite on the Via
Tiburtina had been chosen in the fourth century as the
place where young men and young women would conse-
crate themselves to God, and pronounce the vows of chastity. These scenes are represented on certain devotional
medals, two of which are here reproduced.

The first, discovered in 1636 in the Catacombs of Cyriaca
together with a glass cup upon which the heads of St. Peter
and St. Paul were designed in gold leaf, was purchased by
Claude Ménétrier, and offered to Cardinal Francesco Barberini. A bad mould of the lost original is exhibited in the
Vatican Library. It represents the consecration to God, on
the grave of St. Lawrence, of a girl named SVCCESSA. The
second, the origin of which is not recorded, represents sym-
bolically the sacrifice of Abraham, practically the offer made
to God by URBICVS of his son GAVDENTIANVS, the consecration taking place, as usual, at the grave of the Levite.

These scenes help us to understand the meaning of the
verses of Prudentius ; in which he does not indulge in poetical allusions, but mentions an historical fact, viz., the
abjuration of the Vestal Claudia in the Basilica of St.
Lawrence, and the iteration of her vows of chastity not to
Vesta but to the true God.

The Catacombs of Cyriaca, in the heart of which St.
Lawrence was buried, contain many authentic documents of

[1] Marucchi in *Nuovo Bullettino di arch. cristiana*, 1899, p. 206.

these " Gottgeweihten Jungfrauen," [1] such as the tombstones of Lavinia, VIRGO DEI INIMITABILIS, who died April
3, 409, in her thirty-fifth year; of Prætextata, VIRGO SACRA,
who died August 6, 464; of Adeodata, VIRGO DIGNA ET
MERITA, " who lies here in peace by the will of her heav-
enly Spouse," and others. This is the reason why one of
the most favorite subjects for symbolic paintings in these

Medals of devotion of the sixth century, commemorative of the
consecration to God of boys and girls, and of their vows of chastity pronounced at the grave of St. Lawrence.

special catacombs of Cyriaca is the parable of the wise and
foolish virgins. Now we cannot ascribe to a mere chance

[1] Monsignor Giuseppe Wilpert, one of the leaders of the Roman school of
sacred archæology, has adopted this title for his learned treatise on Christian
Virgins published at Freiburg in 1892.

the finding, in these same crypts, of an epitaph inscribed with the following verses : —

> " Claudia nobilium prolis generosa parentum
> Hic iacet : hinc anima in carne redeunte resurget
> Æternis Christi munere digna bonis."

(Here lies Claudia, daughter of noble parents, waiting for the day of the Resurrection, to receive from Christ the gift of perpetual happiness.) The Claudia of patrician birth, buried among the virgins of God near the grave of St. Lawrence, is manifestly the same noble girl whose secession from the altar of Vesta is recorded by Prudentius, and whose name is erased from the pedestal. By a fortunate coincidence the first letter of the name erased can still be made out, and it is a C, the initial of Claudia.

I have said that records of time, of important events, and of prodigies were kept in the Regia. Time was recorded by means of the " Fasti consulares," events by means of the " Fasti triumphales " and of the " Annales maximi," while prodigies were registered by means of minutes compiled by the inquiring officers.

For nearly four centuries and a half after the foundation of Rome the knowledge of the calendar was possessed exclusively by the priests. One of them, the Rex sacrorum, on the calends of each month announced to the people assembled in the Curia Calabra, when the nones of that month would fall (on the 5th, except in March, May, July, and October, when they fell on the 7th); and on the nones the people were again gathered in the Arx to be told what feast-days fell in the remaining part of the month. In like manner, all who wished to go to law were obliged to inquire of the priests on what day they might bring their suit, and received the reply as from the lips of an astrologer.

The whole of this lore, so long a source of power and profit and therefore jealously enveloped in mystery, was at length made public by a certain Cn. Flavius, scribe to Appius Claudius Cæcus, who, having gained access to the pontifical

The Regia, from the Sacra Via.

books, copied out all the requisite information, and exhibited it in the Forum for the use of people at large. From this time forward such tables became common, and were known by the name of " Fasti," [1] closely resembling a modern almanac.

Many of these Fasti have been found, in a more or less fragmentary state, in my lifetime, the most important replica being the one discovered at Cære in 1873 by Luigi Boccanera, the only one in which mention is made of the birthday of Rome (April 21):

<p style="text-align:center">ROMA · CONDita
FER<i>iæ</i> · CORONATIS · OM<i>nibus</i></p>

---

[1] William Ridgeway, in Smith's *Dict. of Antiq.* vol. i. p. 828.

More complete are the copies found in the sixteenth century, when ancient monuments had not yet suffered irreparable injury at the hands of modern vandals.   They are known by the name of Fasti Pinciani, Venusini, Maffeiani, Esquilini, Prænestini, etc., from the place in which they came to light, or to which they were removed.   The calendars are properly called Julian, because they are later than the great reform of the year made by Julius Cæsar B. C. 46, and were destined to make the people of Rome and of the surrounding towns acquainted with the new computation. We owe to the same circumstance the composition of the celebrated Fasti of Ovid, a poetical " year-book " or " companion to the almanac " published to illustrate the reform of the dictator.   Ovid's work, however, is incomplete, and deals only with the first six months of the year.

From these various elements Professor Mommsen was able to reconstruct in 1863 the complete set of the " Commentarii diurni," giving every possible detail for each day of the year, one of the greatest epigraphic and archæological achievements of the age.[1]

There is no doubt that the original copy of the reformed calendar must have been engraved on the walls of the Regia, the official residence of the reformer ; and yet while we are in possession of a considerable part of the Fasti exhibited in the same place, not a fragment has been found of the calendar.

These Fasti were discovered in 1546, during the memorable campaign of destruction initiated by Paul III. in 1540 to provide materials for the " Fabbrica di S. Pietro."   The remains of the building were first seen at the bottom of the trench on the fifteenth day of August ; a month later not a

[1] *Corpus Inscr. Lat.* vol. i. pp. 382–410.   Second edition by Mommsen and Huelsen, 1893.

vestige was left to tell the tale. Panvinio and Ligorio, both witnesses of the proceedings, say that the beautiful building was so far intact at the moment of the discovery that a whole column or page of the Fasti, engraved in the space or panel between two pilasters, was still in situ (" loco antiquo mota non fuerat "), so that Michelangelo and Ligorio himself found no difficulty in designing the plan and the architectural details of the structure. Other inscribed blocks having been found out of place, a careful search was made in various directions by means of tunnels bored in the bank of rubbish. Ligorio adds that the find was made half way between the arch of Fabius and the temple of Castor. The vandals of the " Reverenda Fabbrica " did not even tarry to reach the ancient level to indulge in their destructive errand, but sold the exquisitely carved blocks to limeburners and stonecutters as fast as they appeared in the trench. Some were hammered into chips and thrown into the limekiln, others sawn into slabs or transformed into new shapes. The reader may form an estimate of the irreparable losses inflicted on the Regia between August 15 and September 14, 1546, from the fact that the few architectural fragments reproduced on pages 70, 71 are the only ones, as far as I know, that escaped destruction ; and yet so indifferent were the learned men of the age to the fate of the glorious ruins of Rome, that Panvinio himself ends his account of these sad events by raising a canticle of praise to Paul III. under whose " felicissimus principatus " they had taken place.

The Fasti consulares et triumphales would probably have shared the same fate but for the intervention of Cardinal Alessandro Farnese, who rescued them from the hands of the contractors, and removed them to his own garden of La Farnesina, according to Metellus — to his palace, accord-

Fragments of the architecture of the Regia.

ing to Marliano. Such a valuable set of historical records,
however, was not destined to remain long in private hands.
Yielding to a request of the city magistrates, that kind
prince of the church made a present of the set to his
fellow-citizens, and the Fasti were thus removed to the

middle north room of the Conservatori Palace on the Capitol, with the help of Michelangelo for the architectural part, while the epigraphical was entrusted to a committee of learned men, Antonio Agostino, Gabriele Faerno, Ottavio Pantagato, Bartolomeo Marliano, and Tommaso Cavalieri, presided over by Gentile Delfini.

We cannot, however, take the word of Panvinio and Ligorio in too strict a sense, as if the builders of St. Peter's

Fragments of a frieze, probably of the Regia.

had found the Regia intact, and as if they were the first to lay hands on the sacred edifice. The destructive process had been inaugurated long before the time of Paul III. A fragment of the Fasti (from A. U. 386 to 396), after having served as threshold for the church of S. Maria in Publicolis, in the fifteenth century, had been saved from destruction by the sacristan, and set into the wall of the adjoining house belonging to Prospero di Santa Croce ; [1] another, dated A. U. 766, was seen by Fra Giocondo da Verona about 1485, in the house of Antonio dei Rustici ; a third, dated from the first Punic war, was copied by Mazo-

[1] Compare Huelsen, *Corpus Inscr. Lat.* vol. i. second ed. 1893, p. 1.

chio in 1511, in the house of Francesco de' Fabii, etc.   The
present excavations of the Forum have supplied us with
another proof that marbles were removed from the Regia,
even before the fire and pillage of Robert the Norman, A. D.
1081, when the Forum was still free from all accumulation
of rubbish.   In clearing away a section of the Basilica
Æmilia which had been occupied by a public office (for the
collecting of taxes?) about the time of Charlemagne, a
valuable fragment of the same records was found, used, as
in the case of S. Maria in Publicolis, for a threshold.   The
block of marble, which must have originally contained
some thirty lines of consular names, has been so mutilated
by the chisel of the stonecutter, and so worn away by the
rubbing of feet, that only the names of the " tribuni mili-
tum " for the year 374, and of the consuls for the years
422–424, can be read.   Yet the fragment, mutilated as it
is, enables us to correct both Livy and Diodorus as regards
the number and the names of the tribuni.   Diodorus, xv.
50, mentions only seven, Livy, vi. 27, only six; the newly
found fragment from the Regia mentions nine, with names
and genealogy in full, ending with the record that towards
the end of that year Cincinnatus was appointed .dictator
to defend the City from the attack of the Prænestinians.
Record is also made of the dictatorship of Cnæus Quintius
Capitolinus A. U. 423, " clavi figendi causa."   This very
old custom of driving a nail into the right side of the cella
of Jupiter's temple on the Capitol, on September 13, originated from the Etruscans, who used to keep account of
the years in this primitive fashion.   In progress of time the
ceremony was performed only under extraordinary circumstances, to avert the spreading of the plague, to expiate a
great crime, to call back to obedience the disaffected plebeians, and the like.   The occasion for driving the nail

A. U. 423 was found in a sudden and terrible influx of mortality among the patrician families. Doubts were at first entertained as to whether the mortality was due to natural causes, or to a murderous conspiracy. The theory of wholesale poisoning prevailed as usual in these contingencies, and one hundred and seventy matrons of noble birth were sentenced to death. It is the old story of the *Untori*, so impressively described by Manzoni in connection with the Plague of Milan of 1630. This valuable fragment of the

Remains of a mediæval building occupying part of the Basilica Æmilia, where an important fragment of the Fasti has been found, used as a threshold at the point marked A.

history of republican Rome was discovered at the point marked A in the preceding illustration.

To return to the excavations of 1546, we learn from Panvinio another curious particular, viz., that the Regia had been occupied in the darkest period of the middle ages by a double colony of marble-cutters and limeburners, both of

The entrance to the Regia, from the east.

which companies had left traces of their sinister work. Panvinio saw a limekiln of considerable size, with a layer of half-charred marble blocks at the bottom, while others had been spared from the fire to be sawn in slabs, " on which were carved birds, flowers, Solomon's knots, and other barbarous and utterly senseless ornamentations which we see so often carved on the panels of pulpits and choirs in mediæval churches." Panvinio obviously refers to the workshop of a Roman " marmorarius " of the eighth or ninth century, who, for the sake of the *materia prima*, had established himself amidst the marble buildings at the east end of the Forum. Giacomo Boni has discovered in this same neighborhood a block showing, on one side, a cross of the Carolingian age, with the four branches bent apart in the form of a spiral, and, on the other, exquisite mouldings of the time of the Flavians.[1]

[1] See Boni's article in the *Nineteenth Century* for April, 1900, p. 637.

Notwithstanding these antecedents, it is evident that if the contractors for the " Fabbrica di S. Pietro " had not met with the remains of the Regia in their ferocious campaign of 1546, we should now behold not the bare, shapeless platform shown on page 74, but a tasteful little architectural jewel, not unlike the one reproduced in the accompanying cut from a sketch by Pirro Ligorio, who claims to have made it while the building was being pulled to pieces.

Another duty which devolved on the College of the Pontiffs was to inquire into the prodigious manifestations and strange incidents by which the gods were supposed to

The Regia, from a sketch taken in 1566, by Pirro Ligorio.

forewarn men of impending calamities ; and because these calamities were believed to threaten the nation more than single individuals, the Senate also took a share in the inquest and in the selection of the rites, sacrifices and expiations best calculated to appease the wrath and avert the

vengeance of the gods. Livy's chronicle of the " prodigia "
which marked the advent of every new year at the time
of the Punic wars is quite extraordinary; but we must
acknowledge, in justice to him, that he does not rely much
on the trustworthiness of the reports which he had collected
from the pontifical archives. Speaking of the wonderful
manifestations reported for the year 214 B. C., Livy declares
that in many cases they were the outcome of excited imagi-
nations, ready to find credit among the lower classes terri-
fied by the events of the war. The prodigies were of two
kinds : those that could be traced back to natural agencies
acting under the will of the gods, such as thunderbolts
striking sacred edifices, rivers overflowing their banks, fires,
earthquakes, hurricanes, plague, mortality among the animals, etc., and those essentially supernatural and miraculous
which manifested the direct will of the gods.

The records for the year 214 B. C., the fifth of the second Punic war, include the following entries. In Rome
the Tiber twice submerged the lower quarters and the suburbs, carrying away houses and farms with a great loss of
men and cattle. The vestibule of the Capitol and the temple of Vulcan were struck by lightning, as well as a walnut-
tree in the Sabine hills, and the walls and one of the gates
at Gabii. In Rome, likewise, a shower of blood fell in the
Forum Boarium ; a jet of water burst out in the street of
the Insteii with terrific force ; and an apparition of hostile
legions hurrying to storm the city was seen on the Janiculum. Ravens had built their nest inside the temple of Juno
Sospita at Lanuvium; the pool of the Mincio, by which
Mantua is surrounded, had suddenly taken a bloody color ;
a shower of lapilli had fallen at Cales ; the spear of Mars in
the temple at Præneste had been seen to move ; an infant
had been heard to cry out " Io triumphe ! " while still " in

utero matris"; women had been turned into men at Spoleto; and lastly, celestial figures, clad in white garments, had been seen at Hadria among the clouds, gathered around an altar!

There is a fragmentary treatise, entitled " De Prodigiis " or " Prodigiorum Libellus," containing a chronological entry of these strange happenings from the consulship of Scipio and Lælius, B. C. 190, to that of Fabius and Ælius, B. C. 11. The book — which bears the name, otherwise unknown, of C. Julius Obsequens — is simply an abridgment of Livy, almost word for word, made by an anonymous compiler of the fourth century.

One set of prodigies, the oscillation of the spears of Mars, is strictly connected with the Regia. The formula with which the phenomenon was registered in the pontifical diaries is always the same, if we may trust those that have come down to us, either directly or from the abridg-

The Regia, from the west.

ment of Livy : " hastæ Martis motæ " (B. C. 184) ; " hastæ Martis in Regia motæ " (B. C. 119, 100, 97) ; " hastæ Martis in Regia sua sponte motæ " (B. C. 104). These spears — wooden rods with points of metal — were venerated in a " sacrarium " or inner room of the Regia, as having belonged to the mythical father of the first king and founder of Rome. They were probably two in number, certainly more than one, as they are invariably alluded to by ancient writers in the plural. Giacomo Boni recognizes the innermost sanctuary of Mars, where the hastæ were kept, in the circular structure represented in the accompanying view (page 77), but whether his conjecture is acceptable or not, I agree with him on one point : that the sacrarium was in a certain sense a seismic observatory. We cannot state with certainty how the spears were suspended so as to register the smallest oscillations ; but whatever the arrangement was, we know that their vibration was considered to be the forerunner of disaster, to be averted only by the most solemn sacrifices. Aulus Gellius distinctly affirms that they were shaken by earthquakes; and the fact that several propitiations were offered in succession indicates that fresh shocks were always expected and dreaded. In this respect the hastæ Martis can properly be compared with the " ancilia " or shields kept in the assembly room of the Salii on the Palatine, which were likewise believed to be stirred occasionally by a supernatural power when a special expiatory ceremony was required.

As the official residence of the Pontifex Maximus, the Regia was the home of Julius Cæsar during the greater part of his public life. He did not actually dwell in it, but in a house on the opposite site of the lane, called Domus Publica, or Domus Pontificis, or Domus C. Cæsaris. The living and the official apartments were, however, so

closely connected that what is related of one may be applied
to the other. Pliny describes the spreading of awnings
over the Sacra Via and the Forum " from the house of
Cæsar to the Capitol," on the occasion of a gladiatorial
show which he offered to the people. " Here took place
the scandalous intrusion of Clodius at the festival of the
Bona Dea, which induced Cæsar to divorce his wife Pompeia, though he refused to bring Clodius to law, alleging
as his reason for the divorce that his wife must be above
suspicion. Cicero in a letter to Atticus alludes to a visit
paid by the latter to the Regia, when after the battle of
Pharsalus it had become a necessity to court Cæsar's pardon
or protection." [1]   Here also took place the meetings for the
Julian reform of the calendar, from which point of view
the Regia and its annex, the Domus Publica, bring to
mind the Casino Sora Boncompagni at Frascati, where a
similar operation took place in 1582, in the time of Pope
Gregory XIII. From the same house Cæsar set forth on
the fatal Ides of March, B. C. 44, alarmed by the ominous
dreams of his wife Calpurnia and by other evil presages ;
and hither his lifeless body was brought back from the
lobby of Pompey's theatre, and cremated, as the historians
say, " in the Forum, where the Romans place their ancient
Regia."

A very interesting discovery has been made in connection
with these events. We knew from the description by Suetonius that the partisans of the murdered hero had set up
a column of Numidian marble (giallo antico) on the site
where the pyre had been formed, inscribed PARENTI PATRIÆ
(to the Father of the country). An altar was placed at the
foot of the pillar, which became for some time the centre
of a rather irregular worship, to which one of the consuls,

[1] Nichols's *Forum*, p. 122.

C. Antonius, soon put a stop by hurling down from the Tarpeian Rock those among the worshippers who were Roman citizens, and by crucifying those who were artisans and slaves. At the same time the column and the altar were overthrown by order of the other consul, Dolabella, the son-in-law of Cicero. These violent measures gave rise to a popular outbreak, followed by other executions, until the Triumvirs at last gave satisfaction to the hero-worshippers by raising a temple inscribed DIVO IVLIO, which was brought to completion by Augustus.

The discovery to which I refer is that of the exact spot where the body of the great man was incinerated. (See page 83.) It is marked by an altar — or, to speak more accurately, by the core of an altar — built of concrete with chips of Numidian marble, that is, with the fragments of the original column set up on the site of the incineration and overthrown by Dolabella. If we remember what a prominent place belongs to Cæsar in the history of Rome, in the history of the world, we cannot help feeling a deep gratification at being able to behold again this plain slab of stone which has actually been in contact with his mortal remains, and which marks the beginning of his second life as a deified man, as a god of the Roman Olympus.

It has been observed that, whatever may have been the sentiment of Eastern or Hellenic nations on the subject of attributing divine honors to their heroes, who had lived mortal lives, the Romans hesitated for many a century to adopt the fashion. They were more bent on worshipping abstractions than individuals ; but towards the end of the Republic, under the influence of Asianized Greek ideas, they began to believe that, while all souls were immortal, those of the great and good were divine. Antistius Labeo actually wrote a book about this time on gods that had

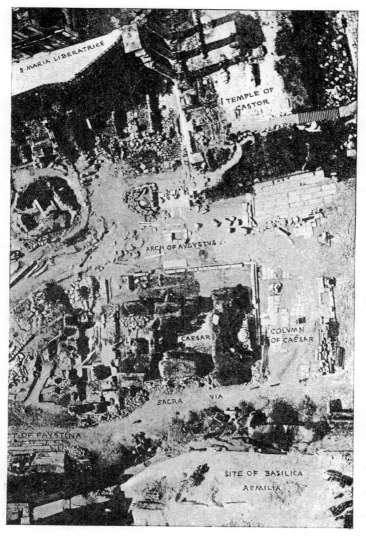

THE TEMPLE OF CÆSAR AND ITS SURROUNDINGS

(From an aerial photograph taken by Captain Moris, R. E.)

been men (*de diis animalibus*), and little by little the ideas
of the few and enlightened became the ideas of the " vulgus
profanum." The time was fully ripe for deification to be
practised in Rome, and the man came. Julius Cæsar's
brilliant military exploits abroad, and his overthrowing the
tyrannical aristocracy at home, made him the adored of
the people. When Octavian Augustus celebrated in his

The exact place where the body of Cæsar was cremated.

honor the games of Venus Genetrix, considered to be the
ancestral goddess of the Julian family, and a comet appeared in the heavens, described by Dion Cassius, xiv. 7,
the opinion that Cæsar had become a god became universal.

Next year, 43 B. C., Cæsar was solemnly enrolled among
the gods by a law of the Senate, called " lex Rufrena," [1]
under the name " Divus Julius." From this time down-

[1] *Corpus Inscr.* i. 626 ; ix. 2628.

wards the name " Divus " acquired the specific meaning of a god who had been a man, while "Deus" was a god from the beginning.   It is still alive in some branches of the Christian church as an epithet of saint ; in fact, as Boissier remarks in his book "La Religion romaine" (vol. i. p. 180), apotheosis among the ancients corresponds in many respects with Christian canonization.

It is high time, however, that we should leave the Regia and continue our peregrination up the " Clivus Sacræ Viæ " towards the summit of the ridge on which the arch of Titus now stands.   The aspect of the ascent is quite different to-day from what it appeared two years ago, before the beginning of the present excavations ; we seem to be crossing a district fresh from pillage and devastation, levelled to the ground by the violence of man combined with the destructive powers of nature.   And yet this section of the Sacred Way was once the most fashionable rendezvous of Roman society, lined by the richest and most fascinating shops of the Capital.   On the right of the ascent were those of the jewellers and goldsmiths and makers of musical instruments, while florists, chemists, and perfumers displayed their goods on the opposite side.   Here were also the consulting rooms of fashionable physicians ; and here, partly on the site of the present Basilica Constantiniana, rose the Horrea Piperataria, an institution of the time of Domitian, the scope of which was to provide the City with a general storehouse for the preservation and sale of spices, such as are described by Pliny in the twelfth book, and especially of pepper, which the Romans had learned to use after the conquest of Greece.   The pepper came from the East Indies by the way of the Red Sea, and was probably landed at Berenice or at Myoshormos, from whence caravans carried it to Coptos, called by Pliny " Indicarum Arabicarumque mer-

cium Nilo proximum emporium" (the emporium on the
Nile, for Indian and Arabic wares). The road travelled
over by these caravans, 257 miles long according to Pliny,
258 miles according to the itineraries of Antoninus and
Peutinger, was provided with reservoirs of water in the
intermediate halting-places of Apollonos, Compasi, and so
on, and with military outposts against the robbers of the
desert. These particulars have been made known by the
inscriptions discovered by Maspero at Kuft, in March, 1883,
and commented upon by Mommsen in vol. v., 1884, of the
" Ephemeris Epigraphica."

The Romans used black as well as white pepper, and
obtained the variety by the different treatment of the berry.
The spice was served in elegant " piperatoria " or pepper-
boxes, which ancient writers describe among the silver
plate. The only one of these objects with which I am
acquainted is, in fact, of silver, in the form of a Nubian
slave wearing a hooded cloak, bored with small holes. It
was discovered at Cahors, in France, in 1885, and is now
exhibited in the British Museum. Pepper was held in
such esteem that the chronographer of A. D. 354 registers
as a singular event of the reign of Augustus the arrival of
a ship from Alexandria, carrying " 400 measures of wheat,
pepper, paper, and the obelisk which is now in the Circus
Maximus."

The Horrea Piperataria of Domitian were destroyed in
the fire of 191, shortly before the death of Commodus, together with the entire quarter crossed by the Clivus Sacræ
Viæ. The texts of Galenus, of Dion Cassius, and of Herodianus, which describe this catastrophe, have been collected
and illustrated by Nibby.[1] Galenus, whose consulting

[1] *Sopra l' edificio volgarmente chiamato Tempio della Pace.* Rome, de Romanis, 1819.

rooms and pharmacy were located on the same street, and almost in contact with the Horrea, lost in the fire the manuscript of his first two books, which he had inadvertently left on the desk.

The Horrea Piperataria never rose again from their ashes after the second conflagration. Maxentius changed the aspect of the whole district. He began by spreading on the spot the materials of the gutted buildings, thus raising the level of the Clivus Sacræ Viæ by about six feet. Over this bed of rubbish, by which the last remains of the Horrea were concealed from view, he laid out his new street, to which we ought to attribute the praise bestowed by Caracalla's biographer on his new street Antoniniana : " pulcherrima inter Romanas plateas " (the finest of Roman avenues)! Instead of a narrow tortuous lane, without sidewalks and lined with shops, Maxentius carried a magnificent road up the slope of the Velia, — a road perfectly straight, 181 metres long, 23 metres wide,[1] lining it on the north side with the temple of his son Romulus and with a basilica or court-house, on the south side with a stately portico, called Porticus Margaritaria from the jewellers whose shops opened under its arcades. And although the road and its surroundings must have had the same heavy and clumsy aspect which seems to be characteristic of the public structures of the Constantinian age, it was nevertheless unique of its kind in Rome — " latissima," if not " pulcherrima inter Romanas plateas." The noble avenue is no more. It has been obliterated to the last vestige to lay bare the pavement

[1] Including the sidewalks, which are 8.20 metres and 2.50 metres wide respectively. Its first discovery took place in 1818, as described by Nibby, Fea, and de Romanis. It has since been laid bare under my personal direction, partly in 1878–9, partly in 1882, an operation which I have described and illustrated in the *Notizie degli Scavi* for 1879, pp. 14, 113, pl. vii., and for 1882, p. 216, pl. xiv.–xvi.

The Clivus Sacræ Viæ of the time of Domitian, discovered June, 1899.

of the Sacred Way of the time of Commodus or Domitian.
What we have left to remember it by are the official account
and maps published in the " Notizie degli Scavi " for 1879
and 1882, sheet twenty-ninth of my " Forma Urbis," and a
narrow belt or section in front of the temple of Romulus,
which is also destined to disappear.

The basilica raised by Maxentius on the site and over
the remains of the storehouses for oriental spices was called
at first the Basilica Nova. It seems that when Maxentius
lost his life in the battle of Saxa Rubra, October 27, 312, the
building was nearly completed, because a silver medallion
bearing the legend MAXENTIUS P(ius) F(elix) AVG(ustus)
was discovered in 1828, embedded in a block of masonry
fallen from the vaulted ceiling of the nave ; the Senate,
however, changed its name of Nova into that of Constantiniana to please the victorious prince. It was known in
the middle ages as the Temple of Peace, — a name which is
still attached to the street leading from the basilica towards
the Carinæ (Via del Tempio della Pace). Nibby gave back

to it its classic and genuine denomination, not without opposition from his colleague, Carlo Fea; the correspondence they exchanged, and the pamphlets they wrote on this subject, are so filled with bitterness and vituperation, especially on Fea's side, that one would think they were engaged in a political discussion.

There are a few points in the history of this edifice but little known to students. I have found in the city archives a deed of 1547 by which the city magistrates give permission to Eurialo Silvestri from Cingoli to lay out a garden on the roof of the north aisle, which he filled with works of statuary. The hanging garden and the grounds by which the basilica is surrounded on the east side became later on the property of Cardinal Rodolfo Pio da Carpi, towards the end of the century, and of Cardinal Alessandro de' Medici, who collected within their precincts such a number of statues, busts, pedestals, and inscriptions that few other private museums in Rome could stand comparison with these "giardini di S. Maria Nuova."

Another interesting chapter could be written about the fate of the eight columns of Proconnesian marble which supported the vaulted ceiling of the nave of the basilica, and of the four columns of porphyry which decorated its side entrance. The broken shafts were made use of for the rebuilding of St. Peter's; one whole column was removed to the Piazza di S. Maria Maggiore by Paul V. in 1613, and set up in honor of the Virgin Mary. The diameter of these pillars was so great that Simone Maschino of Carrara was able to cut out of a single block the group representing the Duke Alessandro Farnese crowned by a Victory, with the allegorical figures of the river Scheldt and of Flanders at his feet, which group is now exhibited in the great hall of the Farnese palace.

The newly discovered ascent of the Sacred Way is connected with a more or less legendary event of the apostolic age, the flight and the fall of Simon the Magician. Two facts concerning the career of this extraordinary adventurer are accepted as historical facts by Tillemont, Fabiani, and de Rossi, on the authority of Justin, of Irenæus, and of the " Philosophumena," namely, that he did profess occult sciences in Rome at the time of Nero, and that he came in contact and in opposition either with Peter alone or with Peter and Paul. The incident of the flight, however, is a later addition, of the end of the third or of the beginning of the fourth century. It appears for the first time in the Acta Petri cum Marcello and again in the pseudo-Marcellus. According to these apocryphal documents, Simon, the Samaritan sorcerer from Gitton, the arch-heresiarch, the father of *simony*, named by the people " that power of God which is called great," annoyed at the behavior of the Romans who were abandoning him to follow the teaching of St. Peter, announced that he would ascend to heaven to complain of their conduct to God his father. A large crowd gathered on the Sacred Way to see him fulfil his promise ; and he had actually begun to lift himself up in the air, when Peter prayed God to unmask the impostor before the crowd, and let him fall without great injury to his limbs. The request of the apostle was granted, and Simon dropped on the lava pavement of the road, breaking his right leg in three places. His followers removed him in a stretcher first to Aricia, later to Terracina, where he died under the care of the attending physicians.

This legend must be relegated among the many similar ones, composed and circulated in Rome after the peace of the Church, to please and interest the lower classes, — " le populaire," as Duchesne calls them, — still wavering between

the religion of their ancestors and the Gospel. These
pious novels of the fourth century, the pseudo-Linus, the
pseudo-Marcellus, the Acta Apostolorum, the Passiones
Martyrum, the Acta Petri cum Simone, etc., while they
imagine or alter *facts,* are perfectly genuine as far as topographical details are concerned ; and the reason is clear.
While nobody could challenge their accuracy as regards
events which had taken place in bygone times, especially in
times of persecution, any blunder about places and monuments would be at once detected by the reader. The more
these novels respected topographical exactitude, the more
chance they had to pass as genuine.

This story of Simon the Sorcerer, brought down in his
audacious flight by the superior power of Simon the Apostle, took Rome by storm, and from Rome spread through
all the provinces of the Empire, never losing its popularity
down to our own times. It is mentioned in book ii. of
the Apology of Arnobius, written about A. D. 303, in the
contemporary Acta Petri cum Simone, in the letters of the
Legates of Pope Liberius to Eusebius, bishop of Vercellæ
A. D. 355, and in the " Hæreses " of Epiphanius, where the
accident is described to have taken place " in the middle
of the city of the Romans." These documents agree in
stating that the evidence of the prodigy could be gathered
" to the present day " (*usque in hodiernum diem*) from the
paving-stones of the Sacred Way itself, one of which bore
the marks of the knees of St. Peter and St. Paul, when they
knelt to beg God to unmask the impostor ; while another,
of extraordinary size, had been miraculously coagulated, as
it were, out of four paving-stones upon which the limbs of
Simon had been scattered by the fall.

Speaking of these details, de Rossi says [1] that while the

[1] *Bull. Crist.,* 1867, p. 71.

silence of Justin, of Irenæus, and of the Philosophumena impels us to deny the truth of the legend as far as the apostles are concerned, it seems certain, on the other hand, that a man skilled in the secrets of nature, a student of aeronautics, a classic precursor of Montgolfier, a man used to performing on the stage the part of the " Deus ex machina," had attempted to imitate before the Emperor Nero the flight of Icarus. The inventor and his machine came to grief, but it is only at the end of the third century that Peter and Paul are made to appear on the scene, and cross the path of the sorcerer.

The alleged miraculous stones with the impression of the knees of St. Peter were removed from the pavement of the Clivus Sacræ Viæ to the church of S. Maria Nova, now S. Francesca Romana, about A. D. 1375. Before that time they were shown to the pilgrims in their original place, where they had given rise to the following superstitious practices. On stormy days the rain water descending the steep slope of the clivus would fill up the two cavities, where, according to the statement of Gregory of Tours, ailing pilgrims drank it or signed or washed themselves with it, with the most satisfactory results ; " haustæque mox sanitatem tribuebant ! " The stones are still visible at the right end of the transept of S. Francesca Romana, set into the wall near the tomb of Gregory XI. Unfortunately the recent discovery of the Clivus Sacræ Viæ proves that since the attempt of Simon the Magician, certified by Dion Cassius, Suetonius, and Juvenal, the pavement of the road has been destroyed, relaid, and raised to a higher level at least twice ; and that the one on which the alleged marks of the prodigy were shown to mediæval pilgrims had been made *ex novo* by Maxentius some 225 years after the prodigy had taken place !

CHAPTER III.

THE SACRED GROVE OF THE ARVALES.

THE first gods to whom divine honors were offered by the builders of the Palatine city were those who supplied their hearthstones with fire, made their crops prosper and ripen, protected their flocks and their ancestral fields from the rapacity of men and of beasts of prey, helped them to quench their thirst, or get rid of their ailments at the pure healing springs, and to find shelter and shade in the fragrant groves with which their hillsides were clothed. All is simple and pastoral in the tribute of gratefulness that the primitive Romans were wont to offer to the merciful beings, whose protection they enjoyed ; and never the lyre of classic poets has found a sweeter rhythm than when the canticle is addressed to the sacred springs and to the sacred groves.

> "O Fons Bandusiæ, splendidior vitro,
> dulci digne mero," etc.

"Spring of Bandusia, more clear than glass, worthy of pleasant wine and flowers withal, to-morrow shalt thou be presented with . . . the offspring of the playful herd . . . Thou to oxen wearied with the ploughshare, and to the wandering herd, dost afford a delicious coolness. Thou also shalt become one of the ennobled fountains, when I sing of the ilex-tree set upon the hollow crags, from whence thy babbling brooks dance down." [1] So Horace addresses the spring flowing by his farmhouse of Digentia, the ruins

[1] Horace, *Od*. iii. 13, Lonsdale and Lee's translation, London, Macmillan, 1874, p. 64.

of which are still shown in the upper valley of the Licenza, above the village of Roccagiovine.

Pliny, speaking of the great love for nature displayed by noble Romans, mentions Passienus Crispus, orator, consul, husband of Agrippina, and Nero's stepfather, who owned a grove on a hill near Tusculum named Corne,[1] where lived a tree which he cherished and worshipped above all things. He would embrace it, and lie under its shade, and pour wine on its roots. The same grove contained another venerable ilex-tree, thirty-four feet in circumference, which, at a great height from the ground, divided itself into ten branches, each equalling a large trunk in size. Pliny calls

The valley of the Anio near Roccagiovine.

this ilex a forest by itself. There is no doubt that love of nature and appreciation for natural beauty were instinctive among the Greeks, and, in a lesser degree, among the Romans. It is revealed in the graceful shape of their temples, in the harmony of their polychrome ornamentation, in the arrangement of their floral decorations, and above

[1] The present Villa Cavalletti, west of Frascati.

all in the selection of sites for their places of worship. In this last respect they remain unrivalled. The following lines were suggested to Chateaubriand by the sight of the temple of Minerva on the promontory of Sunium. "The Greeks," he says, "excelled not less in the choice of the sites of their edifices than in the architecture of the temples themselves. Most of the promontories of the Peloponnese, of Attica, Ionia, and the islands of the Archipelago were crowned with temples, trophies, and tombs. These monuments, surrounded by woods and rocks, viewed in all the accidents of light, sometimes enveloped in sable thunderclouds, sometimes reflecting the soft beams of the moon, the golden rays of the setting sun, or the radiant tints of the dawn, must have imparted incomparable beauty to the coasts of Greece. Thus decorated, the land presented itself to the mariner under the features of the ancient Cybele, who, crowned with towers and seated on the shore, commanded her son Neptune to pour forth his waves at her feet.

"Christianity, to which we are indebted for the only species of architecture conformable to our manners, also taught us the proper situations for our structures. Our (mediæval) chapels, our abbeys, our monasteries, were scattered among woods and upon the summits of hills, not that the choice of sites was always a premeditated design of the architect, but because art, when in unison with the customs of a nation, adopts instinctively the best methods that can be pursued."

And speaking of the present degeneration of feeling on this point, especially in connection with civic edifices, he adds : "Did we ever think, for instance, of adorning the only eminence that overlooks Paris ? Religion alone thought of this for us." [1]   He could have mentioned likewise Notre

[1] *Travels in Greece, Palestine,* etc., by F. A. de Chateaubriand, translated by Frederic Shoberl, 2d ed., London, Colburn, 1812.

Dame de Fourvières at Lyons, Notre Dame de la Garde at Marseilles, Notre Dame of the Haute Ville at Boulogne, and many others, which appear to the pilgrim and to the mariner in the same glorious light as the shrines and temples which once crowned the headlands of the Ægean and the Tyrrhenian seas.

Were we to take a survey of the Campagna, and of the various ranges of mountains by which it is framed, from a lofty point of vantage, — from the dome of St. Peter's, for instance, or from the belfry of S. Maria Maggiore, — we should be surprised at the number of high peaks consecrated to the Deity in ancient or mediæval times, but which the modern generations have deprived of their beautiful ruins and their beautiful clothing of green. From the Mons Albanus, upon which stood the federal temple of Jupiter, to the Mons Afflianus, crowned by the temple of the Bona Dea, and to Soracte, once sacred to Apollo, each summit once bore a white temple visible from every corner of the old land of Saturn, or a mediæval abbey, under the roof of which the weary pilgrim might find rest, help, and protection. Temples and churches have equally disappeared ; and woe to the lonely traveller seeking shelter from the fury of the storm, or advice about his lost track. Silence and desolation reign alone on the abandoned peaks !

Early Roman religion can best be studied in two institutions which date from the beginning of the City, the sisterhood of the Vestals and the priesthood of the Arvales. I have spoken at length of the first in chapter vi. of " Ancient Rome," and I have nothing to add to the account already given. Before entering, however, into the subject of the Arvales, I must mention another branch of rural worship, that of the gods who protected the ancestral field from the encroaching of the neighbor.

The early settlements in the lower valley of the Tiber, Antemnæ, Fidenæ, Collatia, Veii, Gabii, Ardea, and Rome, were all organized on the same system, as far as division of property was concerned. Their walls or palisades or earthworks enclosed an area ten times as large as that required by the number of inhabitants, because they shared it with their flocks, and each hut, made of a framework of boughs and covered by a thatched roof, had its own orchard and sheepfold. This condition of things has been admirably illustrated by the discoveries made at Veii and Antemnæ, under my personal supervision, where traces of huts (hard-trodden, coal-stained floor within a ring of rough stones) have been found at a considerable distance from each other. The city of the Palatine was not different from Veii and Antemnæ; in fact, the characteristics of the "agellus" and the sheepfold must have been even more prominent in Rome, because its population was essentially pastoral. The village had two gates, the names of which have come down to us: one, leading to the Rumon (river), was called "Rumanula;" the other, leading to the pasture lands of the Oppian, was called "Mugonia," from the lowing of cattle.

The agellus attached to the huts contained also the family tombs. The neighborhood of the River-gate was called "ad Statuam Cinciæ" because there was the "sepulcrum familiæ" and the "casa" of the Cincii.[1] In this state of things it was necessary to define and protect the limits of each piece of ground which had become hereditary, because it had been cultivated and settled upon by one single family for a certain lapse of time. The trees growing nearest to the boundary line became, therefore, "arbores finales et terminales," sacred to Terminus or to Silvanus; and when there were no trees available for the purpose,

[1] The family tomb and the family hut.

The cliffs of Veii at the Ponte Sodo.

they would make use of stones, or of wooden posts called "stipites oleagini" or "pali sacrificales." The setting up of these boundary marks was consecrated by a sacrifice ; a trench was dug, a victim was slain, its blood was cast into the trench, together with corn, fruit, incense, honey, and wine ; the whole being consumed by blazing pine-brands. On this bed of ashes the stone or post was set up. The "Terminalia" or annual feast of the Terminal gods fell on February 23 ; and was celebrated among neighbors, as well as by the city in general. The public festival was performed at the sixth milestone of the Via Laurentina, probably because this was originally the extent of the Roman territory in that direction.

To explain the evolution of these shapeless stones and posts into the beautiful "hermæ" of later times, we must refer to the Greek custom on this subject. There were to be seen in many parts of Greece heaps of stones at the crossings or roads, or on the boundaries of land, called ἑρμεῖα, ἑρμαῖα, ἑρμαῖοι λόφοι, because Hermes was the presiding god over the common intercourse of life, traffic, journeys, roads, boundaries, and so forth. The heaps of stones were succeeded in progress of time by a single block, the sacred character of which was acknowledged by pouring oil upon it and adorning it with garlands of wild flowers. The first attempt at an artistic development of the rude block was the addition of a head, in the features of which the characteristics of the god were supposed to be expressed. This is the origin of the " hermæ " or " hermuli " statues composed of a head placed on a quadrangular pillar, the height of which corresponds to the stature of the human body. They became very popular objects among the Greeks, who lavished them in front of their houses, temples, gymnasia, palestræ, libraries, porticoes, at the corners of streets, at the crossings of highroads as signposts with distances inscribed upon them, etc. So great was the demand for these hermæ that the word ἑρμογλύφος became the synonym for a sculptor. They retained their original name even in case the head or bust represented no deity at all, but the portrait of an illustrious man. This last class was in great demand among the wealthy Romans for the decoration of their gardens and villas, in which places, strange to say, they were brought back to their original scope, being used as posts for wooden railings, on the border line between the paths or avenues and the lawns or shubberies or pine groves. In this case they were commonly crowned with the portrait busts of philosophers, historians, poets, tragedians, each being inscribed with the name of its subject. It is easy to understand what benefits the science of iconography has derived from these labelled portrait heads ; in fact, one of the first archæological handbooks produced in the sixteenth century is the " Imagines Virorum Illustrium " of Fulvio Orsino, published in 1570 by Antonio Lafreri with more than a hundred exquisite illustrations.

The wealthy and learned Romans of the last century of

The Pianella di Cassio near Tivoli.

the Republic or of the Golden Age of Augustus, who covered the hillsides of Tusculum, Tibur, and Præneste and lined the shores of Antium, of Formiæ, and Bajæ with their magnificent country seats, paid this tribute of honor to every one who had obtained fame in the literary and scientific world, none excepted. We remember, for instance, the excitement caused in 1896 by the discovery of the fragments of the poems of Bacchylides, which were so beautifully reproduced in facsimile by F. G. Kenyon. There is no use in denying that the name of the great lyrist, born at Julis, in the island of Ceos, towards the middle of the fifth century

B. C., considered by the ancients as a worthy rival of Pindar, was almost ignored or forgotten at the time of the discovery. Not so in ancient times. The Romans offered to Bacchylides the same honors they were wont to pay to Pindar.

The evidence of this fact, not generally known to students, is to be found in the discoveries made in 1775 at the " Pianella di Cassio " among the ruins of the Villa of Brutus, one mile east of Tivoli, or the road called di Carciano or Cassiano. To the substructures of this delightful villa, built partly in opus incertum, partly in the so-called Pelasgic or polygonal masonry, age has given a golden-brownish hue, such as is seen in the late fall in our forests, when the setting sun strikes the half dried leaves of the oak or the chestnut. The gardens are now represented by groves of olives, two or three centuries old, the quiet green of which harmonizes well with the color of the ruins. (See page 99.)

As the sixteenth century can boast of the finds made by Paul III. in the Baths of Caracalla, the seventeenth of those made by Innocent X. and Clement X. in the palace of the Valerii on the Cælian, so the following one will be remembered forever for the discoveries obtained in this Villa of Brutus. Visconti describes the search as " uno dè più insigni scavi dè nostri tempi." Seventeen statues were brought to light from the ruins of a hall of basilical type, and twenty hermæ from the site of the gardens. There were the portrait busts of Antisthenes, Bias, Periander, Æschines, inscribed with their names, and the headless hermæ of Anacreon, of Chabrias, of Pittacus with the motto " Know the time, " of Solon with the motto " Not too much," and of Cleobulus with the motto " Keep an even mind." There were seven plinths or pedestals of hermæ bearing the names of Pisistratus, Lycurgus, Archytas, Hermarchos, Diogenes ; and lastly of Bacchylides and

Pindar. All these marbles are now exhibited in the Sala delle Muse in the Vatican Museum.

In respect of discoveries and excavations the reign of Pope Braschi will remain quite unrivalled. Instead of fettering or forbidding private enterprise and of grudging to private collectors every fragment, however indifferent, of antique marbles or terracottas, Pius VI. invited landowners and excavators to collaborate with him in the recovery of works of art and of epigraphic documents. I am just now perusing the registers of the Vatican Museum of the last quarter of the eighteenth century, and I simply wonder

The motto " Know Thyself " in a mosaic floor in a tomb of the Appian Way.

at the exquisite taste and discernment of the pontiff who would allow no one but himself to decide on the subject of acquisitions for the Museo Pio Clementino, or of exportation of antiques to foreign countries. And whenever exportation was denied, or an embargo put on a statue or on an inscription, he declared himself ready to purchase the object at a just price. No wonder that his call should have been answered by many, and that the greatest activity should have prevailed in the field of discoveries.

Were we to accept in a strict sense Roman religious traditions, the brotherhood of the Arvales and the worship of the Dea Dia ought to be considered even older than the worship of Vesta and the sisterhood of the Vestals. These referred their institution to the time of Numa, the Arvales to the time of the founder of the City. The Arvales formed a college of twelve priests whose duty it was to offer sacrifices for the prosperity of the fields (*arva*) and to implore the blessings of heaven on the produce of the soil. The legend says that when Acca Larentia lost one of her twelve sons, Romulus allowed himself to be adopted in his place, and called himself and the other eleven " fratres Arvales ; " but, as I have remarked in chapter i. of " Ancient Rome," legends are not necessary to prove the extreme antiquity of the brotherhood. In the commentaries, or minutes of its periodical meetings, of which I shall speak presently, it is said that, whenever iron tools were brought into the sacred grove of the Dea Dia, as for engraving the annual records on the base of the temple, or for the lopping and felling of the trees, expiatory sacrifices were performed " ob ferri inlationem," or " elationem," that is, to purify the temple and the grove from the unlawful contact with the metal. This practice shows that the worship was instituted in the age of bronze, before the introduction of iron. The abhorrence of the use of iron, however, is not the only recollection of prehistoric ages to be found in the Arvalian ritual. It was known that at the time of the foundation of the City, the

inhabitants used pottery and domestic earthenware made
by hand and baked in an open fire, exactly like the one
which is found in the necropolis of Alba Longa buried
under three strata of volcanic sand, lapilli, and other erup-
tive materials. In memory of this primitive state of things
the use of earthenware was obligatory, or at any rate preferred in sacrifices and libations. Even the sacred fire of
Vesta was kept burning in an earthen receptacle. Juvenal
describes the " Simpuvium Numæ," the drinking cup of
Numa Pompilius, — a relic preserved down to the fall of the
Empire, — with exactly the same words we should use in describing the fossil pottery of Alba Longa. Now in the Acta
Arvalium the following record is engraved more than once :
" ollas precati sunt " (they have addressed their prayers to
earthen jars). In reading this statement we could not help
thinking of the worship of Numa's drinking cup ; still, no
evidence of the fact could be produced. In 1870, I do not
remember exactly whether at the foot of the temple of the
Dea Dia or on the highest part of the sacred grove, eighteen
prehistoric cups were found, which, although in a more or
less fragmentary state, could be recognized as absolutely
identical with the fossil pottery of Alba Longa.

The sacred grove and place of meeting of the Arvales
was at the fifth milestone of the Via Campana, now called
Strada della Magliana, on the slope of a hill now occupied
by the Vigna Ceccarelli, at a place quaintly called " Affoga
l' Asino." The writer of the otherwise excellent article in
Smith's Dictionary, vol. i. p. 199[b], speaking of the Arvales
meeting " in luco deæ Diæ via Campana apud lapidem V.,"
says, " There is no road known as the Via Campana, and the
one on which the spot is actually situated leads to the mouth
of the Tiber, and not into Campania. The phrase . . .
probably means country road (Feldstrasse) and may con-

The Vigna Ceccarelli, the former seat of the Arvales.

tain a trace of the process by which the district round Rome has come to be known as the Campagna." This statement is incorrect. The via was called Campana, from the remotest antiquity, because it led to the Campus Salinarum Romanarum, even now retaining its twenty-six centuries old name of Camposalino. I have been able to discover this point in a rather unexpected way.

Before the marshes of Maccarese and Camposalino — the ancient salt work of the Vejentes — were drained in 1889, a boatman used to ferry sportsmen from the local railway station to the shooting-grounds, on the opposite shore of the swamp, and fasten his canoe to a rope attached to a heavy piece of marble, in the place of an anchor. In the winter of 1887 the antiquarian Alberici, while duck-shooting in that boat, noticed that there were letters engraved on the face of the marble. On closer examination it proved to be a valuable document, viz., the plinth of a statuette representing the Genius of the guild of salt-carriers (*Genius saccariorum salariorum*) who carried the salt in sacks from the Campus Salinarum to Porto and to Rome, following the road accordingly named Via Campana. This valuable document is now exhibited in Hall I. of the Museo Municipale al Celio.

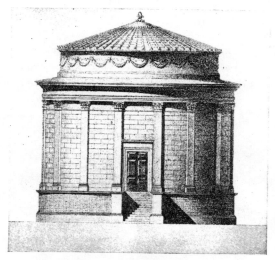

The Temple of the Dea Dia restored.

The first discovery of the seat of the Arvales at the fifth milestone of this road, in a field then belonging to Fabrizio Galletti, seems to have taken place under the pontificate of Gregory XIII., about 1575. Flaminio Vacca has left the following account of the find : " Outside the Porta Portese, at a place called ' affoga l' Asino,' in a cane-field near the Tiber, many statues of eminent personages were dug out, together with the pedestals on which their names were inscribed, and with columns 30 palms long. These were sawn into slabs and made use of in the Cappella Gregoriana at

St. Peter's ; the statues were dispersed among many collectors in Rome." Traces of earlier excavations have, however, been detected in a fly-leaf from the pocket-book of Salvestro Peruzzi († 1573), son of Baldassarre († 1536), which is now preserved in the Galleria degli Uffizi, Florence. Salvestro gives the sketch of a graceful little edifice with an apse and a pronaos, and says that it contained nine statues of emperors wearing the badge of the Order, viz., the " corona spicea," and nine pedestals with dedicatory inscriptions ending with the words FRATRI ARVALI. Salvestro's account is not accurate, unless two pedestals were destroyed or burnt

The head of Augustus as Frater Arvalis.

into lime at once ; contemporary epigraphists mention only seven dedications inscribed with the names of Hadrian, Antoninus Pius, M. Aurelius, L. Verus, Septimius Severus, Caracalla, and Gordianus.[1] The fact that all the predeces-

[1] *Corpus Inscr.* vol. vi. n. 968, 1000, 1012, 1021, 1026, 1053, 1093.

The west wing of Michelangelo's cloisters.

sors of Hadrian are missing, while the set from Hadrian to
Gordian III. is almost complete, shows that the sacred
grove, or at least the Cæsareum, must have undergone at
the beginning of the second century the same fate by which
the House of the Vestals was destroyed at the time of Septimius Severus. The records of the Vestales Maximæ discovered in that house begin with the reconstruction by Julia
Domna, and continue almost without a break to the suppression of the Order in 382. The only iconographic relic
of earlier days pertaining to the Augusteum of the Arvales
is the marble head of Augustus himself, formerly in the
Villa Mattei and now in the Sala dei Busti of the Vatican
Museum (n. 274), which represents the emperor at a ripe
age, with a garland of ears of wheat, the symbol of the
fraternity to which he belonged. I shall not follow in
detail the history of subsequent discoveries from the time

of Salvestro Peruzzi to the present day, because it has already been given by de Rossi and Henzen.[1] These discoveries were splendidly brought to a close in 1868–1871 by Dr. Wilhelm Henzen, then director of the German Archæological Institute, when nearly one thousand lines of the Acta, with other inscriptions and architectural remains of the temple and other edifices, were brought to light, in the " Vigna Ceccarelli di Sopra," near the railway station of La Magliana.　The Acta, purchased by the Italian government in 1873, have been admirably rearranged in chronological order by Dr. Dante Vaglieri in two of the old Cistercian " Hermitages " on the west wing of Michelangelo's cloisters in the Baths of Diocletian. (See p. 107.)

From these records we learn the following details.　The oldest fragment yet found dates from A. D. 14, the last of Augustus, the first of Tiberius.　The calendar of the brotherhood dates also from the same epoch.　We infer from these facts that the system of engraving the minutes of the proceedings on marble must have been taken up soon after the reform of the Order accomplished by Augustus after his election to the pontificate in B. C. 2.

The Arvales, the only Roman religious institution in which the name of " brothers " occurs, were twelve, double the number of the Vestals ; but absence from town, illness, and other circumstances so thinned their ranks that the average number of members attending one meeting is five. The fullest meeting recorded in the space of two hundred years is that of October 12, 59, when twelve members met to offer a sacrifice for the " imperium " of Nero.

The seats were not hereditary, even in the case of imperial personages.　The place of a private nobleman, L. Æmi-

---

[1] De Rossi, " Vicende degli atti Arvalici," in *Annali Instituto*, 1858 ; Henzen, *Acta Fratrum Arvalium*, Berlin, Reimer, 1874.

lius Paullus, was given in December, A. D. 13, or January,
14, to Drusus Cæsar, son of Tiberius; and that of his
grandson, Drusus the younger, again to a private individual,
P. Memmius Regulus, A. D. 38.

The president (*magister*) of the fraternity was elected
on the second day of the feast of the Dea Dia, at the beginning of May, and his tenure of office lasted for a year. It
was his duty to entertain his colleagues at dinner in his own
house, during the same May celebrations; but if the house

FERIAE·ET·SVPPLICATIONES
AD·OMNIA·PVLVINARIA
Q·FD·CAESAR·AVGVST·IN SICILIA·VICIT

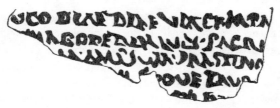

Two specimens of the Acta Arvalium of the first and third centuries.

was too small or otherwise unfit for the reception of the
noble guests and their attendants, the tables were set up
elsewhere, — for instance, in the Augusteum (A. D. 218).
At all events, when we hear of the brothers banqueting at
such and such a house, we need not be afraid that the host
had to meet the expense of the proceedings; he simply
supervised the arrangements. These banquets were costly
enough; one hundred denarii a seat.[1] The minutes of the
year were engraved on the marble stylobate of the temple,

---

[1] About seventy shillings, or seventeen dollars.

proceeding from left to right at the end of each " magisterium " or presidency, viz., after the 17th of December. The following incident shows that they did not tarry long in transferring the minutes from their books to the marble panels of the stylobate. The Emperor Vitellius ended his presidency on December 17 of the year 69, and was murdered before the end of the month. Now as his name is erased from the minutes in consequence of the " memoriæ damnatio " pronounced by the Senate soon after his death, it is evident that they must have been inscribed between the 17th and the 31st.

Comparing the chronology of the Acta with the precise spot in which they have been found, Professor Henzen has been able to follow the progress of their incision on the various marble surfaces available in the grove. As I have said above, advantage was taken at the beginning of the base of the temple, with little or no concern for space, devoting probably each marble panel to the records of one year ; no matter whether they covered the whole space or left a blank. The writing surface on the base of the temple lasted until the time of Antoninus Pius. Later on, the blanks were filled up with no respect to chronology, so that the records of the year 213 were engraved at the foot of the panel of A. D. 155, those of the year 219 at the foot of the panel of A. D. 90, etc. Fortunately the grove contained other marble edifices, like the Cæsareum, where the images of deified emperors were kept and worshipped ; the Tetrastylum, where meetings were held and banquets celebrated ; and a Circus, where races were run on the second day of the May festival. These edifices, the Cæsareum and the Tetrastylum at least, were resorted to for the engraving of the Acta ; those of A. D. 218 were actually written on a table or " mensa," and those of 220 on a marble chair or " cathedra."

The dispersion of these valuable documents all over the
City and the Campagna is really astonishing. Fragments,
nay, whole panels, have been found at S. Prisca and at S.
Sabina on the Aventine, in the Villa Negroni-Massimo on
the Esquiline, in the foundations of the apse and sacristy
of St. Peter's, in the pavement of St. Paul's, in the Villa

The church of S. Marina at Ardea.

Wolkonsky, in the catacombs of Hippolytus and Callixtus,
in the bed of the Tiber. This scattering of the Arvalian
marbles is manifestly connected with the great religious
evolution of the fourth century ; in fact, we know that
when the doctrines of Christ began to gain ground in the
outskirts of the metropolis, and in the farm lands of the
Campagna, the grove of the Arvales, as the oldest suburban
centre of superstition, became one of the main points of
attack. The evangelization of the country, however, had to
overcome far greater obstacles than that of the City. The
Latin peasants were — and are still — an ignorant race,
tenacious of old habits and traditions. They clung to the
religion of their fathers because it pleased them to know

and to feel that their interests were intrusted to the never failing care of local spirits, their own personal friends as it were, and because they saw in the commonest phenomena of nature the manifestation of a superior power. Springs, rivers, caves, trees, forests, hills, and mountains all appeared to those simple minds fraught with life, and visible embodiments of divine agents. They divided these salutary and beneficent beings into two classes : one comprising the higher gods of nature, Apollo, Diana, Silvanus, Pan, etc. ; the other restricted to local spirits, nymphs, fauns, and the "genii loci." The belief in this last category dates from an earlier stage than the conception of deities with wide provinces and multiple functions. The primitive settlers in the woodlands of Latium divinized every hill, or tree, or brook, more distinct personality being attributed to the nymphs, because the abundance or scarcity of water was more important than anything else in nature, to the herdsmen and to the laborers of the soil. The various groups of nymphs had their special haunts and abodes in watery glades, in groves, among the frowning crags, or in the dark recesses of grottoes, where sacrifices were offered to them of goats, lambs, milk, and oil, but never of wine. Some of these "nymphæa" were private, and reserved to the peasants of one single farm ; others public, the gathering-place of a wide neighborhood. These were selected on certain days of the year for the celebration of joyful processions and of rural sports, and for thanksgiving after the successful close of harvesting, sheep-shearing, of the vintage, and so on. For this purpose special calendars or almanacs were made up for the use of the peasantry and set up at the crossings of country roads. Such is the so-called "Menologium Rusticum," formerly in the possession of Mgr. Colocci, and now in the National Museum at Naples.

This rustic almanac contains as many columns as there are months in the year, each marked by the corresponding signs of the Zodiac. Then follow the names of the months, the number of their days, the determination of the nones

The campanile of Castel S. Pietro above Palestrina struck by lightning.

(and indirectly of the ides, which fell eight days after), the length of days and nights, the name of the sign through which the sun passes, and the god under whose care the month was placed. For instance : —

" The month of May. Thirty-one days. The nones fall on the 7th. Length of day fourteen and a half hours, of

night nine and a half. The sun enters into the constella-
tion of Taurus. The month is under the protection of
Apollo."

The various agricultural operations of the month of May
are subsequently specified, such as the winnowing of the
cornfields, the shearing of sheep, the washing of wool,
the breaking of oxen, etc. The column ends with the religious duties to be performed in May, viz., the lustration of
the crops, and certain sacrifices to Mercury and Flora.

It is easy to conceive what obstacles the preachers of the
gospel must have found in these deeply rooted superstitions
in consequence of which the Campagna remained essentially
pagan long after the gods had been expelled from their
temples in the City. The study of local traditions, of folk-
lore, of the origin of many suburban sanctuaries and
shrines, would help us greatly to make out how the religious
transformation of the Campagna was gently brought about.
To facilitate it great care was taken to assimilate practices
which were not absolutely objectionable, — for instance, the
Ambarvalia, which were transformed into the Rogations, —
and to substitute parallel figures with an affinity of names to
the gods of rivers, of springs, of mountains, and of forests.
Thus the places of Apollo and Silvanus were taken by St.
Silvester, on the forest-clad peaks of Soracte, of the Monte
Compatri, of the Monte Artemisio, and of the Vulturella ;
S. Marina or S. Marinella became the protector of mariners
at Ardea (see p. 111), at Ostia, and at Punicum ; St. George
became the driver away of plague-spreading dragons ; while
the points struck by lightning, whether of church towers or
of mountains, were consecrated to Michael the Archangel.

The picturesque shrines which the explorer of the Campagna and of the Sabine and Volscian districts meets at the
crossings of roads and lanes have not changed their site

A wayside shrine.

or purpose ; only the crescent which once shone on the forehead of Diana the huntress is now trodden by the feet of the Virgin Mary, who also appears crushing the head of the snake once sacred to Juno Lanuvina ; but the wild flowers still perfume with their delicious scent the " iconetta," as the shrine is still called in the Byzantine fashion among our peasantry (small εἰκών), and the sweet oil, instead of being poured over the altar, burns before the image of the Mother of God in quaint little lamps. The month of May, once sacred to the Dea Dia, has become the month of Mary.

We are not acquainted with the particulars of the " Chris-

tianization " of the sacred grove of the Arvales, the records of the brotherhood ending with the reign of Gordian
III. (about 238 A. D.). The portrait statue of the same
emperor is the last, chronologically speaking, discovered
among the ruins of the Cæsareum. We may assume,
therefore, that the institution, ten centuries old at the time
of Gordian III., died of sheer decrepitude towards the
middle of the third century, when the Christians appear on
the spot, or rather under it, honeycombing the hill with
the winding galleries of their cemetery of Generosa.

I have already spoken of these small but interesting catacombs in chapter vii. of " Pagan and Christian Rome "
(p. 332). The name of Generosa pertaining to them indicates that the ground under which they ramify, or where
their entrance was, belonged to a lady of that name.
Without assuming that this lady Generosa had purchased
part of the old Arvalian property, it may be simply a case
of an enclave within the boundaries of the grove. And,
moreover, the first Christians, the first illustrious victims of
the persecution of Diocletian, were not laid to rest in crypts
purposely cut out of the rock, but in common sand-pits, to
which entrance was gained from the side of Generosa's farm.

One of the curiosities of this underground cemetery is
a painting of Christ in the character of the Good Shepherd,
on the edge of whose tunic we see twice the sign 卐, called
" crux gammata " because it is formed by the grouping of
four Γ (gamma). The sign never appears in the catacombs
so long as that of the anchor remains in favor. Its first
representation is to be found, if I remember right, in the
celebrated painting of Diogenes the fossor of the crypts of
Domitilla, whose tunic is embroidered with the mystic device, instead of the usual " calliculæ " and " clavi." Now
as the 卐 is the primitive Asiatic symbol of happiness, the

"svastika" of the Brahmins and Buddhists, certain writers have attempted to find in it a link between Buddha and Christ, between the Indian religion and the gospel. Enough to observe that the svastika, as a mere ornamental combination of lines, appears in prehistoric pottery of the æneolithic period, in the coins of Gaza, Corinth, and Syracuse, in the fibula of Cære, in the so-called Samnitic tomb at Capua, in Roman mosaic pavements, etc.

Among the many symbols of the cross adopted by the

The Good Shepherd with the svastika.

faithful in the age of persecutions, with which they could mark the grave of the dear ones without betraying the secret of their faith, there was the Phœnician letter *tau*.

From the tau, +, to the crux gammata, 卐, the transition is hardly perceptible.

There is no doubt that while these things were going on underground in the cemetery of Generosa, the grove of the Arvales, the temple, the Cæsareum, the Tetrastylum, were kept in good repair by the state, although practically abandoned by the brotherhood. Possibly the action of the state was limited to preventing the neighbors from trespassing over the boundary line of the grove and damaging its buildings and stealing away their marble decorations. Certainly not the smallest fragment of the Acta has been found used by the Christians in the adjoining catacombs. But granted that men did not lend a helping hand to the slow destructive powers of nature, we can easily imagine what the state of the place was after a century and a half of neglect, when it was given up altogether to Pope Damasus as Church property. If a fig-tree could have found time to set root and grow on the pediment of the temple A. D. 183, as described in the minutes of that year, at the time of the greatest prosperity of the Order, we may imagine what masses of arborescent vegetation must have covered the roof at the end of the fourth century. The grove, also, must have shown traces of neglect, exposed as it was to the fury of storms, so violent in this district between Rome and the sea that the minutes mention over and over again trees struck by lightning and felled to the ground. I am afraid that it also gave shelter to outlaws, as shown by the wholesale slaughter of Julius Timotheus, schoolmaster, and seven of his pupils, made by a gang of highwaymen on the very edge of the grove, as described in " Ancient Rome," p. 212.

It seems as if Pope Damasus had watched with impatience the moment he could take legal possession of the place, and build aboveground and on the highest and most conspicuous point a memorial chapel, *sanctis martyribus simplicio Faus*TINO VIATRIC*i*, whose graves had made the catacombs of Generosa a favorite place of pilgrimage. The oldest dated epitaph found within this chapel of Damasus belongs to A. D. 382, the very year in which the worship of the gods was officially abolished by Gratian, and the property of temples confiscated or transferred to the Church.

The grove of the Arvales was not the only one which brought back to the Romans of the late Empire the memory of the primitive state of their soil and of the veneration which their ancestors professed towards the sylvan gods. Rome had been founded in a well-wooded country, each of the seven hills being distinguished by a special growth of trees from which they were sometimes named. A forest of laurels grew on the Aventine the recollection of which lasted to the end of the Empire in the streets named " Lauretum maius " and " Lauretum minus " respectively. The valley between the Aventine, and the Palatine is said to have derived the name of Murtia from the myrtle grove which surrounded the shrine of Venus Murtea.[1] The Cælian, likewise, was called Querquetulanus from its forest of oaks (quercioli); the Oppian, Fagutalis from its forest of beeches; the Viminal from its reeds (vimina); the Campus Codetanus from its *Equisetum arvense* (codeta); the Corneta from its cornelian trees, etc. With the growth of the City many of these landmarks disappeared, their memory being perpetuated by a cluster of trees which were held in great veneration, and to which sacrifices were offered. There is a large map of these sacred groves, published by Agretti and Visconti in 1838,[2] and a good account of them is to be

---

[1] Compare, however, Becker, *Topographie*, p. 467, n. 971.

[2] *Pianta dell' antica città di Roma con i suoi boschi sacri*, Roma, 1838.

found in Brocchi's " Stato fisico del Suolo di Roma," p. 24 sq. Agretti and Visconti have marked the site of forty-four groves, but the existence of some of them is not sufficiently authenticated. At the end of the Empire probably there were only twenty or twenty-five left.

Such being the sylvan nature of the Roman soil, no wonder that one of the first gods to be worshipped by the semi-savage inhabitants of the Septimontium should be Faun, whose prophetic warnings and mysterious voice they imagined were heard from the recesses of the forests. The Bona Dea, the supposed bride of Faun, had also a share in the divine honors, and was herself called Fauna. Silvanus, however, was the special protector of woods and trees, especially of pines and cypresses ; hence his name of Silvanus dendrophorus, the " bearer of a tree." Woods sacred to the deity were called " luci " in opposition to " silvæ " or " nemora," which names designate an ordinary forest.

It is remarkable, indeed, that one of these luci should have survived through the events of centuries, and should still be flourishing, still venerated, still called by its classic name of " Bosco Sacro." I allude to the cluster of fine ilexes on the west side of the valley della Caffarella, near the so-called grotto of the " ninfa Egeria " and the church of S. Urbano. Inscriptions discovered in that neighborhood[1] show that these lands once belonged to Annia Regilla, wife of Herodes Atticus ; that after her death in childbirth the lands were consecrated to the gods ; that they contained wheat-fields, vineyards, olive groves, pastures, a village named Triopium, a temple dedicated to Faustina under the title of New Ceres, a burial plot placed under the protection of Minerva and Nemesis, and lastly a grove sacred to the memory of Annia

[1] Ennio Quirino Visconti, *Iscrizioni greche Triopee, ora Borghesiane*, Rome, 1794. See Bibliography in *Pagan and Christian Rome*, p. 288.

The sacred grove of Annia Regilla.

Regilla. The remains of the Triopium are to be seen in the Vigna Grandi ; the family tomb is represented by the exquisite little building known as the " tempio del Dio Redicolo," the temple of Ceres and Faustina by the church of S. Urbano. As regards the sacred grove, there is no doubt that the present trees continue the tradition and live on the very spot sacred to the memory of Annia Regilla, " cuius hæc prædia fuerunt."

Modern Romans, alas, have not inherited from their ancestors the feeling of respect for the sylvan gods. I do not belong to the party which has taken up the habit of condemning whatever has been done in Rome since 1870 ; far from it. I believe, and I am proud to assert, that the little we have lost is nothing in comparison with what we have gained in health, in cleanliness, in comfort, in purposes of life, in self-respect. The only point of regret is the one concerning the green, the shade and the vegetation, against which rulers and ruled, magistrates and citizens, clergy and laity seemed at one time to have developed an equal share of contempt, if not of hatred. When the beautiful Villa Corsini was purchased by the City in 1876 to be turned into a public park, the splendid old ilexes lining the crest of the hill were cut down under the plea that they obstructed the view. When a considerable part of the Monti Parioli was likewise purchased in 1887 for the laying out of the great Parco Margherita between the Via Flaminia and the Salaria, the oaks and the ilexes of the Villa Bosio were sold to a charcoal-burner. When a government delegate took possession of the administration of the City in 1892, he inaugurated the restoration of the finance department by cutting down the small garden of the Piazza Mastai, the keeping of which involved an expense of nearly three pounds a year! Another picturesque corner of the Parco Margherita, the " Sassi di S. Giuliano," — weatherstained crags plunging into the Tiber a little above the Ponte Molle, — has just been stripped of its crown of evergreens to allow a private contractor to quarry stone ; and the ragged outline of the rocks has been cut and smoothed to an angle of 45°, like a railway embankment. With such examples coming from official quarters, no wonder that owners of private villas should have sold them to the first comer who offered money enough to satisfy their greed. It is true that the sale and the destruction of the historic Roman villas has brought luck to none ; sellers as well as purchasers are equally bankrupt ; but this well-earned retribution does not give us back what we have lost. Let me say, however, that a decided change for the better has taken place of late in this branch of public administration. Over ten thousand trees are planted every year in Rome and the suburbs, and if the " Arbor day " shall be celebrated for some years to come with equal zeal, the City will be framed again in green as in the palmy days of its history.

I must at the same time remark that the feeling of respect for *single* trees, like the cornelian of the steps of
Cacus, the fig-tree of the Comitium, the chamærops of the

A picturesque corner in the new Passeggiata del Gianicolo.

Capitol, the *Diospyros Lotus* of the Vulcanal, the olive-tree
and the vine of the Forum, has survived through the middle
ages, and is still alive in Rome. In the middle ages whole
quarters of the City were named from single trees conspicuous in the wilderness of the ruins. Such is the origin of
the name of the ninth ward, the "Rione della Pigna" (pine-
tree), and also of the streets and squares called del Fico,
della Gensola, dell' Olmo, dell' Arancio, del Lauro, etc. A
lemon-tree is shown in the garden of S. Sabina planted by
St. Dominic himself when he took possession of the adjoining convent at the time of Pope Honorius III. (1216–1227).
In the garden of S. Onofrio, which now forms part of the

Passeggiata del Gianicolo, stands Tasso's venerable oak, under the shade of which the poet used to retire for meditation and study. It was partly blown down by the hurricane of October, 1842, but several branches have since sprouted out of the trunk. I have in my collection of prints a spirited etching by Strutt, representing the oak before its fall. The same fate befell in 1886 Michelangelo's cypresses in the garden of la Certosa, two out of four being destroyed, and the others mutilated. (See page 107.)

Perhaps the most touching instance of care and respect towards old trees is to be found in the Alban hills, in the avenue which leads from Albano to Castel Gandolfo, known by the name of " Galleria di Sotto." Wherever one of the old giants — ilexes, oaks, or elms — planted by Sixtus V. at the end of the sixteenth century shows signs of decrepitude and begins to lean and bend as if asking for help and support, its branches and its trunk are propped by means of columns of masonry. The person who shows such delicate feelings towards the noble trees of Castel Gandolfo is Pope Leo XIII., himself a splendid specimen of vitality at an age which it is seldom given to mankind to reach.

I have spoken up to the present time of sylvan gods and goddesses who were beneficial to mankind. Let us now turn our attention to the evil geniuses, whose pernicious influence those simple dwellers on the Palatine hill sought to avert, and whose wrath they strove to appease, by special propitiations.

The evil genius was symbolized amongst the Eastern nations, especially amongst the Chaldeans, by the serpent; and the Bible represents the first and bitterest enemy of mankind under the same form. Bossuet, in his " Elévations à Dieu," speaking of the fall of man, remarks : " Pourquoi il [Dieu] détermina cet ange superbe à paraitre sous cette

forme, plutôt que sous une autre ; quoiqu'il ne soit pas néces-
saire de le savoir, l'Ecriture nous l'insinue, en disant que le
serpent était le plus fin des animaux ; c'est à dire celui qui
. . . représentait mieux le démon dans sa malice, dans ses
embûches, et ensuite dans son supplice." [1]   Step by step the
serpent conquered divine honors.   In Egypt it was made
to personify the principle of evil conquered by Osiris.   In
the paintings or in the hieroglyphic papyri of the earliest
dynasties the symbol of two serpents springing at each other
is often seen, one of which seems to snap at a ball which
the other holds in its mouth : an evident allusion to the

Tasso's oak by S. Onofrio.

dualism in Eastern religions.   At a later period the theo-
gonic condition of the serpent improved, and it became ultimately a symbol of the Sun and of Life.   In the belief of

[1] " Though it is not necessary for us to know why He decreed that that
proud angel should appear in this shape, rather than in another, the Scriptures
hint at an explanation in saying that the serpent was the most subtle of all animals . . . and therefore the one that best represented the devil in his malice,
in his treacheries, and finally in his punishment."

Latin aborigines, long before the foundation of Rome, the serpent symbolized the "genius loci," and as the oldest Latin gods were worshipped through their respective geniuses [1] the serpent became the living symbol of some of them,

The young Hercules strangling the serpent.

— of Æsculapius, the god of medicine; of Minerva, the goddess of wisdom; of Mercury, the god of subtleness; and, above all, of the Juno called Lanuvina from Lanuvium, the seat of her worship. The sacred serpents of Lanuvium are still alive, and I am sure it will interest my reader to know some curious details collected on this point by Professor Tommasetti, a great explorer of the Roman Campagna.[2]

[1] The Genius Jovis, the Genius Junonis Sospitæ, the Genius Deæ Diæ, etc.

[2] "Nuove ricerche sulla spiaggia latina," in *Atti Pontif. Accad. di Archeologia*, 26 Nov., 1896.

The serpent of Juno of Lanuvium was not an abstract symbol; a live specimen of a particular species was kept in a cave, within the sacred grove adjoining the temple of the goddess; pilgrims and devotees offered it food and votive e m b l e m s ; and whenever doubts were cast on the honesty of a young girl she was compelled to undergo the judgment of the serpent, by which she was devoured if guilty. The behavior of the sacred animal

The Juno Lanuvina.

was also taken as an omen for the coming harvest. These human sacrifices, the evidence of remote antiquity in the worship of the goddess, lasted at least up to the second century of the Christian era, when Ælianus wrote his well-known account (x. 16). According to Prosper of Aquitania, the institution was still flourishing in the fourth and fifth centuries, but the live serpent of classic times had been superseded by a mechanical contrivance of tremendous power. This artificial serpent was of great size; from its eyes, made of precious stones, darted fiery sparks; it held a sword in its mouth; and when the unsuspecting girl descended the steps of the cavern to lay her offering before the dragon, she unconsciously touched a spring which set the mechanism in motion and made the sword fall on her neck. The fraud was discovered at last by a Christian hermit, a friend of Stilicho, who, having obtained admission somehow into the cave, felt his way at every step with a cane, until he succeeded in touching the spring, and in making the sword fall without injury to himself. On hearing of the monk's discovery the Christians of the neighborhood invaded the cave, destroyed the dragon, and probably levelled the temple of Juno to the ground.

We have the evidence of these extraordinary events not only in the magnificent statue of the goddess herself, now in the Rotunda of the Vatican, but in the actual existence of a special kind of serpents in the territory of Lanuvium.

Cicero, " De Divin." i. 79, describes how the nurse of Roscius discovered him wound in the coils of a snake in a field called Solonium, " qui est campus agri Lanuvini." Atia, the mother of Augustus, born according to the tradition alluded to by Suetonius (Aug. 6) in the neighborhood of Velitræ and Lanuvium, bore a serpent's mark on her skin. The Solonium mentioned by Cicero is actually called Dragone and Dragoncello, the Field of the Dragon; and a church built there in the middle ages was dedicated to St. George, the driver-away of dragons. Professor Tommasetti thinks that the peculiar kind of serpents bred within the precincts of the temple must have been dispersed after the abandonment of the sanctuary, but that they did not migrate too far. In the farm of Carrocceto, right under the hill of Civita Lavinia, there is to be found the largest species of

THE MONTE DELLO SERPENTE, AVENTINE

(inoffensive) serpents known to live in the Roman Campagna, and these serpents are actually called by the peasantry " Serpenti della Regina," a manifest allusion to Juno magna Sospita Regina, as the goddess of Lanuvium was officially named. But I have myself something to add to Professor Tommasetti's interesting remarks. I have just found in some long-forgotten records of the state Archives that the section of the Aventine hill upon which stands the church of Santa Sabina was called in the middle ages " Lo Monte de lo Serpente," a manifest reminder of the great temple of Juno Regina, on the remains of which — shattered by the earthquake of A. D. 422 — the church of S. Sabina was built by Peter the Illyrian in 425.

CHAPTER IV.

THE TRUTH ABOUT THE GRAVE OF ST. PAUL — THE BASIL-
ICA PAULLI IN THE FORUM, AND THE BASILICA PAULI
APOSTOLI ON THE ROAD TO OSTIA.

SPEAKING of the fire which swept over the Forum in the
year 210 B. C. under the consulship of Marcellus and Lævi-
nus, Livy says, xxvi. 27, 3, that the flames leapt directly
from the public square upon the private houses around
"because they were not screened, as they are now, by a
belt of basilicæ." In fact, the first edifice of this kind was
erected only in 184 by M. Porcius Cato the elder, under
the name of Basilica Porcia. The institution became at
once so popular that, before the end of the Republic, five
more "regal halls" were built for the accommodation of
the habitués of the Forum : the Sempronia in 169 on the
line of the Tabernæ Veteres, the Opimia in 121 by the
temple of Concord, the Fulvia in 179 by the Argiletum,
the Æmilia in 54, and the Julia in 46 (rebuilt and enlarged
by Augustus in the year 12).

The basilicæ are identified generally with our law-courts,
but such was not their exclusive purpose. They were
used not only for the administration of justice but also for
exchanges, or places of meeting for merchants and men of
business. The two uses are so mixed up that it is difficult
to say which was the principal one. We, "laudatores
temporis acti," are in the habit of seeing things rather
idealized whenever we speak or think of bygone times,
and we like to picture the Forum of Republican Rome

as an august and mighty place, in which the destinies of the world were discussed and decided upon, where state trials were conducted, slaves tortured, and the bodies of state offenders, who had undergone capital punishment, exposed on the Gemonian steps, until the executioner would hook them to a chain and drag them across the pavement to one of the openings of the Cloaca Maxima.

The Forum was altogether a much gayer, a more vulgar and matter-of-fact centre of life; used for military reviews and parades as well as for public banquets, gladiatorial fights, and shows of every kind, including exhibitions of works of art, paintings, statues, panoramas, and wonders of nature, such as the serpent fifty cubits long, exhibited at the time of Augustus. Whenever one of these celebrations took place, the shops and the porticoes were hung with shields and tapestries lent to the Ædiles by private collectors, and stands were erected, with seats for hire, much to the annoyance of the populace, whose accommodations were thus considerably reduced. C. Gracchus put an end to this practice by setting fire, in the darkness of night, to the stands.

As regards the every-day city life, we may take the Forum as a place of rendezvous and intrigue; where all kinds of transactions were practised, from the hiring of waiters and flute-players for "at homes" to the borrowing of large sums of money. The shops, originally rented to butchers and schoolmasters, became in time more attractive and ornamental. Civil and criminal cases were tried at the statue of Marsyas, the meeting-place of lawyers, witnesses, and clerks; while auctioneers and slave-merchants usually met by the Argentariæ. The Canalicolæ, a drunken and sharp-tongued race, complainers of everything and everybody, were to be found along the gutter by which the rain-water was drained into the cloaca. Well-to-do citizens preferred the lower end of the Forum and the Sacra Via, lined by the beautiful shops of jewellers, perfumers, and makers of musical instruments. The neighborhood of the Vortumnus at the entrance to the Vicus Tuscus (Via di S. Teodoro) bore an ill fame, and so did the lower Subura, the notorious headquarters of pickpockets and receivers of stolen goods. Copyists, booksellers, and shoemakers had established themselves along the Argiletum, fruiterers and florists on the Summa Sacra Via, and vendors of bronze vases near the temple of Janus.

The basilicæ, likewise, were haunted by a special and generally disreputable set of men, such as fishmongers, who poisoned the vestibules and colonnades with the offensive smell of their merchandise; the " subbasilicani," concocters and propagators of false news and spicy gossip; and, above all, the bankers and brokers with their usual retinue of usurers, money-lenders, and shady men of business. The arcades of the Julia and of the Æmilia and the middle section of the street " ad Janum " may truly be called the Bourse and the Exchange of ancient Rome.

Before the beginning of the present campaign of exploration it was known that the Basilica Æmilia, the most beautiful of Roman structures of the golden age, lay buried under the block of houses on the north side of the Forum, between the churches of S. Adriano and S. Lorenzo in Miranda; but what its plan and size were, what its state of preservation, what the style of its architecture, no one could tell. The results of the excavations have been rather disappointing to the general public, who labored under the delusion that the place had never been excavated before, though not to us students, who had foreseen the state of despoilment of the basilica in reading the accounts of the search for

THE WEST COLONNADE OF BASILICA JULIA, FROM THE VICUS JUGARIUS

Site of Basilica Æmilia before excavation.

marbles made at the time of Paul III. by the architects of
St. Peter's. The history of the place is briefly this : First
constructed in 179 B. C. by the censors M. Fulvius Nobilior
and M. Æmilius Lepidus, under the name of Basilica Fulvia,
it was repaired a century later by another Æmilius, consul
B. C. 78. His son, L. Paullus, having received from Julius
Cæsar a gift of 1500 talents, rebuilt the hall from the foundations. The work lasted twenty-five years, and the third
dedication of the " Æmilia Monumenta," as Tacitus calls it,
took place in 34. A fourth restoration is mentioned under
Augustus, a fifth and the last under Tiberius. Classic
writers, while expatiating in general terms on the marvellous beauty of the building, give no particulars, except that
it was " columnis e Phrygiis mirabilis," that is, that it was
admired for its columns of pavonazzetto, the purple-veined
marble quarried near Synnada, in the heart of Phrygia.
We owe this particular to Pliny the elder, xxxvi. 24, 2, who

published the Natural History in A. D. 77, after the fire of Nero (A. D. 65) and before the fire of Titus (A. D. 80). We know, therefore, that the basilica had not been damaged on the former occasion ; but did it escape uninjured on the second ?   And what was its fate in A. D. 283, when another great conflagration, which goes by the name of Carinus, raged from one end to the other of the Sacra Via, destroying the Basilica Julia, the Senate House, the Græcostasis, and the Forum Julium, that is to say, the edifices by which the Æmilia was surrounded on every side ?   Probably it suffered a certain amount of damage, which must have been made good soon after, because we find the basilica mentioned again towards the middle of the fourth century.   And here our information ends.   What became of it after that time is only a matter of conjecture.   Yet it is not improbable to suppose that its spoils were made use of in the construction of the Basilica Pauli Apostoli on the road to Ostia in A. D. 386.

I have already described, in " Pagan and Christian Rome," p. 150, how the memorial church raised by Constantine over the grave of the Apostle was too small and inadequate for the accommodation of pilgrims who flocked to it in vast numbers from all parts of the world where the doctrines of Christ had been made known.   Constantine had had no intention of placing St. Paul in an inferior rank to that of St. Peter, or of showing less respect for his memory ; but, while the position of St. Peter's grave in relation to the circus of Nero and the cliffs of the Vatican was such as to give Constantine perfect freedom to extend the basilica in all directions, especially lengthwise, the case with that of St. Paul was remarkably different, because the highroad to Ostia — the channel by which Rome was fed — ran only a hundred and fifty feet east of the grave itself.

THE EXCAVATIONS OF THE BASILICA ÆMILIA

The Triumphal Arch of Honorius at St. Paul's.

Hence the necessity of limiting the size of the church within these two points.

In 386 Valentinian, Theodosius, and Arcadius wrote to Flavius Sallustius, prefect of the City, declaring that if the S. P. Q. R. would give their consent for the suppression of a certain old road which ran back of the apse of the Constantinian church, they were ready to rebuild the church *ex novo*, changing its front from east to west, and extending it towards the Tiber, so as to make it vie in size and beauty with St. Peter's. The consent was willingly given, and the reconstruction, begun in 388, was completed in 395 by Honorius, as certified by the verse

THEODOSIVS CÆPIT PERFECIT HONORIVS AVLAM

which we read on the " triumphal arch " at the top of the nave, together with the name of Galla Placidia, sister of

Honorius, and wife of Atawulf, king of the Goths, at whose expense the arch was covered with the glorious mosaics.

I need hardly say that the new edifice was erected at the expense and with the spoils of older ones, which had once formed the pride and glory of imperial Rome. In fact, we cannot find among the sacred and profane buildings of the fourth and fifth century a single one which could not be compared in this respect to Æsop's crow. If the S. P. Q. R. themselves, to perpetuate the memory of Constantine's victory over Maxentius, erected an arch by the Meta Sudans with the marbles of two or three older ones, and of several patrician mausoleums, the builders of churches did not hesitate, to be sure, to follow the example and lay hands on whatever pagan edifice best suited their purpose. From this point of view our churches can be divided into two groups : those built with the spoils of only one classic monument, such as S. Maria Maggiore, S. Pietro in Vinculis, and S. Lorenzo fuori le Mura, the columns of which were removed from the Macellum Liviæ, the Porticus Tellurensis, and the Opera Octaviæ respectively ; and those built at the expense of several, like St. Peter's, the Lateran, S. Agnese, S. Clemente, etc.

The church of St. Paul of the time of Theodosius and Honorius belongs really to both classes, because although its pavement was patched with nearly one thousand inscriptions stolen with equal freedom from Christian as well as from heathen cemeteries, and although the columns dividing the inner from the outer aisles were of unequal size and quality, yet the twenty-four columns of Phrygian marble, by which the nave became renowned all over the world, beautifully matched in color and finish and crowned with capitals of the same exquisite cut, must have been removed from one and the same edifice.[1]

---

[1] The columns of the nave were forty in all, all fluted and well matched ;

Archæologists have inquired as to their place of origin. Nicolai and Piale contend that they were removed from the Mausoleum of Hadrian; Fea and Nibby identify them with the "columnæ Phrygiæ" which, according to Pliny the elder, made the Basilica Paulli in the Forum "mirabilis" and unique. The controversy has by no means died out. It was taken up again in 1888 by de Rossi and Huelsen

The Basilica Pauli Apostoli, destroyed by fire in 1823.

against myself, and after a debate which took up two whole sittings of the Archæological Institute (January 27 and February 3), it ended, as parliamentary debates do, by each side retaining its own view.[1]

of those nearer to the arch of Placidia, nine on the right and seven on the left were of white marble, the rest of pavonazzetto, a marble as beautiful as it is easily tarnished by the combined action of dust and damp. Cardinal Antonio Finy († 1743) caused ten columns to be cleaned at his expense. His example was followed by other cardinals. The last four were polished by order of Benedict XIV. They measured 10.25 metres in height, 1.19 metres in diameter, with an intercolumniation of 1.81 metres.

[1] Compare *Mittheil.* 1889, p. 242 ; Thédenat, *Le Forum*, p. 161 ; *Bull. arch. Com.* vol. xxvii. 1899, p. 169.

At the beginning of the present campaign we felt sanguine that the spade would be more successful in clearing up the matter than all our reasoning, but unfortunately the search was given up when hardly two fifths of the basilica had been laid bare. Of one thing, however, we are sure, — that a considerable section of the building was dismantled and levelled to the ground at the end of the fourth century, that is, at the precise time when the church of St. Paul was raised on the road to Ostia.

We must remember that shortly after peace and freedom were given to the church, and the doors of temples began to be closed, it became the fashion among the victorious Christians to place pagan buildings under the protection of saints whose names sounded more or less like those of the gods just expelled from the structure or of the founders and former owners of the place. For instance, if a chapel was erected within the precincts of a palace or of a villa which had belonged to one of the Cæsars, or to the imperial domain in general, it was dedicated to St. Cæsarius. Thus we find a church Sancti Cæsarii in Palatio on the Palatine; another of the same denomination in the villa near Velletri, where Augustus passed his youth; and a third at the eighteenth milestone of the Via Labicana, where Maxentius owned a large estate. Temples of Jupiter were dedicated to St. Jovinus or Juvenalis, temples of Saturn to St. Saturninus, temples of Apollo to St. Apollinaris, etc. On the door of the church of S. Martina, built on the alleged site of the Martis forum (Marforio) the following play upon words was engraved: —

MARTYRII GESTANS VIRGO MARTINA CORONAM
EIECTO HINC MARTIS NUMINE TEMPLA TENET.

No wonder, then, that the materials of the Basilica Paulli should have been chosen to adorn the grave and the memorial church of the apostle of the same name. The two names, in fact, seem to have been purposely put, as it were, in opposition, or rather in comparison, as shown by the following incidents. Towards the beginning of the fourth century it became the fashion to fasten on the neck of run-away slaves and dogs a brass ring from which hung a label giving the name and the address of the owner, with the request that, in case of a renewed attempt to escape, the fugitive should be arrested and brought back to his mas-ter. These small keimelia are of great interest on account of the topographic indications they contain, such as " ad ædem Floræ ad Tonsores," " in regione quinta in area Macari," " ad Mappam Auream in Abentino," " de regione XII ad balineum Scriboniolum Romæ," etc. Nineteen such addresses are registered in vol. xv. p. 897 of the " Corpus Inscr. Lat." The collars of slaves are distin-guished from those of dogs by the formula " servvs svm " (I am the slave of . . .) with which they begin. Two labels, one undoubtedly of a dog, the other probably so, contain the following words · —

Corpus n. 7138 : AD BASILICA(*m*) APOSTOLI PAVLI ET DDD NNN FILICISSIMI
PECOR(*arii*) ;

n. 7189. TENE ME QVIA FVGI ET REBOCA ME IN BASILICA PAVLLI AD LEONEM ;

which mean respectively : " I am the dog of Felicissimus, shepherd of the Basilica of the apostle Paul, (rebuilt by) our three Lords " (Valentinian II., Theodosius, and Arcadius), and, " Hold me because I ran away and take me back to Leo (the porter ? of) the Basilica Paulli." These two labels have been quoted by de Rossi as if they prove that the two basilicas were in existence at the same time, and there-fore that the columns of the pagan could not have been made use of in the Christian, but there is no evidence of synchronism. In fact, the dog of Felicissimus the shepherd is by some years the younger of the two, as shown by the palæography of their respective labels.

The latest document certifying the existence of the basilica in the Forum is to be found in the pedestals of Gabinius Vettius Probianus, who was prefect of the City in 377, nine years before the reconstruction of St. Paul's. This energetic magistrate took a leading part in the removal of the statues of gods from temples to civic buildings, such as forums, baths, and courts of justice, where they were set up again and exhibited as mere works of art.[1] Seven or eight such pedestals have already come to light, some on the Sacra Via in front of Faustina's temple, some from the Basilica Julia, some from the Æmilia. Those of the Julia declare expressly how Probianus " has put up this statue to ornament the Basilica Julia which he has lately restored," those of the Æmilia contain the more vague formula, "statuam conlocari præcepit quæ ornamento *basilicæ* esse posset *inlustri*." Together with these and other pedestals a set of plinths has been found, with inscriptions which show their respective statues to have been the work of Praxiteles, of Polycletus, of Timarchus, of Bryaxis, etc. Could we behold once more, could we catch only a glimpse of this marvellous array of masterpieces, by which the Sacred Way of the decadence was transformed into the finest art gallery the world has ever seen, where every famous artist and school was represented by its best productions! Unfortunately they were not chiselled in marble but cast in bronze, which means that they all are beyond hope of rediscovery.

It is to be regretted that the excavation of the Æmilia has been given up, at least for the time being, when the section laid bare amounts scarcely to two fifths of the total

---

[1] "Stabunt et æra innoxia quæ nunc habentur idola ! " Prudentius, *Peristeph.* ii. v. 479, 480.

area. As far as we can judge at this imperfect stage of exploration, the noble building comprised three parts : a central hall divided into nave and aisles by a double line of columns ; a row of rooms or offices on either side of the hall, opening on the outside porticoes ; and these last - named porticoes, which decorated the longitudinal sides of the building.

The rooms, or offices, each 5.41 metres wide, 7.15 metres deep, the pavement of which is inlaid with white and polychrome marbles in graceful and sober design, were identified soon after their discovery with the "Tabernæ Novæ" of the republican Forum — unnecessarily, I believe.

The rooms form part of the essential plan and frame of the basilica,

A " candeliera " or marble pilaster of the Basilica Æmilia.

corresponding in width to the arcades of the portico on which they open ; in other words, there are as many rooms as there are arcades in the façade. Edifices of this kind must have had plenty of meeting and sitting rooms for jurors, judges, lawyers, clerks, and witnesses; others in which records and " pièces à conviction " were kept. It may be possible also that some of the apartments were let to bankers and money-lenders, called "argentarii" and "nummularii" respectively. Well known are the nummularii of the Basilica Julia, like T. Flavius Genethlius, a Thracian by birth, who took to banking after having been a rider in the circus, or L. Marcius Fortunatus, who married the girl Zoe when only sixteen years of age.[1] If this sort of people showed partiality for the Julia, it is easy to conceive what a competition there must have been about renting rooms in the Æmilia, which stood right in the "Wall Street" of classic Rome.

The existence of bankers (*argentarii*) at Rome can be proved as early as 309 B. C., although silver (*argentum*) was not coined in Roman mints before 268 B. C. Their name, however, can be very well explained if we regard them as the changers of foreign (especially south Italian and Etruscan) silver coins into Roman bronze currency. In progress of time the money-changing business passed into the hands of an inferior class of agents, called "nummularii," while pure banking-affairs, like the opening of current accounts, the receiving of deposits, the making of loans, was reserved to the argentarii. They acted in a strictly private capacity, and whenever in early times we hear of public or state bankers, we may be sure they were appointed for a special emergency, under the name of "tres viri mensarii," chiefly to lend money to private individuals during a financial crisis, such as those which occurred in B. C. 351 and 216. When the public treasury lent aid to business men in a similar stress A. D. 33, Tiberius seems to have done it through ordinary bankers, who at all events were always considered to exercise a public function. Just as stockbrokers in London are licensed by the Lord Mayor, and in Dublin by the Lord Lieutenant, so in Rome the bankers were under the super-

[1] *Corpus Inscr.* vol. vi. 9709, 9711, etc.

vision of the prefect of the City, and in the provinces under that of the governor.

The business transacted in their offices were the " permutatio," or the exchange of foreign for Roman coin, subject to the payment of a small agio — the drawing of bills of exchange payable by correspondents abroad, an operation which made it imperative for the banker to be acquainted with the current value of the same coin in different countries and at different times, and the keeping of sums of money for clients. If the money was deposited by the owner as a " depositum," that is, to save himself the trouble or danger of keeping it and making payments, then the banker paid no interest, but simply honored the cheques of the client as long as there was a balance in his favor ; but when the money was deposited, as a " creditum," at interest

A marble panel from the Basilica Æmilia.

for a specified lapse of time, the banker was allowed to use and invest it as he thought best for the common interest.

In case of failure the law enacted that the claims of the " depositarii " should be satisfied before those of creditors who had money at interest in the bank. " Of all this business," says Professor L. C. Purser,[1] " of the receipts as well as of the expenditure the bankers kept accurate accounts in books called 'codices,' 'tabulæ,' or 'rationes,' and there is every reason for believing that they were acquainted with what is called in bookkeeping 'double entry.'"

The central hall of the basilica, where justice was dispensed, was divided into nave and aisles by two rows of columns, of which many pieces have been found. The pavement, quite well preserved, is inlaid with slabs of giallo, portasanta, africano, cipollino, etc., all rectilinear and arranged so as to harmonize in design with the site of the columns.

The peculiarity of this pavement is that it has been found covered from one end to the other with loose copper coins of the end of the fourth century. And as this abnormal dispersion of coins was either contemporary with or very soon followed by a raging fire (ashes, coals, and burnt matter in general have been found all over the place, forming the first and lowest layer of the stratified rubbish) many of them have been melted and welded together into a shapeless mass of metal. These masses, as well as single coins, have also been cemented against the slabs of the pavement, which appears all marked with spots of verdigris. I do not know how many thousand specimens of this worthless currency have been put aside just now ; but what I know is that, great as their number may be, we are only collecting what the Cinquecento excavators have left for us to pick, after appropriating the better part of the spoils. Bartolomeo Marliano, contemporary with the looting of the basilica in 1531, mentions " magnam æreorum nummorum copiam " (a great quantity of copper coins) found by the marble-cutters and limeburners of his days. This band of devastators did irreparable injury to the

[1] In his excellent article in Smith's *Dict.* vol. i. pp. 179–183.

basilica, reaching the lowest level of its foundations in their
quest for building materials, and wrenching from their sock-
ets even the tufa blocks upon which the columns of the
nave stood. The spoliation of the Basilica Æmilia can be
compared only to that of the temples of Cæsar and Vesta, of
which merely the cores of the foundations remain to mark
their respective sites. That of the Æmilia must have

The oldest known view of the ruins of the Forum, now in the Escurial.

begun at a very remote period, probably before the end of
the fourteenth century, when we hear of a great limekiln,
called the " calcaria ecclesiæ sancti Adriani," established
among its ruins, and fed with its marbles. A second campaign of destruction was inaugurated in 1431, when Pope
Eugenius IV. granted leave to Filippo di Giovanni da Pisa,
stonecutter, to demolish the " old walls known to exist
in the place called Zeccha antiqua," by which name the
" ciceroni " of the fifteenth century used to designate the
neighborhood of S. Adriano. According to Flavio Biondo,

an eyewitness, it took ten years to uproot the foundations
of the basilica and to burn into lime whatever materials
had escaped the kilns of the preceding century ; but in
fact the destruction lasted many years longer, through the
pontificates of Calixtus III. and Pius II.

Towards the end of the century nothing was left standing except a corner of the edifice, to which the name of
" Forinbuaro " (Forum Boarium) had been applied, for the
same reason that Metella's mausoleum is still called " Capo
di Bove," that is, on account of the bulls' heads or skulls
sculptured on the frieze. This noble ruin had probably
been spared by the Quattrocento vandals out of respect for
the saint, whoever he was, under whose protection they were
placed and whose chapel they contained. Cardinal Adriano
Castelli da Corneto, however, did not carry his scruples so
far ; he simply laid hands on the last remnant of the basilica
in 1496, making use of the marbles for his palace (now Tor-
lonia-Giraud) in the Borgo di S. Pietro.

Bramante, Antonio da Sangallo the elder, Fra Giovanni
da Verona, and Baldassarre Peruzzi have left most interesting drawings of what they saw discovered and destroyed
on this occasion, which I have reproduced in facsimile in
my Memoir on the Senate House in the " Atti dei Lincei "
for January, 1883, vol. xi.

After this long tale of disasters we should feel inclined
to believe that the wretched spot was left in peace ; but we
have yet to deal with the worst gang of depredators, those
of Paul III., whose deeds positively cast into the background
those of the so-called barbarians of Alaric, Genseric, and
Robert the Norman. I have related in " Ruins and Excavations," p. 247, how sentence of death was passed on the
monuments of the Forum and of the Sacra Via on July 22,
1540, by a brief of the genial Pope Farnese by which the

Commissioners for the rebuilding of St. Peter's were given absolute liberty to search for ancient marbles wherever they pleased, to remove them from antique buildings, and to pull these buildings to pieces if they thought it best for their purpose. They started from Faustina's temple in 1540–41 and reached the opposite site of the valley by the Vortumnus and the Augusteum nine years later, carrying off, burning into lime, crushing into fragments every vestige of the stone-work and marble decoration of the arches of Fabius and Augustus, of the temples of Cæsar and Vesta, of the Regia, of the Augusteum, etc. As regards the Æmilia, it seems that, to revenge themselves for their disappointment at finding the place looted already, they uprooted out of pure wantonness the foundations down to the level of spring water, because the possession of a few blocks of tufa certainly could not have repaid the trouble and expense of boring such deep trenches.

By a singular chance two marble blocks, containing only eight letters, escaped their attention ; but these eight letters, PAVL . . . and REST . . . , tell a long and decisive tale. They bring back to our memory the last episode in the history of the building, the RESToration made at the time of Tiberius by a PAVLus (Æmilius), descendant of the founder. Other marble fragments have been found near the site of the limekiln, or else lying on the pavement of the Via ad Janum. They all belong to the true golden age of Roman art.

Let us now turn our attention to the discoveries made quite lately in connection with the basilica and grave of Paul the Apostle, whose figure appeals to us more forcibly than any other in the history of the propagation of the gospel in Rome. I do not speak so much of reverence and admiration for his work, as of the sympathy and charm

inspired and conveyed by his personal appearance. In all
the portraits which have come down to us by the score,
painted on the walls of underground cemeteries, engraved
in gold leaf on the love-cups, cast in bronze, worked in
repoussé on silver or copper medallions, or outlined in mosaic, the features of Paul never vary. He appears as a
thin, wiry man, slightly bald, with a long, pointed beard.
The expression of the face is calm and benevolent, with a
gentle touch of sadness. The profile is unmistakably Jewish ; in fact, although born in a gentile city, and of parents
who had acquired by some means the Roman franchise,
although brought up to speak and write with freedom and
mastery the Greek language, and made to feel the influence and the atmosphere of a cultivated community, Saul
was essentially a Hebrew of the Hebrews. As to the air of
refinement which pervades his countenance, we must remember that, though he was a σκηνοποιός or tentmaker by
trade, we are not obliged to believe that he was actually
compelled to manual labor. The province of Cilicia in
general, and Tarsus, his birthplace, in particular, were
known for the manufacturing of a goat's-hair cloth called
cilicium, largely used for tents. It is not impossible that
Saul's father may have owned one such establishment, in
which the future apostle underwent his apprenticeship.

The picture I have attempted to sketch does not differ
essentially from the one drawn by Conybeare and Howson [1]
from elements gathered from Malalas, Nicephorus, and the
apocryphal " Acta Pauli et Theclæ." Conybeare and Howson ascribe to the apostle a short stature, a long face with
high forehead, an aquiline nose, close and prominent eye-
brows. " Other characteristics mentioned are baldness,
gray eyes, a clear complexion, and a winning expression. Of

[1] *Life and Epistles of St. Paul*, p. 762[b].

The road by which St. Paul approached Rome.

his temperament and character St. Paul is himself the best painter. . . . We perceive the warmth and ardor of his nature, his deeply affectionate disposition, the susceptibility of his sense of honor, the courtesy and personal dignity of his bearing, his perfect fearlessness, his heroic endurance." [1]

I believe that the attempt made by Jowett some forty years ago, to demolish what he calls a blind and undiscriminating admiration for Paul, by representing him as a man whose appearance and discourse made an impression of feebleness, out of harmony with life and nature, a confused thinker, expressing himself in broken words and hesitating form of speech, with no beauty or comeliness of style, has met with but little success.

St. Paul saw Rome for the first time in the month of January of the year 61. After his eventful journey across the sea, from Adramyttium to Fair Havens and Malta, his shipwreck on the coast of that island, and a second crossing to the Bay of Naples, he landed at Pozzuoli, and following

[1] Smith, *Dictionary of the Bible*, ed. 1863.

the Via Campana to Capua, and the Via Appia to Forum Appii, Tres Tabernæ, and Bovillæ, entered the city by the old Porta Capena.[1]

Julius, the centurion of the eleventh legion Augusta, who had accompanied him by order of Porcius Festus, governor of Judea, handed him over to Afranius Burro, prefect of the Prætorium. He was given a sort of bail, with freedom to preach and evangelize, under the supervision of a police officer. After a lapse of two years, no accuser having come forth to challenge his appeal to the emperors, he underwent his trial in the " consilium principis " and was restored to full liberty and the full enjoyment of his rights of Roman citizenship. The trial probably took place in November or December, 63.

Here ends the evidence of the Acts of the Apostles, which St. Luke is supposed to have finished in the spring of 64. Other particulars about St. Paul's travels and apostolic life may be gathered from the Epistles. He visited Rome for the second time in the year 66, and after a long term of imprisonment was executed at the Aquæ Salviæ on the Via Laurentina, on June 29, in either 67 or 68.

In examining the various details concerning St. Paul's visit to Rome, his execution, his burial, we must sift what is pure and conclusive biblical or archæological evidence from what does not go beyond the limits of a pious tradition or a devout legend. For instance, when we are told that the hired house in which the apostle " mansit biennio " (lived for two years), preaching the gospel freely (" docens quæ de domino Jesu Christo sine prohibitione "), is the one. the remains

---

[1] Compare, among others, Smith, *Voyage and Shipwreck of St. Paul,* 3d ed., London, 1866 ; Farrar, *Life and Work of St. Paul,* London, 1879, vol. ii. chap. xliv., xlv. ; Ramsay, *St. Paul the Traveller and the Roman Citizen,* London, 1895, p. 315.

THE PLACE WHERE ST. PAUL WAS EXECUTED

of which are to be seen under the church of S. Maria in
Via Lata, we must not give credit to the statement; [1] because those remains belong, not to a private dwelling, but
to a great public edifice, to the Septa Julia, one of the
architectural masterpieces of Agrippa, which extends along
the Corso (Via Flaminia) from the Piazza di Venezia to the
Piazza di Sciarra, including the sites of the palaces di Venezia, Bonaparte, Gavotti, Doria, Simonetti, and others. It is
impossible to believe that a private citizen could have lived
in the Septa Julia.

Again, when we are told that St. Paul found shelter in
another Roman house, the site of which is actually marked
by the church of S. Paolino alla Regola, Via dei Vaccinari,
that being the Jewish quarter and the proper field for the
apostle's preachings, we must not believe the statement;
because the Ghetto, the Jewish quarter of ancient Rome,
was in the Transtiberine region and not in the Campus
Martius.[2] But when we come to the question of the friendship between the apostle and the philosopher Seneca, Afranius Burro, M. Annæus Gallio, and other eminent personages of the imperial court, — friendship denied by many as

---

[1] " And he abode two years in his own hired dwelling, and received all that
went unto him [xxviii. 30], and preached the kingdom of God, and taught what
concerned the Lord Jesus Christ with boldness, none forbidding him [xxviii.
31]." " We infer, therefore," Canon Farrar says, " that Paul's hired apartment was within close range of the Prætorian Camp."

[2] In the excavations which the American School of Athens carried on in
1898 at Corinth, a marble lintel was found among the ruins of a house of the
Roman period, upon which the letters

$$(συν)ΑΓωΓΗ \; ΕΒΡ(αιων)$$

were engraved. The thought arose that the stone belonged to the very synagogue where Paul " reasoned . . . every sabbath, and persuaded the Jews and
the Greeks." The inscription, however, is much later than the apostolic age ;
it simply proves that the meeting-place, made famous by the preaching of
Paul, continued to flourish down to a very late period. Compare Dr. Richard-
son's article in the *Century,* 1899, p. 854.

an impossible occurrence, — archæological evidence shows the fact to be absolutely true. I have already spoken in " Pagan and Christian Rome," p. 16, of the funeral tablet found at Ostia in 1867, inscribed with the words " Sacred to the memory of Marcus Anneus Paulus Petrus, son of Marcus Anneus Paulus," which gives us the proof of the bond of sympathy and esteem established between the Annei — Seneca, the consul suffectus at the time of the first trial of St. Paul; his brother Gallio, governor of Achaia — and the founders of the church in Rome. No wonder that Tertullian, " De Anima," xx., should call the first, " Seneca sæpe noster " (Seneca very often one of ours) !

How strange it seems that students and visitors in general should pay so little attention to the grave of this remarkable man, remains of which have been found at the fourth milestone of the Via Appia, on the left or east side of the road !

L. Annæus Seneca, son of the rhetorician Marcus, a Spaniard by birth, a Roman by residence, banished to Corsica, A. D. 41, on the suggestion of Messalina, was called back to the capital in 49, and made the tutor of the young Domitius. On the accession of his pupil to the imperial throne, under the name of Nero, Seneca became one of his chief advisers, exerting his influence to check his vicious propensities, but taking advantage at the same time of his place of trust to amass an immense fortune. His suburban villas of Alba, Nomentum, Bajæ, etc., vied in extent and magnificence with those belonging to the crown, especially one, located four miles outside the Porta Capena, which Juvenal calls " magni horti " and Tacitus " suburbanum rus." The conspiracy of Piso, A. D. 65, gave Nero the long-sought-for pretext to get rid of the ill-tolerated adviser ; and although there was little or no evidence of his being a party to the plot, his death was decided upon. Seneca, suffering from asthma, had stopped for rest, on his return from Campania, at his villa on the Appian Way, when Granius Silvanus, tribune of one of the prætorian cohorts, surrounded the estate

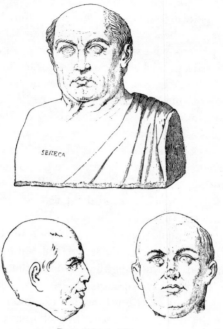

Portrait bust of Seneca.

with his men, and showed the doomed man the death warrant. Without betraying any emotion, "Seneca cheered his weeping friends by reminding them of the lessons of philosophy. Embracing his wife, Pompeia Paulina, he prayed her to moderate her grief, and to console herself for the loss of her husband by the reflection that he had lived an honorable life. But as Paulina protested that she would die with him, Seneca consented, and the veins in the arms of both were opened. Seneca's body was attenuated by age and meagre diet, perhaps also from his attacks of asthma; the blood would not flow easily, and he opened the veins in his legs. His torture was excessive; and to save himself and his wife the pain of seeing one another suffer, he bade her retire to her chamber. His last words were taken down in writing by persons who were called in for the purpose, and were afterwards published. Seneca's torments being still prolonged, he took hemlock from his friend and physician, Statius Annæus, but it had no effect. At last he entered a warm bath, and as he sprinkled some of the water on the slaves nearest to him, he said that he made a libation to Jupiter the Liberator. He was then taken into a vapor bath, where he was quickly suffocated. Seneca died, as was the fashion among the Romans, with the courage of a Stoic, but with somewhat of a theatrical affectation which detracts from the dignity of the scene." [1]

When the Appian Way was excavated in 1852–53 by order of Pius IX. some reminders of the philosopher's fate were discovered in the neighborhood of the fourth milestone : the lid of a sarcophagus representing the death of Atys, son of Cresus (a subject evidently chosen as a veiled allusion to the death of Seneca himself), a marble head showing a remarkable likeness to his well-known features, and other fragments of a tomb of the first century. All these relics were set up by Canina on the spot on which they had come to light, as shown in the accompanying illustration. However, as Seneca was almost certainly cremated and not inhumated, the sarcophagus cannot pertain to him, though the resemblance of the head to the inscribed portrait of the Villa Mattei cannot be questioned. Another

[1] Marindin, in Smith's *Classical Dictionary*, ed. 1894, p. 863.

The Via Appia by the so-called tomb of Seneca.

reminder of the same event is to be found in the inscription discovered by Nibby and Gell, while surveying this section of the road in 1824, in which mention is made of a Quintus Granius Labeo, son of Marcus, tribune of the third legion.[1] If we recollect that Granius was the name of the officer of the same rank, Nero's messenger of death to Seneca, that he was given in recompense for his services the very villa in which the tragedy had taken place, and that, after his suicide in 66, the property must have been inherited by a near relative, we cannot help connecting the tomb of the Granii with that of Seneca himself.

To come back to the grave of St. Paul: tradition says that his body was claimed from the executioner by the inevitable matron Lucina [2] and laid to rest in certain catacombs

---

[1] *Corpus Inscr.* vol. vi. 3521.

[2] This merciful lady, if we believe the agiographs of a later age, seems to have been connected with the most famous executions of Christians from the apostolic age to the beginning of the fourth century.

which the pious lady owned on the left or east side of the
Via Ostiensis, back of the apse of the present church, where
the sandstone cliffs of the Vigna Salviucci rise to the height
of forty-two metres above the valley of the Tiber. Here
the sacred remains rested in peace until the persecution
of Valerian (253–260), when Christian cemeteries were confiscated for the first time. After a temporary removal to
the so-called Platonia near the present church of St. Sebas-
tian, they were once more deposited in the original grave,
in the rock-cut catacombs of Lucina.

I have already explained [1] that, when memorial churches
were raised over and around the tombs of martyrs, after
the peace of the church, the tombs themselves were never
touched, altered, removed, raised, or sunk. If the rock in
the heart of which the catacombs were excavated stood in
the way, and made it impossible to give the memorial building the required form in length, in breadth, and in height,
the rock was cut away. This was done in accordance with
two rules: first, that the tomb of the hero should occupy
the place of honor in the centre of the apse ; secondly, that
the body of the church should extend *east* of the tomb.

Applying these principles to the case of St. Paul, it was
generally admitted that Constantine the Great had cut away
the spur of rock containing the catacombs of Lucina, leaving only the grave of the Apostle *in situ.* The Liber
Pontificalis adds that the grave was encased by the same
emperor in a strong room or cella, made of solid sheets of
bronze, five feet long, five broad, five high. The belief in
this state of things, viz., that St. Paul was actually buried
in a rock-cut catacomb, was so firmly rooted among Christian archæologists that in 1867 Monsignor Francis Xavier
de Merode, the pugnacious minister of war of Pius IX.,

[1] *Pagan and Christian Rome,* p. 119.

and a great lover of Christian antiquities, purchased the Vigna Salviucci — where the rock stands — with the view of making clear the connection between the catacombs and the present grave.

Several Christian crypts were, to be sure, discovered in the Vigna Salviucci and in its neighborhood, which de Rossi identified with those of Timotheus, Felix and Adauctus, and Commodilla, mentioned in the earliest pilgrim-books, but no trace of the alleged catacombs of Lucina was found, or has been found since. The solution of the problem has been obtained within the last few months in the following way.

The scheme for the sanitation and drainage of Rome, which has been carried into execution at a great cost since 1870, involves the construction of two main sewers about ten miles long, one on the right bank of the Tiber running parallel with the Via Campana and emptying into the river at la Magliana, one on the left bank running parallel with the Via Ostiensis and joining the Tiber at Torre di Valle.

This last leaves the City at the western end of the Protestant cemetery by the pyramid of Caius Cestius, crosses the road to Ostia a thousand yards outside the gate, and runs between the apse of St. Paul's and the rock where the apocryphal catacombs of Lucina were said to be, cutting the disputed ground at the depth of thirty-four feet. Such a deep excavation, so near the grave of the Apostle, was expected to give us the solution of the many problems connected with it. However, before giving the account of what has been found and of the results obtained, I must bring back to the memory of the reader the discoveries made before the present day.

The marble casing of the grave of the Apostle was seen for the first time on July 28, 1838, when the altar above it, injured by the fire of July 15, 1823, was demolished to make room for the present one. A marble floor was discovered composed of four slabs, on which the dedication

PAVLO APOSTOLO MART(yri)

is engraved in large letters of the time of Constantine. The slabs and their precious inscription were left visible under the new canopy, and I have myself had the privilege of studying them at leisure (on December 1, 1891), by lowering myself on hands and knees through the " fenestella confessionis." Two things we must bear in mind : first, that the slabs inscribed with the name of Paul are not in their original position, but appear to have been replaced over the grave most negligently, in a slanting direction ; secondly, that the inscription is mutilated at the right end, the last three letters of the word MART(*yri*) being missing.

Other discoveries took place in 1850, when Pius IX. was laying the foundations of the new canopy ; they are of paramount interest for the question we are investigating. It was then ascertained that Paul's grave stands on the margin of an old road, paved with blocks of lava, amidst other tombs of purely pagan type. According to the evidence of an eye-witness, Father Paul Zelly, who was then abbot of St. Paul's, the old road runs at a distance of fifteen feet west of the grave, and at an angle of about 14° with the Via Ostiensis, into which it runs lower down. Besides the Apostle's grave there were the remains of a columbaria or square sepulchral chamber with pigeonholes for cinerary urns. This tomb was found almost intact, but it seems that no attention was paid to it, no drawings taken, and no copies made of the inscriptions which probably accompanied each pigeonhole. I have lately come into possession of some notes, taken at the time of these finds by Vespignani

the elder, who acted as assistant to Luigi Poletti, the re-
builder of St. Paul's, but they are of no special importance.
The objects put aside " nel cavo della seconda confessione
in settembre 1850 " [1] were the tombstones of a C. Julius
Berullus and of a
Priscilla, both pre-
ceded by the invo-
cation Diis Mani-
bus ; two Christian
ones, several brick
stamps from the
kilns of Faustina
the elder, and one
from the Officina
Fauriana. They do
not throw much
light on the ques-
tion; and yet we
are sure that if
proper attention
had been paid to
these excavations,
and a more careful
search made among
the tombs and
columbaria which

A view of the tomb and canopy of St. Paul.

lined that bit of road, we should now know the name of
the personage who had given the first disciples of Christ in
Rome the permission to bury St. Paul in his own family
burial-plot.

The cutting for the main sewer has revealed the following facts. First, there is no connection whatever between

[1] In the foundations of the new Confession, September, 1850.

the grave of St. Paul and the many Christian catacombs with which the rock of the Vigna Salviucci is honeycombed.

Secondly, these catacombs belong at all events to a much later period than the apostolic age. Boldetti claims to have read in one of them the date of the year 107, marked with the consulship of Sura and Senecio, and that of the year 111, marked with the consulship of Piso and Bolanus. These are certainly the oldest dates ever discovered in Roman catacombs; but even granted that Boldetti has made no mistake, they are at all events forty years more recent than the execution of St. Paul.

Thirdly, the whole neighborhood, from the foot of the rock to the middle of the fields in which the basilica stands, is thickly covered with pagan tombs of the first and second centuries. In the space of a few weeks not less than 183 of them have been discovered in the cutting of the drain alone.

Fourthly, these tombs are placed and oriented on the lines of two Roman roads; namely, the Via Ostiensis — which fits exactly into the modern one — and a branch road which connects the towpath on the left bank of the Tiber with the same Via Ostiensis. To this branch road belongs the pavement discovered in 1850 in the foundations of the canopy.

In the fifth place, the person who claimed the body of the Apostle after the execution, be it the matron Lucina or not, owned not a catacomb, but a burial-plot in the open — " sub diu " — in the angle formed by the junction of the two roads. Here, nearer to the side lane than to the main road, a tomb was raised to St. Paul. We do not know of what nature, size, shape, the tomb was; whether it bore an inscription or not. If we are to believe the Liber Pontifi-

calis, the authority of which after the recent edition of
Duchesne is above suspicion, the grave itself must have
been small. "Eodem tempore fecit Constantinus basilicam
beato Paulo Apostolo . . . cuius corpus ita recondit in ære,
et conclusit sicut Beati Petri."[1] Now the case of solid
metal, inside of which Constantine sealed the body of St.
Peter, was five feet long, five wide, five high. Five Roman feet equal 1.478 metres. The mean height of the
human body being 1.58, the case appears too small. It is
impossible to think that the body of Paul was incinerated,
and the ashes preserved in a cinerary urn ; and even granted
that he was of a stature below the average, the coffin in
which he was laid to rest would certainly have exceeded the
measure of five feet. I agree with Stevenson that the figures have been altered by the carelessness of early copyists
of the Liber Pontificalis.

Another explanation offered for the short measure of the
case is that the Apostle having been beheaded, the head
may not necessarily have been placed in its right position.
If I remember rightly, twice tombs of beheaded men have
been discovered since the revival of classic studies : one
at Cuma, one in the Vatican district, when Pope Paul III.
was digging for the foundations of the Bastione di Belvedere. This bastion occupies part of the site of the ancient
cemetery of the Via Triumphalis. Among the many tombs
and columbaria discovered on that occasion, one belonged
to a decapitated person. Ligorio describes the find in
the following words ("Bodleian," p. 139): "There was
also a sepulchral chamber decorated with stucco reliefs and
paintings, in which a walnut cut out of an agate was discovered ; . . . it was lying near a skeleton which had the

---

[1] " At the same time Constantine built the church of St. Paul, enclosing his
body in a case of solid metal, as he had done for St. Peter."

skull not in its proper place, but across the legs ; and where the skull should have been, there lay a perfect and beautiful plaster mould of the head of the buried man. This plaster mould was removed to the private collection of the Pope."

In the sixth place, it has been ascertained that the mean level of the tombs which line the two roads is eleven feet lower than the level of the modern road, and about nine feet below that of the nave and aisles of the church.

Comparing these data with the finds of 1850, Stevenson

The Via Ostiensis flooded by the Tiber.

comes to the conclusion that the grave itself must lie about twelve feet and six inches below the floor of the transept, and only eleven feet above the mean level of the Tiber, which runs close by. Now it is a known fact that the Tiber reaches that height fifteen times a year at least, not to speak of extraordinary inundations, like the one of 1870, in the course of which the waters rose twenty-six feet above the level of the grave. We may safely conclude, therefore, that the Apostle was buried in a low, damp, almost swampy field, permanently exposed to the overflow of the river, unless precautions had been taken to keep the waters off by means of levees and embankments and sluices, of which we know absolutely nothing. The metal case of Constantine may have saved the grave from the inflow of water after the erection of the church.

Has the venerable grave come down to us intact since the time of Constantine ? The question is more easily put than answered. The church, to be sure, went safely through the barbaric invasions, being considered an inviolable asylum even by the Goths and the Vandals. Of this fact we have the evidence in Epistles 54 and 127 of St. Jerome, where he déscribes the fate of Marcella, the founder of monastic life in Rome. " This noble matron was left a widow after seven months of marriage, and being pressed by the Consul Cerealis to marry again, determined to sever all connection with the world for the rest of her life. Following the rule of St. Athanasius, Bishop of Alexandria, she dressed herself in simple garb, gave up the use of wine and meat, and divided her time between the study of the Scriptures, prayers, and pilgrimages to the tombs of apostles and martyrs. St. Jerome became Marcella's spiritual adviser ; such was the serenity and beauty of her character that in one of her letters she is addressed as ' the pride of Roman matrons.' However, when Rome became the prey of the Goths, the barbarians broke into her peaceful retreat and tortured her in an attempt to discover the secret hiding-place of her treasures, — treasures that she had long before given up to the needy. Fearing more for the safety of

Principia, whom she had adopted as a spiritual daughter, than for her own life, she threw herself at the feet of the Gothic chieftain and begged to be conducted to the church of St. Paul outside the walls, which, like St. Peter's, had been set apart by Alaric as a refuge for women and children."

The Saracenic invasion of 846 makes, however, an exception to the rule. It would be impossible to discuss within the limits of the present chapter all the arguments brought forward to prove or disprove the profanation of the tombs of Peter and Paul in 846. Leaving aside the question of Peter, of which I have spoken at length in " Pagan and Christian Rome," p. 148, and in " The Destruction of Ancient Rome," p. 131, there is unfortunately no doubt that the infidels plundered at their leisure the Basilica of St. Paul, and laid their hands on the venerable tomb. We find the evidence of this fact in chapter xxii. of the Life of Benedict III., in Duchesne's edition of the Liber Pontificalis, vol. ii. p. 145 : SEPULCHRUM [Pauli Apostoli] QUOD A SARRACENIS DESTRUCTUM FUERAT PERORNAVIT !

The question is, what did the Saracens actually destroy, — the altar erected high above the grave, the canopy or ciborium which covered the altar, or the grave itself ? I believe that the expression of the Liber Pontificalis is not to be taken in too literal a sense ; for why should Benedict III. have restored and redecorated the group formed by the grave, the altar, and the canopy, if the grave itself had been profaned and its contents scattered to the four winds ? And besides, we know that the word DESTRUCTUM, " destroyed," is an exaggeration ; because the marble slab with the epitaph PAVLO APOSTOLO MART(yri) is still in existence, and it is the original of Constantine's time, not a copy made by Benedict III. The tomb incurred another risk in

The new façade of St. Paul's.

the sack of 1527, when the scum of the soldiery from Spain, Germany, and northern Italy pillaged the City and its sacred edifices for the space of several weeks. L. Mayerhofer, in the " Historisches Jahrbuch," 1891, p. 721, has published a letter written by an eye-witness, a clerk from Speyer named Theodoric Vafer — alias Gescheid, and dated June 17 of that eventful year, in which he expressly says : " We have (or they have) profaned all the churches of Rome ; men and women have been slain over the altar of St. Peter's ; the tomb or coffin inside which the remains of Peter and Paul had been laid to rest has been broken open, and the relics dispersed " (*Urnam sive tumbam, in qua requiescebant ossa S. Petri et Pauli effregerunt et ipsas reliquias profanarunt*). One thing is certain, however : none of the many hundred published or unpublished accounts of the sack of 1527, consulted by Gregorovius,

Grisar, Orano, and other specialists, mention this incident, which, considering the extraordinary devotion of the Romans to the founders of the church, would have caused them greater grief than all the horrors, massacres, tortures they endured in those days. Briefly my opinion is this : The grave of St. Paul has come down to us, most likely, as it was left by Constantine the Great, enclosed in a metal case. The Saracens of 846 damaged the outside marble casing and the marble epitaph, but did not reach the grave. As to the nature of the grave itself, its shape, its aspect, its contents, I am afraid our curiosity will never be satisfied.

This most fascinating of Roman churches is closely connected with England and especially dear to the Anglo-Saxon race. As the emperor of Austria was the protector of St. Peter's, the king of France of St. John Lateran, the king of Spain of S. Maria Maggiore, so the kings of England were the defenders of St. Paul outside the walls. In the shield of the abbot, above the gate of the adjoining cloisters, we still behold the arm grasping the sword, and the ribbon of the Garter with the motto : " Honi soit qui mal y pense ! "

CHAPTER V.

STRANGE SUPERSTITIONS IN ROME.

In perusing the first part of the sixth volume of the " Corpus Inscriptionum Latinarum," which contains about a thousand dedications to gods and goddesses,[1] found in Rome or in its immediate vicinity, we are struck by the variety and strangeness of names which appear in the roll. No nation has ever shown such liberality in opening the gates of its Olympus to newcomers as the Romans have done. What the Gospel says of the centurion detached at Capernaum, and of his inquiries into the Jewish religion, may be applied to a great many other officers and magistrates in charge of Roman interests in the far-away provinces of the Empire ; in fact every soldier, every sailor who came back to his native place, on receiving the " honesta missio," carried with him fresh superstitions gathered from the more or less civilized lands in which he had kept garrison. Another source of corruption of the simple old Roman religion may be found in the harbors of Ostia and Portus, where thousands of ships landed every year from every corner of the Mediterranean, the crews of which were allowed to worship in their own fashion, under the guidance of their consul, or " proxenos," who was invested at the same time with the functions of " archiereus," or high priest. The authorities at Rome, both clerical and civil, tried to stop the invasion of foreign deities and the import of for-

---

[1] Pars prima *Inscriptiones Sacræ*, pp. 1–150, nn. 1–871 (appendix, nn. 3671–3744*). Two or three hundred more have been found since 1876.

eign mysteries, with little or no result. I was present many years ago at the discovery of a foreign lodge, or " megarum," in the harbor of Porto, where the adepts of the worship of Isis and Serapis held their meetings; and in giving an account of the find (in " Bullettino dell' Instituto " of 1868, p. 227) I was led to inquire into the legal condition of these adepts in respect to Roman religious legislation. I must acknowledge that no decided line of action was ever followed in dealing with these intruders. Periods of tolerance succeeded outbursts of persecution, and vice versa, until the adepts were almost forced to seek safety in secrecy.

Hence the great number of " Mithræa," " Metroa," " megara," sacred caves and lodges, found daily in Rome and its neighborhood. We must also remember that when the garrison and the police of Rome were no longer allowed by Septimius Severus to be drafted from the ranks of Roman citizens, but from the semi-barbarian tribes of the lower Rhine and of the lower Danube, the men brought over with them their own gods, their θεοὶ πατρῷοι, whom they could worship in their barracks with absolute impunity. This state of things has been beautifully illustrated by the finds made in the barracks of the " Equites Singulares," in that part of the old Villa Giustiniani, near by the Lateran, which is now crossed by the Via Tasso.

These " Equites Singulares Augusti " formed a select body of horsemen, attached to the person of the Emperor, like our life-guards or " cuirassiers du roi." They were drafted mostly from amongst the Thracians, the Batavians, the Pannonians, and the Mœsians, in contrast to the Prætorians, who were taken in preference from the Spanish and Gaulish provinces, and even from Italy. The Equites Singulares, who wore helmets without plumes, and carried oval shields, swords, and lances, formed a regiment

THE BACCHUS DISCOVERED IN THE BARRACKS OF THE
EQUITES SINGULARES

one thousand strong, divided into two squadrons, quartered respectively in the old barracks (*castra priora* or *vetera*) discovered between 1885 and 1887 in the Via Tasso, and the new barracks (*castra nova* or *Severiana*) discovered in 1733 or 1734 in the foundations of the Corsini Chapel at the Lateran.

We may gather an idea of the extent of these barracks from the fact that the present church of St. John Lateran and the adjoining palace of Sixtus V. occupy only a section of the last named barracks,[1] and we may appreciate the splendor of their fittings and decorations from the works of art which have come to light within their boundaries. Such are the marble chair, now in the Corsini Library, the low reliefs of which represent a procession of warriors, a boar hunt, and sacrificial ceremonies, the work of a Greek chisel ; and the marble statue of Bacchus now in the Villa Maravini at Lugano, an illustration of which is here given.

The greatest and happiest event in the life of a Roman soldier was his receiving the " honesta missio," or honorable discharge, after serving the required number of years. During the Republic the legionaries were bound to serve from sixteen to twenty campaigns, the horsemen only ten. Under Augustus the term for the legionaries was reduced to sixteen years, while the city garrison served for twenty, and the auxiliaries for twenty-five ; but as a matter of fact we find soldiers commonly retained in the service as " evocati " long after their legal enlistment had expired, such as T.

[1] The church is cut in two by a Roman street, which runs parallel with the transept of Clement VIII., passes under the canopy of Urban V., and leads to a postern in the walls of Aurelian below the " Giardino dei Penitenzieri." Constantine, after disbanding (the Prætorians and) the Singulares, made a present of their empty barracks to Pope Miltiades in 313, for the erection of the " Mother and Head of all the churches of the city and of the world," and gave up also a small section of his own imperial Lateran palace, west of the street.

Cillius from Laranda, who died at the age of seventy after serving thirty-eight years in the eleventh legion, and Claudius Celer from Verona, who had enlisted at twenty and died at sixty-three, without giving up his commission.[1] After Hadrian's time soldiers did not obtain their discharge till they had seen twenty-five years' service, but during the last five years they were released from the harder duties. There were three kinds of discharges : the " honesta missio," when they received the full recompense for their long and faithful services ; the " causaria," when they were dismissed for physical incapacity or sickness ; and the " ignominiosa," when they were ignominiously cashiered and drummed out before the whole army.

The day of the honesta missio, when the men secured either a piece of land or a lump sum of five thousand denarii, or nine hundred dollars, besides the rights of citizenship and of contracting a regular marriage (*civitas et connubium*), was celebrated by the gallant veterans with a loud display of loyalty towards the Emperor who had signed the decree, and of gratitude towards the gods who had preserved their lives through the hardships and dangers of so many campaigns. As a rule, the veterans discharged on the same day and by the same decree joined forces, and each contributed his own share towards the erection of a monument which took generally the shape of an " ædicula " or shrine when offered to the gods, or that of a statue and a pedestal when offered to the sovereign.

I shall never forget the wonderful sight we beheld on entering the vestibule of the old barracks of the Equites Singulares in the Via Tasso. The noble hall was found to contain forty-four marble pedestals, some still standing in their proper places against the wall facing the entrance,

[1] *Corpus Inscr.* vol. iii. nn. 2834, 2818.

some upset on the marble floor, and each inscribed with the dedicatory inscription on the front and with the list of subscribers on the sides. Some bear dedications to the Emperor commander-in-chief, as, for instance: "To the Genius of our Emperor Antoninus Pius. The Thracians

A statuette of Epona discovered at Albano.

honorably dismissed from the regiment of the Equites Singulares after twenty-five years of service, and whose names are engraved on the sides of this pedestal, have raised by subscription this marble statue on March 1st, the

Emperor and Bruttius Præsens being consuls for the second time (A. D. 139)." Then follow thirty-nine names, of which one is original, — Seutheus, — the rest are Latinized.

More difficult must have been the wording of the dedications to the gods, because each of the subscribers had his own " santo protettore," as we Italians say, and wanted to tender to him, personally, the expression of his gratitude. Sometimes not less than eighteen names of gods occur on a single stone raised by thirty or thirty-five men, of which some are borrowed from the Roman temples, some from the dolmens and menhirs of their native lands. To this last class belong Epona, the goddess of stables and beasts of burden, whose name of Celtic origin is derived from *epus*, horse ; the Fatæ, corresponding in number and nature to the Roman Fates, to the Greek Μοῖραι, and to the German Nornir; the Matres or Matronæ, also three in number, haunting the forests watered by the Rhine and the Danube, like the Sulevæ or Suleviæ, female geniuses of those dark and mysterious leafy recesses, addicted to the kidnapping of children ; Noreia, the genius of the ancient capital of the Taurisci in Noricum ; Toutates and Hercules Magusanus, worshipped by the Batavi ; Deus Sabadius, worshipped by the Mœsians; and Beelefarus, worshipped by the dwellers in the land of Moab, conquered by Trajan in 106, and annexed to the Empire under the name of Northern Arabia.

Among the vast crowd of foreign deities worshipped in Rome I shall select three as a subject of study for the present chapter, the Great Mother of the gods, Mithras, and Artemis Taurica, because recent excavations have allowed us to enter over and over again into the secret dens where their worshippers assembled, and to unravel to a certain extent the mysteries of their worship.

For the convenience of those among my readers who have

THE TEMPLE OF CYBELE ON THE PALATINE

not made a special study of ancient mythology, I shall briefly state, in regard to Rhea or Cybele, that she was supposed to be the mother by Chronos of Hestia, Demeter, Hera, Hades, Poseidon, and Zeus. Hence her Roman title of Magna deûm Mater, the Great Mother of the gods.

Mithras, the god of the sun among the Persians, became popular in Rome under the name of Sol Invictus. He is represented in innumerable works of art as a handsome youth, wearing the Phrygian attire, and slaying a bull which he has brought to the ground.

The Taurian Artemis was an hyperborean goddess, whom the Romans identified with Diana. Her worship was mystic and orgiastic, and connected — at least in early times — with human sacrifices ; in fact, all strangers shipwrecked the coast of Chersonesus Taurica were mercilessly slain on her altar.

Cybele became known to the Romans in 206 B. C., when a meteoric stone considered to represent the goddess was brought over from Pessinus, and placed in a temple raised expressly on the west corner of the Palatine Hill, where its ruins, shaded by a grove of ilexes, stand to the present day. In its first observance the feast of the Great Mother of the gods was a mere thanksgiving for the aid granted to the Roman armies in the Second Punic War ; later on it became a display of the most audacious superstition, and gave origin to the gathering of secret societies, imbued with the Phrygian mysteries, in which the beautiful Atys played also an important part. The myth of this youth is rather vague. The version current at Pessinus was that Agdistis, the androgynous offspring of Uranus and Earth, having been mutilated by the gods, an almond-tree sprang from her blood, the fruit of which was gathered by Nana, the

daughter of the river-god Sangarius.   She bore a son, the
fascinating Atys, reared by goats in the mountains, who
afterwards fell in love with the royal maiden Sagaritis.
Agdistis or Cybele, stung with jealousy, drove him des-
perate, so that he mutilated himself under a pine-tree, into
which his spirit passed.   Violets sprang at its foot from
the blood.   The pine-tree, therefore, wreathed with violets
became a sacred emblem of Atys in the wild festivals of
Cybele, whose priests were eunuchs.[1]

Their joint festival in Rome began on March 15, with
a procession of men and women carrying the sacred reed
of Atys.   On March 22 the sacred pine was borne to the
temple on the Palatine.   March 24 was kept as a " dies
sanguinis," a day of blood, of fast and mourning, when the
high priest cut his arm with a knife to commemorate the
self-inflicted wound of the god.   March 25 was a day of
rejoicing, when banquets were given, the extravagance and
luxury of which became so intolerable that a maximum of
expenditure that would be incurred by the host was fixed
by a decree of the Senate of 161 B. C.   Lastly, on March
25 a procession of priests followed the sacred image to the
first milestone on the road to Ostia, where it was washed in
the waters of the river Almo.

By a singular coincidence my career as an excavator and
as a student of antiquities began in 1867 under the auspices
and with the manifest protection of the Great Mother of the
gods.

On May 14 of that year, while my late friend Carlo Ludovico Visconti and I were resting from our morning work
in the sacred field of Cybele at Ostia, a workman rushed

[1] " The myth symbolizes the growth of life in nature, especially of plant and
tree life, its death and its resurrection, as well as the twofold character of natural production, the male and the female."   Marindin, in Smith's *Classical
Dictionary*, ed. 1894, p. 149.

into our place of shelter with the tidings that a great find was just going to take place. I was then beginning to learn from my companion — the last representative of the Visconti dynasty of archæologists and Pope's "Commissarii delle antichitá" — the gentle art of excavating, for which purpose we used to drive once or twice a week to Ostia, where twenty or thirty hands were employed in exploring those noble ruins: but I had not yet seen with my own eyes a work of statuary come out of the earth.

The sacred field of Cybele is a triangular space of ground, about one acre in extent, with the temple of the goddess at the apex, a colonnade on the right side, and a group of

Cybele's arrival in Rome from Pessinus, from a terracotta bas-relief formerly in the possession of G. B. Guidi.

miscellaneous buildings on the other. The men were at work in a recess at the east end of the colonnade when they saw a bronze hand and a marble head appear above the surface of the rubbish. On reaching the spot we left the marble figure to the care of the men, and took upon ourselves the task of setting free the bronze statuette to which the hand belonged. Like the initiated who used to

gather together in this field for the celebration of the Mega-
lesia, we shed drops of ichor, as our fingers were bleeding
freely at the end of the exhumation.

I need not give a description of the statue, as the accompanying illustration speaks for itself. The original, now
in the Lateran Museum, has been identified by Visconti as
a Venus " Clotho," on account of the spindle which he
thought she was holding in the right hand ; while Helbig
thinks the goddess is simply attending to her toilet. " The
object in her left hand," he says, " was evidently the han-
dle of a mirror, in which she was gazing at her image.
The attribute on the right, much injured by oxidation,
seems to have been a small spatula for laying on rouge." [1]

While we were busy welcoming Aphrodite, the men had
exhumed the recumbent statue of Atys, which, strange to
say, had never left the steps of its altar, nor suffered the
slightest injury from time or at the hands of men. According to the inscription of the plinth, the statue was consecrated to the Phrygian god by Gaius Cartilius Euplus at
the inspiration of the Magna Mater. The bodily form is
delicate, almost womanly ; the face expresses melancholy
resignation rather than suffering. His connection with
vegetation is symbolized by the solar rays (modern, but in-
serted in the five holes originally bored in the marble) round
his head, by the crown of pine cones, pomegranates, and
other fruit, by the wheat ears and fruit in his right hand,
and by the wheat ears springing from the point of the
Phrygian cap. I distinctly remember that at the moment
of discovery the clothing of the figure retained its original
coloring (pink and ultramarine), while the hair, the crescent, and the ears of corn were heavily gilded.

---

[1] Compare Visconti, in *Annal. Inst.*, 1869, p. 216, and Helbig, *Guide*, Eng.
ed., 1895, vol. i. p. 515.

THE VENUS CLOTHO

With the finding of these two statues, the surprises which the sacred field of Cybele held in store for us were by no means exhausted : we had still to explore the *schola* or meeting hall behind the temple, and the *Metroon* or secret cave on the left side of it, both of which places contained an invaluable set of written records, some relating to the " Collegium Dendrophorum " placed under the invocation of Silvanus, some to the " Collegium Cannophorum," worshippers of the Phrygian gods. These records referred mostly

The statue of Atys found at Ostia.

to gifts of silver statuettes (of Mars, the Mother Earth, Cybele, Atys, etc.) weighing from one to three pounds each, offered to the brotherhood by zealous members or else by the " venerables " of the lodge, both male and female. There were also records of " taurobolia " or sacrifices of bulls to propitiate the gods of the sea at the opening of the navigating season. This interesting place has since

been allowed to fall into ruin, and its contents have heed-
lessly been removed to the Lateran museum.

Twenty Mithraic sanctuaries, at least, have been found
and explored in Rome and its vicinity in my time, their
main feature being the extreme care taken to conceal their
entrance from outsiders.   They are to be met with, not only
in cities and villages, but also in the most secluded districts
of the Campagna, where, it appears, servants and farm-hands
were initiated into foreign religious mysteries by their own
masters or allowed by them to assemble in lodges.   In the
spring of the year 1899, while exploring the wild uplands
between the Via Collatina and the river Anio, I was told
by a shepherd in vague and mysterious terms that a figure
of the Madonna had been seen, somewhere in that neighborhood, deep in the bowels of the earth.   It took some
weeks for my companions and myself to make out where
and how the story had originated.   On the border of the
farm of Lunghezzina, towards the hamlet of Corcolle (Quer-
quetula), we were shown a kind of well, overgrown with
shrubs and brambles, which led to the awe-inspiring cave.
Letting ourselves down by means of a ladder, we found a
dimly lighted passage at the end of which a rock-cut staircase descended to unknown depths.   We could not count
the steps, as they were covered with mud and rubbish
brought down by the filtering of rain-water, but there must
have been about forty of them.   The steps led to a door,
also hewn out of the rock, above which we beheld one of
the brightest and best preserved pictures it has been my
fate to come across.   It represents a mystic subject ; and as
far as we could see by the flickering light of a candle and
in an atmosphere darkened by smoke and damp vapors, the
central figure appeared to be Hercules seated on a boulder,

with the club by his side, to whom a winged Victory offers a drinking cup. Cupids were flying above the group in a sky dotted with stars. There is no doubt that the door led into the crypt used as a " lodge " by the adepts ; however, the want of air and of proper light made it impossible for us to proceed farther, and find out the secret of this remarkable cave.

The lodge of the Mithraic brotherhood in the so-called imperial palace at Ostia discovered by Visconti in 1867 could only be entered by a dark, narrow, and tortuous passage, running back of the kitchen and scullery. The other, which I discovered in the same city in the spring of 1888, within the house of the Ægrilii, — the best preserved of all, — stands entirely apart from the living rooms, and can be reached through a corridor built on purpose against all the Vitruvian rules for a Roman dwelling. The same precautions are manifest in the Mithræum of S. Clemente (see illustration on page 197), and in the one of the Via dello Statuto, which I have described in " Ancient Rome," p. 192. The cave which perhaps enjoyed the greatest fame at the time of the renaissance of classical studies is the one of the Capitoline Hill, near the great sanctuary of Jupiter Optimus Maximus. The particulars concerning this Mithræum are rather interesting.

Flaminio Vacca, who has chronicled all the finds made in Rome in the second half of the sixteenth century, says (Mem. 19, ed. Fea, 1790) : " I remember to have seen in my childhood a hole, like a chasm, in the Piazza del Campidoglio ; and those who dared to enter it said that there was a woman sitting on a bull. I happened to mention the subject one day to my master, Vincenzo de Rossi, and he said he had seen the place ; that it contained a bas-relief set into the rock in a cave which cut through the hill from the Arch of Severus to the steps of the Aracœli ; and that the bas-relief represented the Rape of Europa." We can easily forgive those simple explorers for their mistake ; the woman on the bull, the Europa of Master Vincenzo de Rossi, was nothing else but the image of Mithras Tauroctonos, that is, of Mithras slaying the bull. These things happened in 1548. Shortly afterwards, on September 4, 1550, another explorer found his way to the cave. I have discovered a memorandum of this incident in a manuscript note to a copy of Lucio Fauno's " Antichità della città di Roma," now in the possession of the Cavaliere Giulio Vaccai, of Pesaro. The memorandum, which must have been written by a Franciscan brother of the convent of the Aracœli, says : —

" While I was in Rome in the Anno Santo or jubilee of 1550, I descended with some of my brother monks carrying lighted torches into a crypt under the marble steps which lead to our church of the Aracœli. Here we found the mouth of a cave, shaped like a vaulted corridor, from which the wind blew in such force that it was difficult to keep the torches lighted ; and proceeding farther we came to the foundations of the ' Palace of the Cæsars ' [he means of a noble building] where are baths of wonderful beauty, and quite well preserved. Lastly, we entered a hall, the ceiling of which was covered with reliefs in stucco : there were benches and seats round three sides of the hall, while on the fourth side, opposite the entrance door, we saw a great piece of marble representing a bull caught by the horns, etc."

The name of *Lo Perso* given to this cave in the middle ages, is truly surprising, because it betrays an archæological knowledge remarkable for that age, Lo Perso being a manifest allusion to the Persian origin of the god. The name occurs not only in the epigraphic MSS. of Cola di Rienzo,

Nicolas Signorili, and Ciriaco d' Ancona, but also in the legal deeds of notaries and magistrates. I have found, for instance, in the records of Giovanni Angelo de Amatis, a notary of the fifteenth century, the account of a judgment delivered on May 31, 1456, by two city officers, Battista de' Lenis and Paolo Astalli, sitting on a wooden bench . . . " in tribio dicto lo Perso." It seems that before the collapse of the underground sanctuary, which must have taken place soon after the visit of Master Vincenzo de Rossi, the bas-relief was removed to a place of safety. Pignorio saw it in 1606 in the Piazza del Campidoglio. It passed afterwards into the Borghese Collection, whence it was stolen by the French in 1808. It is now exhibited in the Louvre.

The late Commendatore de Rossi has pointed out first of all, I believe, that the existence of many Mithræa and Metroa near or under the great sanctuaries of pagan and Christian Rome cannot be accidental. De Rossi thinks that

The Mithriac bas-relief in the cave of the Capitol.

the members of these brotherhoods sought deliberately and intentionally the contact of the Capitol and of the Vatican, in their attempt to counteract, as it were, the influence of those two great centres of Roman religion. I may add that the Mithræum called Lo Perso, which I have just mentioned, was by no means the only one bored in the rock of the Capitoline Hill. When the carriage road, known as the

Salita delle Tre Pile, — from the three pots, or " pignatte," which form the coat of arms of Pope " Pignattelli," Innocent XII., the maker of the road, — was repaired and enlarged in 1873, I found, on January 3, a staircase cut out of the rock, at the back of the garden which formerly belonged to Michelangelo's house, and a small cave, at the bottom of the stairs, which contained the Mithraic bas-relief published in " Bullettino Comunale," vol. i. p. 114, plate iii.   The cave must have been a private one, judging from its small size, and from the absence of the side benches, where the members usually sat according to the degree they had gained in the lodge.   There were seven degrees in all, marked not by numbers, but by a name in the following order : I. *corax*, raven ; II. *cryphius* (κρύφιος), secret ; III. *miles*, soldier ; IV. *leo*, lion ; V. *Perses*, Persian ; VI. *heliodromus* (ἡλιόδρομος), sun-runner ; and VII. *pater*, the venerable of the lodge.   This is the reason why the pavement of the lodge found at Ostia in 1888 in the house of the Ægrilii is divided by bands of black mosaic into as many compartments as there were degrees of initiation.   The promotion from one to another could not be obtained unless the candidate had successfully withstood certain trials, which are beautifully illustrated in a bas-relief found near Botzen, and published by Layard.

I must acknowledge, however, that the contact between these dens of mystery and the pagan or Christian sanctuaries above ground was not always sought by the sectaries : sometimes the reverse took place, and the sacred caves were given up to the Christians, to be purified under the name of the true God.   Such was the case with the Mithræum of Alexandria, which, having been abandoned for some time by the initiated, was given by the Emperor Constantius to the local congregation in 361.   And while the Christians were searching the place, and investigating how it could be turned into a church, they found a secret passage containing human bones, believed to be remains of human sacrifices. These ghastly relics were shown to the populace, together with the uncanny representations of the Mithras

The lodge discovered in 1870, under the church of S. Clemente.

leontokephalos, Mithras-stone, etc.; but as the population was still essentially pagan, and addicted to all sorts of mysterious practices, the revelation of the secrets of the Mithræum gave rise to the outbreak described by Socrates and Sozomenos, followed by pillage, arson, and murder. The scheme for raising a church on the site of the Mithræum, put aside for the time being, was taken up once more in 389, by Bishop Theophilos, and again the attempt was followed by a revolution, in the course of which hundreds of Christians fell the victims of the infuriated mob.

When the work for the erection of the national monument to King Victor Emmanuel on the Capitol began in

1883, we felt sanguine that the many and vexed problems connected with the topography of the famous hill would soon find their solution. The results have been rather disappointing, except as regards the respective location of Jupiter's temple (Capitolium) and of the Citadel (Arx), which has been made clear, beyond the least shade of doubt. The temple stood on the southwest summit, now occupied by the Caffarelli palace, the Citadel on the site of the Aracœli. The latest link in the chain of evidence was obtained in November, 1892, with the finding of a pedestal, the dedicatory inscription of which begins with the words : " Flaviæ Epicha(ridi) sacerdotiæ deæ virginis cælesti(s), præsentissimo numini loci Montis Tarpei," etc. (To Flavia Epicharis, a priestess of the Dea Cælestis, the protecting deity of the Tarpeian hill, etc.). The grammar of the text is uncertain and the spelling decidedly wrong, but the meaning is interesting. We learn from this inscription that another meeting place of a mysterious sect had been established November, 259 A. D., on the side of the hill, the precipitous face of which was known by the name of the Tarpeian Rock ; that the members of the lodge were of the female sex, except the chaplain, a certain Junius Hylas, who happened to be the husband of Flavia Epicharis herself ; that they were organized in degrees, two of which were named of the *sacratæ* and of the *canistrariæ;* and lastly, that the titular goddess of the lodge was the *Virgo Cœlestis*, a Roman representative of the Phœnician Astarte, and of the Carthaginian Juno, whose worship was first introduced into Rome by Scipio, at the close of the Third Punic War. It is possible that at so late a period as the one to which the inscription of Flavia Epicharis belongs, when religious syncretism was so highly in favor, the name of Virgo Cælestis may have been attributed to Juno, the true Roman

The cliffs of the Capitoline Hill, south face.

Juno, to whom the northeast summit of the hill was especially sacred.

Among the points which these excavations have failed to make clear is that concerning the site of the corner-stone of the great temple of Jupiter, laid on June 1, A. D. 71, and the consequent burial of an enormous mass of gold and silver in the heart of the hill. As the subject is rather new and of considerable interest for the excavators of antique edifices, I beg leave to enter into more particulars.

The old temple of Jupiter, the cathedral as it were of ancient Rome, designed by Tarquinius the Elder, finished by his son, and dedicated by the consul M. Horatius Pulvillus, on September 13, 509 B. C., stood erect for four hundred and twenty-six years. An unknown malefactor, taking advantage of the inflammable material of which the temple was built, set fire to it, and reduced it to a heap of ashes on July 6, 86 B. C.

Its reconstruction was intrusted, first, to Q. Lutatius Catulus, later to Julius Cæsar. The inscription of Ancyra mentions a second restoration by Augustus.

During the civil disturbances of Vitellius the Capitolium was burnt to the ground for the third time. Vespasian inaugurated the works of reconstruction, carrying away on his shoulders a basketful of rubbish, which, according to the direction of the augurs, was dumped into a marsh.

The following details about the laying of the cornerstone, on June 21, A. D. 71, are given by Tacitus in chapter 52 of the fourth book of the "Historiæ."

The space set apart for the ceremony was marked out with masts and pennants, from which hung festoons of evergreens and garlands of flowers. The troops on duty reached the sacred enclosure in the first hours of the morning, under a cloudless sky, carrying branches of palm and laurel instead of the weapons of war. They were soon followed by the Vestal Virgins, clad in their white garments, and attended by sons and daughters of patrician families, sprinkling the enclosure with lustral water which they had drawn from clear springs. The high priest, Plautius Ælianus, then offered the sacrifice of the Suovetaurilia, which consisted of a sow, a sheep, and a bull, while the prætor Helvidius Priscus called down the blessings of the three Capitoline deities, Jupiter, Juno, Minerva, on the enterprise. The prayer being over, Priscus touched the gaily ribboned ropes with which the inaugural stone was bound, and then magistrates, priests, senators, knights, soldiers, and people dragged the great block to the edge of the shaft into which it was to be sunk. The same classes of citizens then marched past the shaft, each individual dropping into the cavity a votive offering, consisting mainly of gold and silver nuggets " as they come from the mines, not worked by hand."

We can easily appreciate the value of the treasure buried in the heart of the Capitoline Hill on June 21, 71 A. D. It represents the spontaneous offering of the greatest city in the world, of a population of about a million souls, full of religious enthusiasm, and impatient to see the august temple rise again from its ashes. Thousands and thousands of pounds' worth of gold and silver must have been sunk at the bottom of the inaugural well. Now it may interest the reader to know that this invaluable treasure has never been discovered to the present day.

The platform of the temple on which the Caffarelli

The Lion cut by Flaminio Vacca out of a block of Pentelic marble from the temple of Jupiter.

palace (now the seat of the German Embassy) was built in the seventeenth century has never been disturbed until comparatively recent times. When Martin Heemskerk drew his celebrated panorama of Rome in 1536, the Monte

Caprino — as the Capitol was then called — was covered with vineyards and gardens. Excavations began after the middle of the sixteenth century, the results of which are minutely described by contemporary archæologists. Blocks of Pentelic marble were found belonging to the peristyle of the temple, of such size that Flaminio Vacca was able to cut out of one of them the great lion now in the vestibule of the Villa Medici. The platform itself was not touched until about 1680, when the Duke Caffarelli removed (partially) the fourteen upper layers of stones. Other damage was inflicted in more recent times.

Now, if the treasure had been detected in one of these excavations we surely should know about it. A find of this sort which requires the connivance of several workmen, and produces a sudden rise in the fortunes of one or more families, cannot be kept concealed ; and if we possess genuine accounts of treasure hunting and treasure trove from the darkest period of the middle ages and from the remotest parts of the City, so much more probably should we have heard of this one, the most amazing of all, in a spot located under the very eyes of the magistrates of the City. And besides, the " Historiæ " of Tacitus, the only document stating the facts of the case, was unknown to literary men before the middle of the fifteenth century, when Poggio Bracciolini discovered the text in the library of Monte Cassino. In all probability, therefore, the vast mass of gold and silver is still awaiting the hand destined to exhume it from its hiding-place.

It is time, however, that we should turn our attention towards the sanctuary of the Scythian Diana at Nemi, the last of the three mysterious deities mentioned at the beginning of the chapter.

The Lake of Nemi lies at the bottom of one of the craters of the Alban range, which measures six miles in circumference at the top of the cliffs and four at the water's edge. Its altitude above the sea is 191 metres, the depth in the centre 36 metres. When the worship of Diana was first established on its shores, and all through the classic period of Roman history, the aspect of the place was very different from its present appearance. There were then no villages teeming with life, no fields yielding the choicest produce of the earth, no villas, no farms, nothing but primeval forests casting their shadows over the silent waters.

The lake was formed many centuries before the extinction of the last volcano of the Alban range (Monte Pila). We may easily imagine what an awe-inspiring place it must have appeared when the mountains around were shaken from their foundations by outbursts of incandescent lava, when the skies were heavy with ashes and smoke, and the thundering of the " boati," reverberating from cliff to cliff, from mountain to mountain, was heard as far as Rome. " Vox ingens," Livy calls it, " vox ingens e luco et summo mon tis cacumine ! " No wonder that such a frightful retreat should have been selected for the seat of a mysterious worship, that of the Scythian Diana, the origin of which is variously explained by Strabo, by Servius, and by Pausanias. The worship seems to have been imported from the Chersonesus Taurica (Crimea), the abode of rude, savage tribes, addicted to piracy as well as to the veneration of Artemis, or, according to their own statement, of Iphigenia. The principal rule of the sanctuary by the Lake of Nemi was, in fact, truly barbaric and worthy of the Scythians ; no one could be elected high priest unless he had slain with his own hands the one who, by a similar deed, had obtained the dignity before him. It is evident, therefore, that the thoughts of the unfortunate priest must have been directed more to the preservation of his life than to the service of the goddess. This extraordinary rite was still flourishing at the time of Marcus Aurelius and Commodus, but the duels were generally confined to runaway slaves, one of whom would escape, for the time being, the fate to which, nevertheless, he was doomed.

In the palace of the Count of Montenegro at Palma, Majorca, there is a bas-relief three and a half feet long and two feet high, of archaic workmanship, discovered in 1791 by Cardinal Despuig near the mouth of the outlet of the lake, at the place called " le Mole di Valle Ariccia," and reproduced by Sir William Gell in his "Topography of Rome," p. 327. It is considered to represent the issue of one of these duels ; the high priest, wounded to death by his rival, lies on the ground holding with his right hand the intestines which are protruding from the gash. The successful antagonist, brandishing the bloody poniard, is surrounded by four female attendants of the temple, in attitudes expressive of the greatest distress. The prohibitory laws of Valentinian II. and Theodosius must have put an end to the practice in A. D. 393.[1]

The temple of the Scythian goddess, to whom human sacrifices were offered in times gone by, rose in the midst of the great forest on the north side of the lake, at the foot of the craggy boulder on which the village of Nemi is now perched. Judging from her figure, as given upon an ancient vase, the statue of the goddess seems to have been an almost shapeless stone, with a rude head, and one arm resting upon a sword. Before the sanctuary expands the lonely lake, fed by the same springs which are now forced up to fill the reservoir at Albano. The temple stands not

[1] Modern archæologists disagree as to the interpretation of the bas-relief.

much higher than the lake, and might have been easily flooded except for a wonderful emissary by which the waters are kept at a fixed level. The emissary, therefore, must be the work of a very remote age, and this explains why no mention of it is to be found in ancient writers. The tunnel is 1,649 yards long, irregular in shape and direction. It is possible that the temple may have been

The Lake of Nemi, with the second ship outlined by means of floaters.

built on the newly claimed land in commemoration of the almost marvellous drainage of the lake.

Though nothing in the present day can exceed the beauty and loveliness of this " Mirror of Diana," as the ancients called it, where fragrant strawberry fields have succeeded to the ancient forest, and life and thrift to the wilderness of old days, its chief celebrity has arisen from the discovery at the bottom of the lake of two ships of great size, and as rich and beautiful as an enchanted palace.

Besides insignificant attempts made frequently by local boatmen and fishermen, a regular search for the mysterious wrecks has been undertaken four times, the first by Leone Battista Alberti, at the time of Eugenius IV. (1431–1439); the second by Francesco de Marchi in 1535; the third by Annesio Fusconi in 1827; the last by Eliséo Borghi in 1895, which has not yet been brought to a close.

Flavio Biondo da Forli, in his " Italia Illustrata," relates that Cardinal Prospero Colonna, who counted among the fiefs of the family both Nemi and Genzano, had often heard from his tenants and fishermen the story of two immense ships sunk deep in the water, so strong and well preserved as to resist all attempts made to float them or to demolish them piece by piece. Prospero being a learned prelate for his days, and very studious of history and ancient remains, determined to find out why two such large craft should have been launched on a narrow sheet of water, enclosed by mountains on every side, and to what causes their wreck should be attributed. He sought the help of the " Vitruvio Fiorentino," the engineer and mechanician, Leone Battista Alberti, who built a raft of beams and empty barrels to support the machinery by means of which the explorations could be made. Skilful smiths prepared hooks, like four-pointed anchors, hung to chains, to be wound up by capstans; and seamen from Genoa, " who looked more like fish than men," were called to adjust the hooks on and around the prow of the first ship. The immense weight of the wreck baffled their efforts; the chains broke; many of the hooks were lost, and the few that were successfully hauled up brought to the surface fragments, which filled the assistants with marvel and admiration. It was seen that the framework of the vessel, ribs and decks, was of larchwood ; that the sides were made of boards three inches thick, caulked with tar and pieces of sail, and protected by sheets of lead fastened with copper nails. Alberti's description of the inside is rather obscure. He says the decks

One of the mooring-rings of the first ship.

were built more to resist fire and the violence of men than to withstand the rain, or the gentle waves of the lake. He speaks of an iron framework supporting a floor of concrete, and also of a lead pipe upon which the name of the Emperor Tiberius was engraved.

Guillaume de Lorraine and Francesco de Marchi renewed the attempt in July, 1535. Guillaume had just invented a diving-bell, or something like it, and was trying experiments on the wreck. De Marchi went down first on July 15, and looking through the convex glass of the spy-holes, which acted like lenses, was horrified at the sight of hundreds of fishes three feet long and as big round as his arm. They were nothing but "lattarini" or "whitebait," sixty or seventy of which are required to make a pound. At his second descent de Marchi remained one hour in the bell. His operations and doings are cleverly described by himself in a curious chapter which is too full of details to be repeated here. He concludes by saying that the ship was

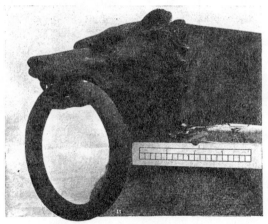

Another mooring-ring of the first ship.

four hundred and seventy-five feet long, two hundred and twenty-eight feet broad, and fifty-three feet high.

It is not necessary to dwell on the absurdity of these figures; but the true ones, as we shall presently see, are none the less surprising if we consider the difficulties of building and launching the huge craft in such an awkward

funnel-shaped hole, and of floating and manœuvring them
in such a diminutive sheet of water.

The third attempt was made in 1827 by Annesio Fusconi,
who has left an account of his doings in a pamphlet which
has become exceedingly scarce. Fusconi sunk some twelve

The Medusa's head from the first ship.

hundred pounds in the experiment, half the amount being
wasted on a threatrical "mise en scène" for the accommodation of diplomatists, noblemen, and prelates, who were to
witness the beginning of the operations on September 10 of
that year.

The enterprise was tried for the fourth time in 1895.
The search made by divers led to the discovery of six
mooring-rings of solid bronze, representing heads of lions,
wolves, and tigers, and one of Medusa, to which objects
a prominent place has already been given in the history of
Greco-Roman art, so exquisitely beautiful are they in
moulding and finish.

Let me declare at the outset that the finding of an ancient ship in good preservation is by no means an extraordinary event among us. Three have already been discovered in my lifetime, — the first in 1876, when the foundations of the iron bridge at " la Ripetta " were sunk in the Tiber by means of compressed air. The craft was so deeply embedded in silt and mud, and the section which fell within the range of the air-cylinder so small, that no investigation could be made.

The second was discovered at Porto d' Anzio in 1884 in the foundations of the Hôtel delle Sirene. The mainmast, part of the rudder, and part of the keel, with fragments of the ribs, were exposed to view. If I remember rightly, Cavaliere Pietro Jonni, the builder of the hotel, had some pieces of furniture made out of the wreck.

In the spring of 1885, about two miles west of Astura, — an island and a castle on the Pontine coast well known in the history of Cicero, Augustus, and Conradin von Hohenstaufen, — and about fifty yards from the shore, which is there very shelving, a fisherman discovered the wreck of a Roman trading-ship, the hull of which was filled with amphoræ, or earthen jars, which were used in the shipment of wine from the islands to the continent.

Crustacea of various kinds had cemented in the course of centuries the whole mass into a kind of coralliferous rock, from which it was very hard to extricate an amphora without breaking it, yet four or five beautiful and perfect specimens were saved, which can be seen at present in the grounds of the Villa Sindici at Porto d' Anzio. See " Ancient Rome," p. 252.

In each of these cases, however, we had to deal with fishing or trading ships of small tonnage and hardly fifty feet in length. Very different is the case of the Lake of

Nemi; and we are not far from right if we compare the vessels which plied on its waters in centuries gone by to the liners which crossed the Atlantic twenty years ago.

The measurements of the wrecks have been taken very ingeniously by the head-diver and his assistant under the direction of the eminent naval engineer Cavaliere Vittorio Malfatti, to whom we are indebted for an excellent report on the subject of these discoveries, and for exquisite illustrations of the ship.[1] Floaters, tied to strings, were fastened at short intervals around the edge of the woodwork, care being taken to draw the string tightly so as to have the floater absolutely perpendicular above the point below. When the operation was finished the people on shore were surprised to see the form, or horizontal section, of a great ship appear on the surface of the lake. (See cut on page 205.)

The exactitude of the proceedings was verified at a subsequent period by measurements taken directly on the wreck

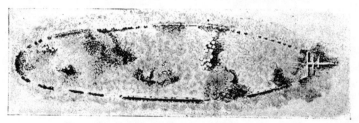

Plan of the first vessel, from Captain Malfatti's survey.

itself. The length between the perpendiculars has been ascertained to be two hundred feet, the beam about sixty feet. The depth of hull cannot be measured on account of the silt which fills it to the level of the deck.

[1] Published in the *Rivista Marittima*, June, 1896, and July, 1897, under the title, "Le navi Romane del lago di Nemi," part i., ii.

The deck itself must have been a marvellous sight to behold. The fanciful naval engineer who designed and built these floating palaces must have been allowed to follow the most extravagant flights of his imagination without regard to time and expense. The deck is paved with disks of porphyry and serpentine not thicker than a quarter of an inch, framed in segments and lines of white, gold, red, and green enamel. The parapets and railings are cast in metal, and heavily gilded ; lead pipes inscribed with the name of Caligula carried the water to the fountains playing amidship and mixing their spray with the gentle waves of the

Some of the decorations of the first ship, from Malfatti's photograph.

lake. There are other rich decorations, the place of which in the general plan of the vessel has not been yet made clear.

The second ship appears to be even larger. One of the beams brought ashore measures eighty-five feet, although broken at one of the ends. The length between the perpendiculars probably exceeds two hundred and fifty feet. An Atlantic liner of such dimensions would have been considered almost gigantic a quarter of a century ago. We knew that the ancients, especially the Syracusans, had built

Timber from the frame of the first ship, landed near the " Casa del Pescatore."

large and wonderful vessels, but we were not prepared to find a monster two hundred and fifty feet long with marble terraces, enamelled decks, shrines, fountains, and hanging gardens in a little speck of water, hardly four thousand feet in diameter. We must remember in dealing with this question that the *quinqueremis*, the typical man-of-war of the ancients, from the end of the third century B. C. downwards, with her complement of three hundred and ten oarsmen, measured only one hundred and sixty-eight feet in length, twenty-six feet in breadth, with a height above water of fifteen feet and a draught of eleven and a half feet.

I am sure the kind reader would be pleased to know why two such great ships should have been launched on "Diana's mirror," between the years 37 and 41 of the Christian era, under the rule of Caligula, whose name is engraved on the water pipes. I am inclined to believe that they were the property not of the state or of the Emperor, but of the sanctuary of Artemis Taurica, the remains of which, excavated by the Frangipani in 1554 and 1737, by the Orsini in 1856, by Lord Savile Lumley in 1885, and by Luigi Boccanera in 1887, are still to be seen commanding the north shore at a place called il Giardino. I believe also that they were used not so much for the conveyance of pilgrims from shore to shore, as for religious ceremonies and for combined processions on land and on water. If we live to see the ships floated again, or beached on the sandy margin of the lake, no doubt they will reveal to us the secret of their origin and of their fate.

CHAPTER VI.

JEWISH MEMORIALS IN ROME.[1]

THE date of the arrival of the first Jews in Rome is not known, but we are told that the first embassy sent by Judas the Maccabee to seek the friendship of the mighty nation was received by the Senate in 160 B. C. Other ambassadors came in 145 in the name of Jonathan, brother and successor of Judas. The final treaty of friendship and commerce was signed only in 139, Simon, the third Maccabee, representing his nation, Popillius Lænas and Calpurnius Piso being consuls at Rome. The connection of this great Hebrew family with Rome is actually recorded by a monument, of doubtful authenticity, it is true, yet very curious and interesting. While the new " Confessione " was being excavated and built at the foot of the high altar in the church of S. Pietro in Vinculis, September, 1876, a marble sarcophagus was found, divided into seven compartments. The sarcophagus itself is an indifferent production of a Christian stonecutter of the fifth century, with bas-reliefs representing five subjects : the raising of Lazarus ; the miracle of the loaves and fishes ; the woman

---

[1] Compare Emmanuel Rodocanachi : *Le saint siège et les Juifs, le Ghetto à Rome*, Paris, 1891 (Bibliography, pp. xiii–xv) ; A. Bertolotti, " Les Juifs à Rome aux xvi, xvii, xviii, siècles," in *Revue des Etudes juives*, 1888, fasc. 4 ; Pietro Manfrin, *Gli Ebrei sotto la dominazione romana*, Roma, 1888–1890 ; Ettore Natali, *Il Ghetto di Roma*, 1887 ; W. D. Morrison, *The Jews under the Roman Rule*, 3d ed., London, 1896 ; A. Berliner, *Geschichte der Juden in Rom*, Frankfurt, 1893 (Bibliography, pp. 220–222) ; A. S. Barnes, M. A., *St. Peter in Rome*, chap. ii., London, Sonnenschein, 1900.

of Samaria at the well; Peter's denial; and Peter receiving the keys.   The partitions were made with slabs of pavonazzetto, marked, I., II., III., IV., IIIII., IIIIII.   Each compartment contained a thin layer of ashes and splinters of bones.   The nature of the contents was explained by two lead labels inscribed with the following words : " In these seven ' loculi ' have been laid to rest the bones and ashes of the seven holy brothers the Maccabees, of their father and mother, and of innumerable other saints." These two labels date from the twelfth or thirteenth century.   In announcing this discovery in the " Bulletino di archeologia di Cristiana," 1876, p. 73, the late Comm. de Rossi said that it required maturer and closer investigation.   Needless to say that the results of his critical inquiry have never been made known.

The Jewish colony on the banks of the Tiber was already

The sarcophagus of the Maccabees.

flourishing at the time of Pompey the Great.   Their presence annoyed Cicero.   " You know what is their number," he says, in " Pro Flacco," xxviii., " their union, the power of their assemblies.   I will speak low, therefore, to be heard only by the judges."   The phrase is purely oratorical, but it bears testimony as to the importance and influence of the Ghetto of those days.   Many Jews had been brought back by Pompey as prisoners of war ; and after their bonds of slavery were loosed by Julius Cæsar, they were allowed to form a separate caste, that of the *Libertini*, a humble but powerful one. The Libertini are mentioned in The Acts vi. 9, as forming a congregation of their own in Jerusalem (ἡ συναγωγὴ ἡ λεγομένη Λιβερτίνων), and probably in the following electoral bill discovered at Pompeii, September 1, 1764 : —

CUSPIUM · PANSAM
ÆD(*ilem*) FABIUS · EUPOR · PRINCEPS · LIBERTINORUM (*rogat*)

De Rossi claims that this Fabius Eupor, who took such a lively interest in the election of Pansa to the ædileship, was but the rabbi of the local Pompeian synagogue ; but his opinion is not shared by the editor of vol. iv. of the "Corpus Inscr. Lat." p. 13, n. 117, nor by Mommsen in "Rhein. Mus." 1864, p. 456.

In Rome the Jews were met haunting the poorer quarters, selling matches, collecting old hats, shoes, and garments, hawking small articles of wear, begging for charity, teaching their children to do the same, and accepting sometimes broken glass instead of pennies. And when the foundations of a modest fortune were laid, they would turn usurers and money-lenders, as graphically described by Juvenal. The murder of Cæsar, who had made them freemen, was mourned by them as a national calamity. " In the general consternation of the city," Suetonius relates, " all the foreign colonies expressed their grief ; the most demonstrative being the Jews, who did not leave the Dictator's pyre even at night."

Augustus, the founder of the Empire, was merciful to the Jews, who showed themselves loyal subjects, and abiding by the Roman laws, to the protection of which they often appealed, as The Acts certify. Their community was numerous. Philon pretends that eight thousand Jews supported or were ready to support his remonstrances to Caligula ; but he, like all other Hebrew annalists, has a tendency to exaggerate the importance of the race. The colony was deeply attached to the mother country ; and every year a rich present was sent from Rome to the temple of Zion. The Jews had their synagogues, their schools, their literature, their poetry, their special quarters, their cemeteries ; yet they possessed no moral or political influence. In the eyes of the Romans they did not differ from the Egyptians, the Syrians, the Cappadocians, and other strangers, whom trading interests had attracted to the banks of the Tiber.

Tiberius did not share the feelings of tolerance of his predecessor ; he determined to exterminate the colony, pushed to it probably by Sejanus, who excited and favored all the bad instincts of his master, hoping to make him more odious and insufferable to his subjects. After the death of the infamous adviser, Tiberius returned to a wiser policy ; the surviving Jews, set free from their confinement in Sardinia, hastened back to the invincible attractions of the capital.

Caligula's bosom friend was the Jew Agrippa, belonging to the family of Herod, who had followed the fortunes of Drusus the younger. He was a frivolous and dissipated young man, who had just run the risk of losing his life in the persecution of Tiberius ; he was perhaps the only representative of his race devoted to Caligula ; the race itself was restive, and the statue of the young Emperor at Jerusalem found no worshipers. He revenged himself in two ways : first by proclaiming Agrippa King of the Jews, — a step which gave rise to the greatest consternation in Judæa, — and then by offering to Philon and his co-ambassadors from Alexandria the grotesque reception of which the imperial gardens on the Esquiline, called the Horti Lamiani, were the scene.

These beautiful gardens were largely excavated under my

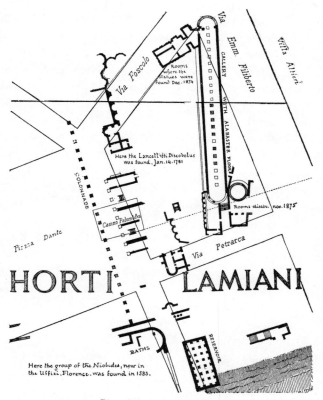

Plan of the Lamian Gardens.

own supervision between 1873 and 1876, and they yielded the richest archæological harvest we have ever been able to gather in Rome from a single spot since 1870. They were an enchanted, fairy-like place, extending over the highest plateau of the Esquiline, from which such a glorious view is obtained of the Alban, the Prænestinian, and the Sabine hills. The Casino, where the Jews were received, contained apartments two stories high, with windows having panes of translucent marble instead of glass. The halls were so large that a portrait of Nero one hundred and twenty feet high (35.64 metres) could be painted in one of them. The huge canvas, twice as large as the mainsail of a frigate, was set on fire by lightning, together with the Casino. " Pictura accensa fulmine cum optima hortorum parte conflagravit." [1] I have myself seen a gallery two hundred and seventy-six feet long, the pavement of which was inlaid with the rarest and costliest specimens of alabastrine-agate,[2] while the ceiling was supported by twenty-four fluted columns of giallo antico resting on gilt bases ; I have seen another apartment paved with large slabs of occhio di pavone,[3] the walls of which were panelled with crusts of black slate covered with graceful arabesques in gold-leaf. I have seen a third hall with the floor made of segments of alabaster, framed in green enamel, around the walls of which were jets of water, four feet apart, which must have crossed each other in various ways, and under striking plays of light. All these things were found in November, 1875.

On Christmas eve of the preceding year, while our men

---

[1] Pliny, *Hist. nat.* xxxv. 7, 33.

[2] A section of this pavement was removed to the Gabinetto delle medaglie in the Palazzo dei Conservatori. Two of the columns have been placed in the passage leading from the Rotunda of the same palace to the Sala delle Terrecotte.

[3] The occhio di pavone is a conglomerate of round shells of the species called *Anomia ampulla*, of various hues, the rarest being the pavonazzo or purplish, of which there are two magnificent columns in the Vatican library.

were excavating the rooms at the corner of the Via Foscolo and the Via Emmanuele Filiberto, at the north end of the gallery mentioned above, the ground gave way, giving us access to a crypt or cellar on the floor of which we found

One of the tritons discovered December 24, 1874, near the
northern end of the gallery.

lying the celebrated bust of Commodus in the character of Hercules, flanked by two tritons or marine centaurs and two statues representing either two maiden daughters of Danaos (according to Helbig) or the Muses Terpsichore and Polyhymnia (according to Visconti). There were also the Venus Lamiana, called by Helbig " a girl binding a fillet round her head " (see illustration, page 223); a

portrait head of young Commodus; a head of Diana; a
Bacchus of semi-colossal size, with drapery of gilt bronze
(missing); and about twenty-five legs, arms, hands, and feet
belonging to statues whose bronze drapery had likewise
been stolen before the concealment.

As regards the furniture of this delightful palace, I find
in the "Bullettino Comunale" of 1879, p. 251, the following description of a piece discovered in September of the
same year at the corner of the Via Buonarroti and the Piazza
Vittorio Emmanuele, eighty or ninety yards from the room
in which the statues were found: "It is not possible to
ascertain the exact shape of this extraordinary piece of furniture, which had the frame of hard wood, encrusted with
gilt metal, and studded with precious stones. Considering,
however, that the piece was supported by four legs exquisitely cut in rock-crystal, connected by horizontal bands encrusted with gilt festoons and bulls' heads like a frieze, we
are led to think it either a state chair or throne, or a state
bedstead. One hundred fragments of the brass work, as
well as four hundred and thirty precious stones, with which
it was studded, have been recovered. There are carnelians,
agates, chrysolites, topazes, lapis lazuli, amethysts, garnets,
all plain; five engraved gems representing the rape of Europa, Venus, a lion, a butterfly, a male bust; and a 'pasta
vitrea,' with two heads, probably of Septimius Severus and
his Empress Julia Domna. One hundred and sixty-eight
fragments of thin crusts of agate were also found in the same
room, but we could not decide whether they belonged to the
same bedstead or to the veneering of the room itself." If
we recall to mind that from these same imperial Lamian gardens come such world-renowned masterpieces as the Belvedere Meleager, the Niobides, and the two Athletes, now in
the Galleria degli Uffizi; the Nozze Aldobrandini, now in the

THE VENUS LAMIANA

Vatican Library; the Discobolos of Myron, in the Lancellotti Palace; the Dancing Women, in the Museo Chiaramonti; the Hercules, removed to England by Colonel Campbell, and many other famous marbles, we may get an approximate idea of what a Roman garden must have been in the palmy days of the Empire, and of the wonders which met the gaze of the Jewish ambassadors on the day of their grotesque official reception by Caligula.

The Lamian gardens acquired fresh notoriety in 1620, when they became the property of the Marchesi di Palombara and the scene of their mysterious meetings with Christina, Queen of Sweden, then engaged in the follies of necromancy, and in the search for the philosopher's stone and perpetual motion. Contemporary chronicles relate [1] how the queen, having taken up her abode in Rome in 1655, set up a laboratory for experimenting in occult sciences, with the help of the most distinguished alchemists of the age. One day a youth from beyond the mountains presented himself before the queen, and asked permission to work in her laboratory, in order to investigate the manner of making gold. Having obtained this, he presented himself again to the queen, after a few days, telling her that he had need of going in search of a certain herb, in order to complete the operation, and entreating her to grant him a hiding-place in which to deposit during his absence two vases of a liquor which, mixed with the herb, would become gold. He wished also that this secret place should be locked with two keys, of different form, one to be kept by the queen, the other by himself. Having obtained his request, he departed.

Some time elapsed, and no tidings being received concern-

[1] The best account by Francesco Cancellieri in his pamphlet, *Sopra la statua del Discobolo scoperta nella villa Palombara*, Roma, 1806, p. 42, n. 2.

ing him, the queen, irritated at being thus deluded, caused the hiding-place to be opened by force, and found the liquor solidified into gold in one vase and into silver in the other.

Among those who frequented the salons of Christina, was the Marquis Massimiliano Palombara, Conservator of Rome for the years 1651 and 1677, and a famous alchemist. Having heard of this incident, he took the queen severely to task for having allowed such a master in this art to escape without revealing his secret.

The marquis was then occupying his Esquiline villa, where, one morning in 1680, he saw an unknown person enter the gate on the side of the Via Merulana, and examine attentively the ground, apparently looking for some mysterious plant. Surprised by the servants, the pilgrim declared that he was in search of an herb of marvellous virtue, and that, knowing how much interested the proprietor of the villa was in the art of making gold, he wished to demonstrate to him that the work, though difficult, was not impossible.

It is easy to imagine how eagerly the marquis welcomed him, and how anxiously he watched his proceedings. The pilgrim crisped and pulverized the herb gathered in the garden, threw it into the crucible, which was full of a mysterious liquor, and promised his host that on the next morning not only would the process be completed, but the secret should be revealed to him.

When the morning came and nothing was seen of the pilgrim, the marquis, fearing that something had happened to him, forced open the door of his room, but neither here nor in the adjoining laboratory were there any signs of him. The guest had, however, liberally kept his promise, for not only from the broken crucible had flowed upon the pavement a long stream of the purest gold, but on the table lay a roll of parchment, upon which were traced and written various enigmas, which, says Cancellieri, no one has been able up to this time to explain, nor ever will.

The Marquis Palombara caused a memorial of the mysterious pilgrim, and the recipes left by him for the manufacture of gold, to be cut in marble and exposed to the eyes of the public. One of the recipes says : " Si feceris volare terram super caput tuum, eius pennis aquas torrentum convertes in petram " (If thou wilt make earth fly over thine head, thou canst convert the waters of a torrent into stone).

Some contain precepts of secret and profound wisdom, like : " Si sedes, non is ! " (If thou sittest, thou advancest not) ; or else : " Quando in tua domo nigri corvi parturiant albas columbas tunc vocaberis sapiens " (When in thine house black crows bring forth white doves, then thou shalt be called wise). Others are an absurd play upon words : " Aqua, a-qua horti irrigantur, non est aqua a-qua horti aluntur," which baffles interpretation. The only sentence adapted to all times is : " Hodie pecunia emitur spuria nobilitas, sed non legitima sapientia " (You can purchase with your wealth a spurious nobility, but not true wisdom).

All these absurdities were actually engraved on the marble posts and lintel of one of the gates of the villa, hence called the Magic Gate. I remember having seen this curious document of human idiosyncrasy in my youth, on the right side of the road which then led from S. Maria Maggiore to S. Croce in Gerusalemme, nearly opposite the ruin called the Trophies of Marius. The door was covered with strange symbols in Latin and Hebrew letters, and astronomical and cabalistic signs of obscure signification ; and every week, when the time for playing the Lotto was nearing, the Magic Gate witnessed an assembly of aged and filthy beggars, trying to get the key to the meaning of the

signs, and secure a good "estrazione" from the wheel of
fortune.[1] It is astonishing to think how the Church authorities could have left this gate standing and claiming such

The Magic Gate of the Palombara Gardens, now in the Piazza
Vittorio Emmanuele on the Esquiline.

a share of popular wonderment, when the august names of
the Trinity, the Blessed Virgin, and the Saviour were mixed
up with profane and cabalistic formulas.

[1] The public lottery is drawn every Saturday at two o'clock, five numbers being drawn from the wheel, which contains ninety in all.

The gate was removed from its place in 1876 and set up again in the square or garden of the Piazza Vittorio Emmanuele, which occupies part of the old Lamian-Palombara estate.

Three other monuments of classic Rome besides the Lamian gardens refer to the Jews: the Arch of Titus on

The Arch of Titus.

the Summa Sacra Via, the triumphal gate of the Circus Maximus, and the Temple and Forum of Peace. There were also a Jewish quarter, and Jewish schools, and many synagogues and catacombs.

The Arch of Titus, on the top of the ridge which separates the hollow of the Forum from that of the Coliseum, is a monument too well known to require a special notice. It was erected after the death and the deification of the conqueror of Jerusalem. Its interest centres in the high relief of the right pier (on the side of the Palatine) on which the spoils from the temple of Zion are represented. These are carried by the victorious soldiers guarding the prisoners of war, all of whom wear crowns of laurel, because even the conquered warriors were compelled to rejoice, at least in appearance, in their own defeat, though their hands are tied behind their backs. The principal trophies of war are the golden table with some of the sacred vessels, the silver trumpets, the ark of the covenant, and the seven-branched candlestick. According to Flavius Josephus these objects were not the original ones, but imitations, or, as it were, emblems of the Jewish defeat, as shown by the fact that the candelabra shows curved branches, instead of branches bent at right angles like those of a trident. Describing the incidents of the triumph of Titus in "Jewish War," vii. 17, Flavius Josephus remarks: "The spoils taken from the temple of Jerusalem had the place of honor among the trophies of war: there was the golden table weighing several talents and the golden candlestick, which, however, differed considerably in shape from the one in use among us, which is formed of a central support standing on a base, and seven branches bent at right angles like a seven-pronged trident." The last objects carried in the triumphal procession were the Tables of the Law.

There is an incident in the history of this arch but little known to students. The Frangipani, having raised their great Turris Chartularia, or "Tower of the Records," on the platform of the temple of Jupiter Stator, close by the arch, had made use of the latter for the main gateway of their stronghold, crowning it with battlements and turrets. No wonder that the weight of these superstructures should have impaired the stability of the arch. And when the architect Valadier was commissioned in 1822 by Pope Pius VII. to demolish the superstructures and restore the monument to its former shape, he began by taking most careful drawings of the joints of the blocks of Pentelic marble, and by marking them with cross-marks ; he then removed such parts as had been disjointed or put out of place or out of the perpendicular, strengthened the foundations, rebuilt the arch, completing the missing parts in plain travertine, and left us the most judicious, the cleverest, and the most laudable specimen of a monumental restoration that could be desired.

The same process had been followed in 1811 by the architect Camporese in pulling down the temple of Vespasian on the Clivus Capitolinus, the columns of which leaned out of the perpendicular by half a diameter, and replacing them straight on more solid foundations. Those, however, were happy days in which sovereigns and governments trusted to men of genius who had won their confidence, and this confidence was not shaken by criticisms of envious rivals or by adverse comments of the press. Should we try the experiment nowadays, we should meet with a different fate, as shown by the following incident, which took place lately in the Forum.

On the southwestern side of this celebrated place, bordering on the Sacra Via, stand eight square pedestals of monumental columns, the shafts of which, varying in size and quality, are lying close by. Describing these pillars in " Ruins and Excavations," p. 258, I had incidentally remarked that if they were raised once more on their pedestals the picturesqueness and the interest of the Forum would be greatly enhanced. The scheme was partially carried out in February, 1899, when the first and second columns, counting from the south, were set up again on their original bases. This simple and matter-of-fact process was proclaimed by the usual critics a " groundless restoration." Deputations waited on the minister to offer their remonstrances, meetings were held, protests sent to the leading papers, and yet there is not a shade of doubt that the.two shafts belong to the individual pedestals upon which they have been replaced. Both were discovered in my presence in 1872. The first, of gray granite, once covered with ornaments of gilt bronze, lay broken in seven pieces, partly on the pavement of the Sacra Via, partly on the stone " margo " of the Forum. The lower half of the second was still lying as it fell, in a slanting position, with the lower end almost level with the top of the pedestal, the upper end nearly touching the Sacra Via. This state of things is shown not only by contemporary photographs, but also by a sketch made by another eye-witness, the late Professor Heinrich Jordan, of Königsberg, who published it on p. 260 of the third volume (1879) of the " Ephemeris Epigraphica."

The conquest of Judæa and the capture of Jerusalem were commemorated on another monument of classic Rome, — the arch at the curved end of the Circus Maximus called the Porta Triumphalis because the winning chariots left the arena through it. Here the so-called Anonymus of Einsiedeln saw, many centuries ago, the original inscription containing the following words : " The Senate and the people of Rome [dedicate this arch] to Titus, son of Vespasian [in the year 81 A. D.], because, acting on the advice and under the auspices of his father, he has conquered the nation of the Jews, and has taken by assault and destroyed the city of Jerusalem, a success which no leader of armies has been able to achieve before." Arch and inscription have long since disappeared.

The third monument connected with the same events is

The monumental columns on the Sacra Via.

the Temple and Forum of Peace, dedicated by Vespasian five years after the fall of Jerusalem, A. D. 75. Josephus ("Jewish War," vii. 5) says: "After the celebration of the triumph, and the establishment of the Roman rule in Judea, Vespasian determined to raise a monument to Peace, which was brought to completion sooner and better than is generally the case with such great undertakings. . . . In this sacred enclosure were collected and exhibited number-less art treasures, to behold which men used to come from all quarters of the earth, and among these the objects of gold (χρυσᾶ κατασκευάσματα) which had been found in the temple of the Jews. The Tables of the Law, and the purple Veils were at the same time deposited by Vespasian's order in the imperial palace (ἐν τοῖς βασιλείοις)."

The art gallery of the Temple of Peace included, among other masterpieces, the celebrated Ialysos by Protogenes, the Scylla by Nikomachos, the Hero by Parrhasios; and, among the works of the chisel, a set of athletic statues from Olympia and Argos; the Ganymedes by Leochares; a group of the Nile surrounded by the sixteen infants, cut out of a single block of reddish basalt; an exquisite statue of Venus by an unknown artist; a bronze by Boëthos, representing a boy strangling a goose; and the celebrated Cow of Myron, praised by Cicero, Ovid, and Pliny, to which not less than thirty-six epigrams of the Anthology are dedicated. The Bibliotheca Pacis, attached to the temple, is mentioned more than once by Aulus Gellius, who says it contained books (for instance, the commentaries of Lælius, the master of Varro, and the letters of Asinius Capito) that could not be found anywhere else. There were, in the last place, vaults and safes in which private citizens could store and deposit their valuables. All these treasures — except the sacred vessels of the Jews, which were perhaps kept in a fire-proof compartment — perished in the memorable fire of Commodus, A. D. 191, vivid descriptions of which are given by Galen, Dion Cassius, and Herodianus. Galen complains of the loss of the first two books of his Treatise, the original manuscript of which he had inadvertently left in his office on the Sacra Via. The office was burnt to the ground together with the great libraries of Peace and of the imperial palace. Dion Cassius says that the fire originated in the middle of the night in a private dwelling, and that after devastating the Forum and Temple of Peace,

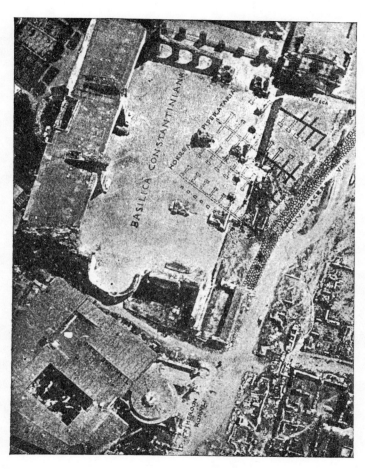

A BIRD'S-EYE SURVEY OF THE CLIVUS SACRA VIA

(Taken by Captain Moris, R. E., from a balloon at a height of 1200 feet)

destroyed the Horrea Piperataria, that is, the shops where the drugs and merchandise from Egypt and Arabia were stored, which I have already described in Chapter II. The vigiles and the prætorians, led by the Emperor himself, did not get control of the flames until the whole quarter was turned into a heap of smouldering ruins.

Herodianus, another contemporary historian (A. D. 180– 238), is inclined to give to the conflagration an almost supernatural cause, and mentions at the same time a shock of earthquake, a thunderbolt, and flames bursting out of the earth. He calls the temple and its surroundings τὸ μέγιστον καὶ κάλλιστον, " the greatest and most beautiful " building of imperial Rome. Its destruction affected morally and materially every class of citizens, on account of the art treasures which no expenditure could ever replace, and of the valuables and personal securities which had been consumed with the safes.

After a lapse of eighteen hundred and nine years, the traces of the fire of Commodus are still visible within and near the sacred enclosure of Peace, and on the line of the Sacra Via, where Galen's office and consulting rooms stood among the stores of Eastern goods. These traces appear at the Templum Sacræ Urbis (SS. Cosma e Damiano) in the brick restorations made by Septimius Severus in the old stone building ; they appear also in the ruins of the Horrea Piperataria, over which the Basilica of Constantine was afterwards built ; and lastly in the line of houses and stores bordering on the Sacra Via, which have been quite lately reëxhumed, giving us a vivid picture of that scene of desolation.

Archæologists and historians disagree as regards the fate of the Forum and the Temple of Peace after the fire.

Nibby and Canina[1] contend that they never rose from their ashes; I cannot see on what ground, as we find the place constantly mentioned in the following centuries. The biographer of the Thirty Tyrants speaks of it in the Life of Victoria, chap. xxxi. The imperial almanac of the time of Constantine mentions it as giving its name to the fourth regio of the City. When the Emperor Constantius visited Rome in 357, he was led to behold among the wonders of the metropolis " urbis templum, forumque Pacis, et Pompeii theatrum."[2] Symmachus speaks of having entered the forum, in the seventy-eighth letter of the tenth book. De Rossi has discovered in the library of St. Gall certain fragments of the Chronicle of Horosius, giving an account of all the wonderful and fearful events which marked the decline and fall of Rome from the fourth to the sixth century. One of these records says: "In the year 408, under the consulship of Bassus and Philippus, underground rumblings were heard in the Forum of Peace for seven days." I believe the true solution of the case is to be found in the following passage of Procopius (Goth. iv. 21): " A drove of oxen was led through the forum which the Romans call of Peace, from a great temple which lies there in ruins, having been struck by lightning in the old times." Procopius therefore makes a distinction between the temple, which had never been rebuilt since the fire of Commodus, and the forum, which had either escaped uninjured, or had been thoroughly restored. We know, for one thing, that two, at least, of the masterpieces, the Cow of Myron and the Ganymede of Leochares, were still to be seen in the forum at the time of the Gothic wars, long after the pillages of Alaric,

[1] *Del tempio della Pace e della basilica di Constantino ;* Dissertazione di A. Nibby. Roma, de Romanis, 1819. Compare Becker, *Topographie*, p. 440.

[2] Ammianus Marcellinus, xvi. 10.

A. D. 410, of Genseric, A. D. 455, of Ricimer, A. D. 472, etc.
For the bronze Cow we have the authority of Procopius
himself (i. 120); as to the Ganymede of Leochares, we
know that the pedestal upon which this celebrated work
of art stood was discovered in the Forum of Peace towards

The Ganymede of Leochares, a late replica discovered
at Fallerone.

the middle of the fifteenth century. This pedestal is now
preserved in the Galleria degli Uffizi. Ligorio, who witnessed the find, saw also a piece of the marble group, repre-

senting the eagle carrying off the beautiful youth to Olympus. Considering, however, that the original group had not been chiselled in marble by Leochares, but cast in bronze, we infer that the bronze had perished in the great conflagration and a marble copy had been substituted in its place. The cut on page 239 represents another copy of the group, discovered at Fallerone (Faleria) in the province of Ancona, and placed in the Galleria dei Candelabri in the time of Pius VI.

It seems hardly possible that the golden vessels from the Temple of Zion, placed in the Temple of Peace among other trophies of war, should have escaped the effects of the fire, the suddenness and violence of which were such that not even the state archives kept in the adjoining fire-proof building (the Templum Sacræ Urbis, now SS. Cosma e Damiano) could be saved from destruction; and yet there seems to be little doubt on the point.

According to Procopius the Jewish spoils were carried off by King Alaric when Rome was looted in August, 410, and tradition adds that when Alaric died in southern Italy, near the city of Cosenza, his followers buried him and his treasures in the bed of the river Busentinus, first diverting the course of the waters, and then letting them flow again over the tomb. The tradition is probably a new and revised edition of the true story of Decebalus, king of the Dacians, which I have already related in " Ancient Rome," p. 391. According to another version, the golden spoils either escaped detection at the time of Alaric or else were only partially looted. The man into whose hands they ultimately fell was Genseric, who stormed Rome in June, 455, at the head of a powerful army of Vandals, with whom were mixed Bedouins and Moors. Genseric appears to have devoted himself mainly to the plunder of the temple of Jupiter Capitolinus; its statues were carried off to adorn the residence of the Vandal kings at Carthage, and the roof was stripped of its tiles of gilt bronze. That portion of the Jewish spoils which had been overlooked by Alaric in 410 was apparently landed in safety at Carthage. Here it was discovered eighty years later by Belisarius, the Byzantine general, and hence it was removed to Constantinople, where it was offered as a present to the Emperor Justinian. Justinian sent it as a pious offering to the church of the Holy Sepulchre at Jerusalem, whence it was carried away in 614 by the Persian conqueror Chosroës.

Whichever of these versions deserves credit, or whether neither one of them is worthy of it, the Tiber is at all events out of the question. The tradition that the seven-branched candlestick was thrown into its muddy bed is very old, and the writers of the Talmud, to make it lie in a more decent place, state that the bottom of the river between Rome and Ostia is paved with sheets of solid metal, stolen from Palestine by the emperors. President Charles de Brosses, in one of his "Lettres sur l'Italie," relates that under Pope Benedict XIV. (1740–1758) the Jews asked permission to drain the river at their own expense, provided they could get undisturbed possession of the treasures which their undertaking might eventually bring to light. According to the same writer the Pope withheld his consent for fear that the stirring up of the mud and silt of the river would generate the plague. *Dignum patella operculum!* The simple-minded president did not perceive that his cicerone was taking advantage of his good faith.

The Ghetto of classic Rome was on the right bank of the Tiber, among the slums of the Trastevere. In the early days of the City, the region between the river and the Janiculum was made so unhealthy by sluggish streams and pools of stagnant water that it was chosen by the Senate as the place of relegation for prisoners of war whom they wished to destroy.   Here were led the inhabitants of Tellene, Ficana, and Medullia after the capture of their villages, and also the leading citizens of Capua, who had sided with Hannibal.   If many of their number perished, many also lived to form in progress of time a poor and unhealthy but populous quarter.   Boatmen, lightermen, tanners, dyers, scavengers, carriers joined the original settlers, together with beggars and vagabonds, and that shady class of strangers who flock to the great cities in quest of fortune or shelter.

The first Jew colonists, driven from their native land by poverty or brought as slaves behind the chariots of Roman conquerors, took refuge in this wretched district, where the Syrians, their neighbors, had preceded them, and where they felt at home among a crowd of pariahs.   Juvenal describes another small Jewish centre, just outside the Porta Capena, in the neighborhood of the sacred grove of Egeria, their furniture being restricted to a basket suspended from a tree and a bundle of straw.

Yet some, if not many, of the Jewish immigrants became wealthy, rose in the scale of society, and, leaving the abject home of their coreligionaries in the Trastevere, settled in the most fashionable streets of the City, where they could make a loud display of their wealth, and built their family mausolea in the aristocratic cemeteries of the Via Appia and the Via Latina.   Of this practice we have a curious but little known piece of evidence, in a sarcophagus now preserved in the court of the Palazzo Spada among other relics discovered by Cardinal Girolamo Spada-Veralli when he restored the church of S. Agnese fuori le Mura after the pillage of 1527.   According to the inscription, engraved in a style characteristic of the Severian age, the sarcophagus belonged to a Jewish lady of rank, named Julia Irene Arista, mother of Atronius Tullianus Eusebius, senator of the empire, " vir clarissimus." The pious lady, faithful to the law of God (*juste legem colens*), after having been delivered from a mortal illness, " Dei virtute et fide mea nobis conservata," lived happily to a green old age, and was buried in the fashionable cemetery

The Trastevere in the middle ages, from a sketch now in the library of the Escurial.

of the Via Nomentana, where probably she and her son owned property. The interest of this remarkable document centres in the title of " vir clarissimus " claimed by the son, of which no other example is to be found in Roman epigraphy : an explanation, however, of this singularity is to be found in the following passage of Ulpianus, " De Officio Proconsulis " : [1] " Septimius Severus and his son Caracalla allowed the adepts of the Jewish superstition to reach the highest honors and offices."

[1] Pandect, *De decurionibus*, leg. 3 d.

The headquarters of the Jews remained, nevertheless, in the Transtiberine district, in the vicinity of the harbor, where vast numbers of Greek, Syrian, Alexandrine, and Carthaginian ships were always moored, allowing them to carry on a brisk trade with the motley crews.[1] Here also were their best schools, their law-courts (Bath-Din), and the central synagogue where the banished sons of Abraham might behold a good yet deceptive reproduction of the sanctuary of Zion.

Nine other synagogues are mentioned in connection with other quarters of the City, viz., those of the Augustans, of the Agrippans [2] of the Campus, of the Campus and Volumnus, of the Subura, of Eleia, of the lime-burners, of the Rhodians, and of the harbor of Rome (Portus Augusti). Their rabbis were called " gerusiarchi," or " archontes," or " archisynagogi." We find also among their dignitaries several "fathers and mothers of the synagogue," and scribes, and patrons, and readers of the law.

The best known of the Jewish suburban cemeteries is the one discovered by Antonio Bosio in the hills of Monte Verde, not far from the present railway station by the Porta Portese. This Columbus of underground Rome explored the long-forgotten crypts on December 14 of the year 1602, and attributed them to the Jewish Transtiberine community on account of the seven-branched candlestick, and of the formula, " Here rests in peace," by which the tombstones were distinguished. Bosio did not carry his exploration very far, probably on account of the crumbling and dangerous state of the crypts. Bianchini, the

---

[1] The Jews themselves did occasionally take to the sea. Several *proscinema* by Jewish sailors have been found engraved on the rocks of the little harbor of Grammata in the island of Syra.

[2] King Herod had given the same names of Augustus and Agrippa to two wings of his palace. See Josephus, *Antiq.* xv. 9, 3.

CHAIR IN THE SYNAGOGUE OF MODERN ROME

great archæological explorer, claims to have entered the same place in the first quarter of the last century.[1] Gaetano Migliore, who followed at a later period Bianchini's footsteps, says : " I could not advance very far on account of the falling stones, yet I saw with my own eyes cubicula, arcosolia, loculi, all utterly devastated, and also, I believe, scattered pieces of Jewish emblems. I did my best to enter the deepest recesses of this old burial-place, but I was obliged to retire because the very sound of my footsteps seemed to hasten the fall of the crumbling rocks." [2] Since Migliore's attempt no one has entered the place ; Padre Marchi tried to rediscover its entrance in 1843, but without success. In 1892 I watched for weeks and weeks the attempts of a man — a painter by profession — to cut a passage through the layer of loose earth at a spot which had been pointed out to him by an old gardener as the entrance to a " subterranean palace." That man had actually cut with his own hands a gallery four feet high and fifteen feet long, when he was compelled to abandon the attempt. I cannot tell whether the rock-cut door which he had reached led to the long-lost Jewish catacomb, or to a Christian one, because the fragments of inscriptions found in the loose earth bore no characteristic religious symbols ; but I am rather inclined to think the latter, because, if we believe what Fioravante Martinelli says in his " Roma ricercata," p. 20, the crypts seen by Bosio were destroyed at the time of Urban VIII., when the new line of city walls was raised on the ridge of the Janiculum. At all events, this ridge is so honeycombed with catacombs that it is difficult to single them out and ascertain their origin. Sixteen years after his first discovery, Bosio found a second catacomb in the

---

[1] *Delle porte Romane*, p. 70.
[2] *Cod. Vatic.* 9143.

same spur of the hill. Benjamin of Tudela must refer to one of these places of entombment when he describes a cave near the Tiber containing the tomb of the "ten martyrs of the kingdom," that is, of the ten Hebrews, preachers of the Mishna, who had given their life for their faith.[1] The whole district outside the Porta Portese has retained its connection with the Ghetto of ancient Rome up to our own days, the plain between the Via Portuense and the foot of the hills being called "Ortaccio degli Ebrei," just as in by-gone times it bore the name of "Campus Iudæorum" or "Contrata Hebreorum." The construction of the new railway station has altered the whole aspect of the place.

Other cemeteries have been discovered on the Via Appia and the Via Labicana, the best of all being the one first entered on May 1, 1859, in the Vigna Randanini, opposite the church of S. Sebastiano. It is still open to visitors. The one found in 1867 on the same road in the vineyard of Count Cimarra is briefly described by de Rossi, "Bullettino di archeologia cristiana," 1867, n. 1. Its inscriptions have never been published in full. Those found in 1883 on the Via Labicana, and in 1885 on the Via Appia Pignattelli have been illustrated respectively by Marucchi and Müller. From their tombstones we gather that some of the Roman Jews kept their own or gave to their children Biblical names slightly Latinized, such as Aster (Esther), Gadia (Gaddi), Ionata, Semoel, Sarah, Lea, etc. Others adopted Greek or Latin names, borrowing the "gentilicium" from patrician families or individuals, to whom probably they had lent money, or rendered service for a consideration.

---

[1] Basnage de Beauval, *Histoire des Juifs*, La Haye, 1716. The vineyard in which Bosio made his discoveries belonged in 1602 to the Ruffini family, and later on to Muzio Vitozzi. See Armellini, *Cronichetta Mensile*, 1879, p. 27.

The Jewish cemetery at the Circus Maximus as seen from the Aventine.

Thus we find two Ælii, one Æmilia, and several Flavii, although this last was the family name of the two hated conquerors of Judæa, Vespasian and Titus. Still more remarkable is the occurrence of many pagan and decidedly profane names, such as Aphrodisia, Asclepiodote, etc.

The head synagogue, mentioned above, is placed by topographers in the neighborhood of S. Cecilia, because the adjoining street was known in the middle ages by the name of "Rua Judæorum." Its precious contents — tapestries woven of gold threads, gold plate, etc. — were plundered by the populace at the time of King Theoderic; but the Jews repaired the damages soon after.

It does not appear that their Transtiberine quarter had a fixed boundary like the Ghetto of later times; but the spirit of brotherhood which seems innate in the Jewish race kept them clustered and huddled together around their temple. It was only after the pillage of Rome by Robert Guiscard, in 1084, that they migrated, with their neighbors the tanners, to the opposite bank of the Tiber,[1] and settled among the remains of the Porticus Octaviæ, the Porticus Philippi, and the Theatre of Marcellus, not far from the Fabrician bridge, which was henceforth named "Pons Judeorum." They continued, however, to bury their dead in the old Ortaccio near S. Francesco a Ripa, until they obtained from the City another "field of death" among the ruins of the Circus Maximus under S. Prisca. This last cemetery is still in existence.

The Jews were not many at the time of this migration. Benjamin of Tudela, who visited Rome in 1165, says : "My fellow-worshippers number about two hundred, all honest men, independent, paying tribute to nobody. Some hold important offices in the court of Pope Alexander III. [1159–1181], like David Magnus, and R. Jechiel, B. Abraham, a bright and courteous youth, who is intendant of the Pope's household." One of the squares of the Rione Regola, destroyed in 1887 to make room for the new Via Arenula, was called Piazza dei Branca, from the illustrious Jewish family of that name — the Branca di Clausura — which flourished in the fourteenth century. The most famous and powerful Roman family of the middle ages, the pillar of the Church, the representative of the Pope's judicial power, the warder of the Pope's state prison, the Pierleoni, were also of Jewish extraction. The grandfather of "Peter son of Leo" (Petrus Leonis, Pierleone) having lent to and gained large sums of money from the Holy See, and seeing the prospect of larger gains and political influence,

---

[1] The latest record of the residence of the Jews in the Trastevere is to be found in a deed of 1515 in the state Archives, vol. 1121, p. 291, where the "Curia Judeorum" is mentioned in the neighborhood of S. Cecilia.

A window of the Pierleoni house, Via di Porta Leone.

abjured the faith of his fathers and was baptized under the name of Benedictus Christianus, which was that of the reigning Pope Benedict IX. (1033–1046). His son was likewise named from the Pope Leo IX. (1049–1055), and his grandson, the real founder of the Pierleoni dynasty, assumed the name of the Prince of the Apostles. The great-grandson became the antipope Anacletus II. ! It seems that this family of mediæval Rothschilds, made barons of the holy Roman empire by their apostolic debtors, were afflicted for generations with the most pronounced Jewish features. They could not get rid of a sallow complexion, a nose like a hawk's, and curly black hair.   Orderic Vitalis describes one of them, who sat in the Synod of Rheims in 1119, as "nigrum et pallidum adolescentem, magis Judeo vel Agareno, quam Christiano similem," and Arnulfus also expatiates on the forbidding Jewish appearance of Anacletus II.

These feelings of repulsion, however, were not shared by the fair ladies of the Roman patriciate, to judge from their anxiety to marry the wealthy sons of Peter.   These had established their headquarters over the remains of the Theatre of Marcellus, where the Palazzo Orsini now stands, while their vassals and servants and gens-d'armes occupied the quarter between the theatre, the Tiber, and the Forum Boarium, which we still call " quartiere di Porta Leone," a picturesque cluster of mediæval houses and towers and lanes but little known to tourists.

The island of the Tiber, crowned with towers, — one of which is still to be seen at the west entrance to the Fabrician bridge (Ponte Quattro Capi, Pons Judeorum), — served as *tête-de-pont*.   Pope Urban II., who had made the Pierleoni warders of the Castle of S. Angelo, died in their house " apud sanctum Nicolaum in Carcere," in 1099.   The constant friendship of the Popes, their high connections by marriage, unlimited wealth, and great political power, made the world soon forget the humble origin of the family.   The Frangipane, as representative of the Ghibelline faction, did not yield to the general feeling ; and their hatred of the Jewish parvenus, who claimed the leadership of the Guelph party, more than once caused trouble and bloodshed within the walls of the City.   At last peace was sealed by marriage and by the common pretense of both families to kinsmanship as collateral descendants of the Anicii.

Tradition says that two Pierleoni migrated to Germany towards the middle of the fifteenth century, where they became the head of the Hapsburg family. This story was credited not only in Rome but also in Austria, until the emperors of the house of Hapsburg found out that their alleged relationship with the Pierleoni would make them seek for their forefathers in the Ghetto of mediæval Rome. By a welcome chance of fate we still possess the tombs of the founder and of the last representative of the great family. The founder died on June 2, 1128, and while the graves of contemporary Popes are all lost, the coffin of the

The tomb of the great Pierleone in the cloisters of St. Paul's.

Hebrew Crœsus still lies under the southern wing of the beautiful cloisters of St. Paul's. It is a marble sarcophagus of the third century, with bas-reliefs representing Apollo, Marsyas, and the Muses, and a panel inscribed with the following words : —

"May Peter and Paul, to whom you were so faithful, protect you, Peter, son of Leo, and welcome your soul into the glory of heaven," etc.

Of the last representative of the family, Lucretia, daughter of Luke, we have a bust and an inscription dated 1582, in the church of S. Maria della Consolazione.[1] Lucretia proclaims herself " the only surviving daughter of the most noble Roman and Austrian race."

In pursuing a mild and lenient policy towards the sons of Israel, the Popes followed the advice of the Fathers of the Church, such as Gregory the Great and Thomas Aquinas;[2] and besides, they were too often in need of financial help to lose the good-will of their bankers. In a document preserved in Cod. Vatic. 7711, the average amount of money borrowed from this source is valued at one hundred and fifty thousand scudi for a period of thirty years. The Jews themselves borrowed considerable sums from Christian bankers at four per cent., lending it in turn to more needy customers at eighteen.

Another reason for their peaceful life in the capital of the Christian world must be found in their skill in medicine, and in their kindness in treating the poor. Towards the end of the fourteenth century a doctor named Emmanuel and his son Angelo rose to such celebrity that the city council in the plenary sitting of May 8, 1385, granted special privileges in their favor, " because they are so brave and merciful in the exercise of the healing art, attending gratuitously the needy." These privileges were confirmed in July, 1392, by Boniface IX. in a letter which begins: " Bonifacius . . . dilecto filio Angelo Manuelis iudei . . . nato Judeo, medico et familiari nostro salutem ! " Martin V. and Eugene IV. were attended in their ailments by the Jew doctor Elihu, Innocent VII. by Elihu Sabbati, Pius II. by Moses of Rieti. Infessura the Diarist relates how Inno-

---

[1] Second chapel on the right.
[2] Gregory's *Epist.* viii. 25 ; Thomas Aq. *Epist.* 363.

cent VIII., at the point of death, yielded to the suggestion
of a Jew charlatan to have his blood rejuvenated with the
blood of three boys. The result of the operation was that
the Pope died as well as the three boys, but the charlatan
saved himself by a prompt flight. The Æsculapius, the
Galen, the Prince of the Jewish medical school in Rome,
was without doubt the Rabbi Samuel Sarfati, of Spanish
extraction, who rose to the much envied position of Pontifical Archiater at the time of Julius II. His wonderful

The Ghetto at the time of Paul V., from a contemporary engraving.

career has been described by Marini in his "Archiatri
Pontificii," vol. i. p. 290.

Paul IV., Caraffa, in opposition to the policy of his pre-
decessors, put an end, for the time being, to the peaceful
state of the colony. His constitution, *cum nimis absur-*

dum, dated July 15, 1555, orders that the Jews must henceforth live apart from the Christians in a quarter of their own, to be surrounded by a wall with but one entrance and one exit. The bishop of Ischia, governor of Rome, enforced obedience to the decree so strictly that on the 27th of the month, that is, twelve days after its promulgation, the Jews were already immured in their pen. Four Christian churches which happened to fall within the enclosure were sacrificed to save them from the unwelcome contact, — S. Lorenzo dei Cavalluzzi (belonging to the Armenians, who received in exchange the beautiful temple of Fortune by the Forum Boarium, Christianized under the name of S. Maria Egiziaca), S. Leonardo de Platea Judeorum, S. Salvatore di Baroncini, and a fourth dedicated to the unheard-of saints Patermuzio and Coppete.

The boundary wall was enlarged from time to time, and the number of gates increased first to five, later to eight. The gates were closed at seven o'clock in winter and at eight in summer. The Mattei family enjoyed the privilege of furnishing the gatekeepers for a yearly remuneration of one hundred and sixty-three scudi and twenty bajocchi. The Ghetto was furnished with a slaughter-house (which I have seen in the place where Prince Orsini now has his stables), and with bakeries for the azim bread. The bakeries were located in the lane called after them delle Azimelle, a congested, evil-smelling alley, demolished in 1888. The Ghetto was a wretched place, and it is one of the glories of the early pontificate of Pius IX. to have destroyed its boundary wall, thrown open its gates, and broken the chains which fettered the faithful Jews. When Gregorovius visited Rome for the first time fifty years ago, the whole Ghetto was inundated by the Tiber as far as the Propylaia of Octavia's portico ; yet the place was not essentially unhealthy :

in fact, more than once it has enjoyed immunity from epidemics which ravaged the rest of the town.

The first Pope who caused the inhabitants of the Ghetto to wear a sign by which they could be distinguished from

Vanished Rome. A street scene in the old Ghetto.

their Christian fellow-citizens was Martin V. The signs varied with time and with the caprice of the ruler. We hear at first of " tabarri rubei," flaming-red overcoats which had to be worn by the unfortunate brotherhood winter and summer, by men and women alike. At Ferrara, where the number of the Jews had increased alarmingly since their banishment from Spain and from Portugal, Duke Hercules selected as a mark the letter O in yellow ochre, to be worn sewed on their breast. Paul IV., their great persecutor, changed the red overcoat for a conical cap of orange hue, not unlike in shape to the one characteristic of our popular mask, Pulcinella ; for which fresh insult the Jews took signal vengeance. On the announcement of Paul's death, which took place on August 18, 1559, the populace, who had tolerated long enough the cruel rule of the Caraffa family, broke into the Conservatori palace and overturned the statue of the Pope, dragging the head through the streets. The Jews took a leading share in this outbreak of popular feeling, and carried the head, in their turn, through the Ghetto, covering the pontifical tiara with the hateful orange cap.

As a rule, common law penalties were applied with more severity in the case of Jews than in the case of Christians, especially when the offence was against public morality. Thus, while Christian " cortigiane " [1] breaking the police regulations were simply punished with fustigation, — much to the joy of the populace, who counted upon such performances as one of the attractions of Carnival, — the Jewesses were generally burned at the stake in the Campo di Fiore.

It is true, at the same time, that Christians who fell victims to the fascination of the brunette daughters of Israel ran the risk of losing their lives, as is proved by the following anecdote.

Sixtus V. having heard that the young Duke of Parma

[1] In Pope Leo X.'s time the number of the cortigiane was equal to about one third of the total of single women or widows within the walls of the city. Their number had diminished to 604 in 1600, to rise up again steadily until the maximum of 1295 was reached in the year 1639.

had lived for a certain time on intimate terms with a Jewess, caused him to be arrested, and on the acknowledgment of his guilt, to be sentenced to the scaffold. As the moment of the execution approached, and when the most powerful intercessions had failed to obtain a mitigation of the sentence from the stern old pontiff, Cardinal Alessandro Farnese, uncle of the young duke, thought of the following stratagem. He caused all the clocks of the Vatican to be put back, with the exception of the Pope's private one, which alone was left to mark the true time. Cardinal Alessandro having entered the audience-room a few moments before the hour fixed for the execution, made a supreme appeal to the clemency of Sixtus V., but in vain. At last the Pope, looking at the quadrant and thinking that all was over, granted the pardon, provided it was not too late. The cardinal rushed to the prison, where the executioner, deceived by the clock, was waiting for the fatal hour to strike. When the stratagem was at last discovered the duke was already beyond the reach of the Pope's police.

Alas! it was reserved to the present generation to see the twenty-two hundred years old Jewish colony dispersed forever. The Ghetto, so quaint in its filth and picturesqueness, is no more. The scheme for the sanitation of the City required its disappearance, and it has disappeared. The Jews of Rome have lost their identity and their personality, scattered as they are among a population of five hundred thousand souls. Yet the poorer ones are still faithful to their old habits; they still pace our streets buying old garments and hawking small articles of wear. The only difference is that they no longer accept broken glass instead of pennies.[1]

[1] "Transtiberinus ambulator, qui pallentia sulphurata [matches] fractis permutat vitris." Martial, *Epigr.* i. 36.

CHAPTER VII.

ENGLISH memorials in Rome, as far as existing monuments are concerned, date back to the first century of the
Empire. In A. D. 51–52, after the capture of King Carac-
tacus and the surrender of his brothers, a triumphal arch
was raised to the Emperor Claudius on the Via Flaminia,
the modern Corso, "for having subjugated eleven kings
of Britain without loss on the Roman side, and for having first of all Romans annexed to the Empire barbarous
trans-oceanic lands." [1] The history of this arch is quite
remarkable. Discovered for the first time in 1562 in that
tract of the Corso which we call Piazza di Sciarra, it took
three hundred and eight years to dig its remains out of the
ground and to fill our museums with its fragments. Four
bas-reliefs, one of the dedicatory inscriptions, and one hundred and thirty-six cartloads of marble were brought to
the surface in 1562. Duke Giorgio Cesarini bought two
bas-reliefs and part of a third, which, after passing through
several hands, are now preserved in the Casino of the Villa
Borghese. The fourth panel was first walled up in front
of the house of Marsilius Caphano in the same Piazza di
Sciarra where it had been found, and was removed in 1593
to the Conservatori palace, where we can see it in the landing of the great stairs. [2] Now three other panels from a triumphal arch of Marcus Aurelius by S. Martina were already
exhibited in the same landing. The city magistrates, think-

[1] *Corpus Inscr.* vol. vi. n. 920.
[2] Helbig, *Guide*, vol. i. p. 407, n. 547.

THE VENUS GENETRIX BY ARKESILAOS

ing it a great pity that the fourth and last should belong to
a different Cæsar, made away with the head of Claudius,
and substituted in its place that of the philosopher Emperor. The one hundred and thirty-six cartloads of Greek
and Luna marble were purchased by the sculptor Flaminio

The conquest of Britain in the inscription of Claudius.

Vacca, who sold them in turn to Pope Clement VIII.,
Aldobrandini. The marbles were sawn into slabs and
made use of in the pavement and in the veneering of the
transept of St. John Lateran.

Other portions of the arch were discovered in 1587, 1641,
and 1870. The only fragment now visible, besides the
four panels mentioned above, is the left half of the dedica-

tory inscription set into the garden wall of the Barberini palace, Via delle Quattro Fontane. The other half supplemented in plaster is altogether wrong. (See page 263.)

If we except a breastplate of British pearls which decorated the statue of Venus Genetrix by Arkesilaos in the forum of Julius Cæsar, and certain masses of pig lead shipped from British mines to the imperial " Horrea plumbaria " on the left bank of the Tiber,[1] there are no other memorials dating from classic times. Those of a later age begin with the following record in the Anglo-Saxon Chronicle, A. D. 688 : " This year King Cædwalla went to Rome and received baptism from Pope Sergius, and in about seven days afterwards, on the twelfth day before the kalends of May [April 20, 689], while he was yet in his baptismal garments, he died and was buried in St. Peter's."

We do not know the details of the hearty reception tendered by the semi-barbaric Romans of the seventh century to the fair-haired and blue-eyed young convert ; but Adhelm, bishop of Sherborne, in a poem written in praise of the royal maiden Bugge, asserts that the king of Essex was received, as it were, in triumph amidst loud demonstrations of joy from the clergy and from the populace. He was buried in the atrium or " paradise " of St. Peter's, and his grave was inscribed with two records, a poem of twelve distichs and a short biographical note. Their text is to be found in Bede's " History," v. 7, and also in the " Sylloge Turonensis," n. 40, edited by de Rossi, " Inscr. Christ." vol. ii. p. 70. The epitaph says, " Here lies Chedual, the same as Peter, King of the Saxons, about thirty years of age. He was laid to rest on April 20th in the Second Indiction, in the fourth consulship of our Lord Justinian the most pious Emperor, and in the second year of the pontificate of our

---

[1] *Corpus Inscr.* vol. xv.[2] p. 987 ; Nibby, *Roma antica*, vol. ii. p. 149.

ANNO dñice incārnātionif fexcentefimo .v. beatī gregoriuf
poft quā fedē Romane & aplice ecclē tredeci annof.
menfef vi. & dief x. gloriofiffime rexit defunctꝰ eft.
atq̃ ao ēnā regni cpleftif fedē ēnf latuf eſr.

OLDEST EXISTING VIEW OF THE FAÇADE OF ST. PETER'S
(From a sketch of the eleventh century in Cod. 124 of the Eton Library)

Apostolic father Sergius the first." According to Giovanni de Deis, who in 1589 published a pamphlet on the "Successors of Barnabas the Apostle," both inscriptions had been composed by Benedict, archbishop of Milan. The same writer declares that the sarcophagus which contained the remains of the king was discovered together with the epitaph in the foundations of the new basilica of St. Peter in the time of Sixtus V. It must have been broken to pieces, and thrown, like the commonest building material, into the building trenches.

According to William of Malmesbury and other chroniclers two other Saxon kings were buried in the " paradise," Offa of Essex and Cœnred of Mercia, both of whom had embraced the monastic life in one of the cloisters near the Vatican. It is uncertain whether King Ina and his queen, Æthelburga, were buried in the same place, or in the national church of S. Maria de Burgo Saxonum, which had been founded or enlarged by Ina himself.[1]

This Schola Saxonum is the oldest and foremost of the foreign colonies which clustered round St. Peter's, in the low and unhealthy ground formerly occupied by the gardens of Agrippina the elder. It dates from A. D. 727, while the Schola of the Langobards was only founded about 770 by Queen Ansa, and those of the Franks and Frisians by Charlemagne towards the end of the same century. It consisted of a hospice for pilgrims and of a chapel dedicated to the Virgin Mary. The chapel is still in existence, near the gate of the Leonine city called Posterula Saxonum (Porta di S. Spirito), although much altered and modernized under the name of Santo Spirito in Sassia. The colony flourished for many years, extending as far as the Ponte S.

[1] Compare Tesoroni's article in the *Proceedings* of the British and American Arch. Society of Rome, March 24, 1891, p. 13.

Angelo on the site of the present Arciospedale di S. Spirito; and the name Burg or Burgh, by which its dwellers designated it, is still in use, Italianized as Borgo.[1]

The reconstruction of this interesting quarter after the fire and pillage of the Saracens in 846 is connected with the establishment of Peter's pence, about which so much information has been given by Garampi, Cancellieri, and de Rossi.[2] To keep the accommodations for pilgrims in good order, to supply them with food and clothing, to nurse them in their ailments, and to offer the Pope a tribute for the maintenance of the places of pilgrimage, a national contribution was established towards the beginning of the ninth century, under the names of Romescot, Romfeah, Rompening, etc., to be shared by every paterfamilias owning a certain amount of property. In 998 the annual subsidy amounted to three hundred marks sterling. A mark contained one hundred and sixty denarii; that is to say, it represented the tribute of one hundred and sixty families. Therefore the three hundred marks put down as the English tribute in the " Liber Censuum " represented forty-eight thousand families, a considerable number indeed, if we recollect what was the state of the British Isles in those days.

Three " ripostigli " or hidden deposits of Peter's pence have been found in Rome: one in the House of the Vestals, one in the belfry of St. Paul's, one at the Aquæ Salviæ or Tre Fontane.

The first, discovered November 8, 1882, in that part of the Atrium Vestæ which had been occupied between 942

[1] Compare Antonio de Waal, *I luoghi pii sul territorio vaticano*, Roma, 1886, p. 14.

[2] Garampi, in *Cod. vatic. latin.* 9022, and *Memorie della beata Chiara di Rimino*, p. 232 ; Cancellieri, in *Giornale arcadico*, 1821, vol. x. p. 264 ; De Rossi, in *Notizie degli Scavi*, decembre, 1883.

11. *Henry Cleen sculps.* *Burgus Roma.* *Philipp Gall excud.*

THE BORGO, TIME OF ALEXANDER VI

and 946 by an officer of the court of Pope Marinus II., contained a gold-piece of Theophilus (A. D. 829–842) and eight hundred and thirty-four silver pennies, representing the tribute of so many families. The pennies all come from English royal or archiepiscopal mints, except four which bear the stamp of the mints of Pavia, Limoges, and Ratisbon. The presence of the four outsiders among the mass of British pennies is not to be wondered at. In " Vol. Miscell. Ashmole," 1820, of the Bodleian, p. 7, there is an account of the discovery in Lancashire, in 1611, of a repository with pieces of Alfred, Edward, Edmund, kings, and Plegmund, archbishop, mixed with foreign pennies, some French, some marked with the name of King Berengarius. Most of the English pieces bore the motto SCI PETRI MO(*neta*) EBORACE CIV, which has nothing to do with Peter's pence, but only shows that the piece was struck in the archiepiscopal mint of York, the cathedral of which was dedicated to St. Peter.

The second ripostiglio was found in 1843, walled in in the old belfry of St. Paul's-outside-the-Walls, the third in 1871 at the Tre Fontane. Both date from the time when the institution of the " denarius sancti Petri " had become general among the nations of western Europe.

I conclude by remarking that the discovery of English coins in Rome is an extremely rare occurrence. There are only a few in the Vatican collection, the origin of which, besides, is not known. Considering this state of things, de Rossi has come to the conclusion that English silver must have been recoined in the Pontifical mint.

The institution of an English college in Rome is connected by modern guidebooks with the old Schola and hospice of the Saxons, but without warrant, for the hospice, after having thrice been burned and plundered, was abandoned in 1204, and its revenues were transferred by Innocent III. to the newly founded hospital of S. Spirito. The institution may with more reason be connected with that of the Jubilee which caused a revival of Anglo-Roman intercourse in 1300. English pilgrims felt the loss of their national hospice ; and it was at this juncture that a London merchant, named John Shepherd, purchased certain houses on the Via now called di Monserrato, and having converted them into an establishment for the reception of pilgrims and travellers under the invocation of the Holy Trinity and St. Thomas, became with his wife the first superintendent of the new institution.[1] According to the original deed in the archives of the present English college, the foundation must have been made about the year 1362. Hospice and church occupied part of the site of the " Stabula Factionis Venetæ," the barracks and stables of the squadron of the charioteers of the Circus who wore the blue colors. The other three squadrons were distinguished, as is well known, by their white (Factio albata), green (Factio prasina) and red (Factio russata) costumes. Each had independent barracks, built with great magnificence, and ornamented with precious works of art, adjoining which there was a field called Trigarium or Campus Trigarius, for the breaking in and training of horses, for which purpose the charioteers availed themselves of the " triga," the untamed animal being harnessed between two trained ones. The barracks of the Greens, the favorite color with the Roman populace, are placed in the neighborhood of the church of S. Lorenzo in Damaso, on account of the denomination " in Prasino " (among the Greens) which the church

---

[1] Compare Henry Foley's vol. vi. of the *Records of the English province of the Society of Jesus*, London, Burns & Oates, 1880, p. xxviii.

bore in ages gone by. The surmise has been shown to be correct through the discovery of a pedestal dedicated to an " agitator Factionis Prasinæ " under the adjoining palace of la Cancelleria, and also of a water-pipe inscribed with the words " Factionis Prasinæ." [1] These beautiful barracks, or whatever parts of them were left standing, were occupied between 366 and 384 by Pope Damasus, who transformed them into an " archivum," or " chartarium Ecclesiæ Romanæ " for the preservation and safe-keeping of books and documents belonging to the Holy See. Barracks and library have disappeared long since. The building, repaired and probably disfigured from time to time, was levelled to the ground four hundred and fifteen years ago (1486) by Cardinal Raphael Riario, nephew of Sixtus IV. Its columns of red Egyptian granite were made use of by Bramante in his wonderful court of the Palazzo della Cancelleria. (See p. 273.) The " Stabula Factionis Prasinæ " were bounded on the west side by a street now called Via dei Cappellari. On the opposite side of the same street, and between it and the Via di Monserrato (also ancient), rose the barracks of the Blues, on a corner of which the English hospice was established by John Shepherd. Many interesting finds are recorded in connection with the place. Pietro Sante Bartoli, pontifical superintendent of antiquities at the end of the seventeenth century, says that a " bellissima statua di un Fauno " was discovered in the foundations of the new college in the spring of 1682, as well as the architrave of a shrine dedicated to the god Silvanus, A. D. 90, by a charioteer named Thallus. The Blues are also recorded in inscription n. 9719 of vol. vi. Corpus Inscr. Latin. (" Crescens . . . natione Bessus, olearius de porticu Pallantiana Venetianorum "), and in n. 10,044,

---

[1] *Corpus Inscr.* vol. vi. n. 10,058, 10,063 ; *Bull. Arch. Com.* 1887, p. 10.

a pedestal erected in memory of one of their great victories (" Victoria Venetianorum semper constet feliciter "). I may add that when the present church of St. Thomas à Becket was commenced in 1870 from the designs of Vespignani the elder, remains of ecclesiastical edifices of the eleventh or twelfth century and of an ancient Roman road were discovered in the excavation for the foundations.

The pilgrim-book of the new college, commencing December 29, 1580, and ending in 1656, has been published by Foley. The hospitable gates of the college seem to have been equally open to Protestants and Catholics, provided the visitors came from the mother country, and brought letters of recommendation. The first entry in the book runs as follows : —

" 1580, December 29. The illustrious Dom. Thomas Arundel, an Englishman of the diocese of . . . was this day admitted as the first guest, and remained with us for three days." This is the celebrated Sir Thomas surnamed the " Valiant " on account of his daring exploits at the battle of Gran, when he took with his own hands the standard of Mahomet. For this action of bravery he was created a Count of the Holy Roman Empire in 1595 and first Baron Arundell of Wardour in 1605. We also meet with the names of the Duke of Buckingham, the Earls of Carnarvon, Devon, Bolingbroke, the Lords Berkeley, Kensington, Howard, Stafford, Hamilton, etc. Of Henry, son of the first marquis of Worcester, it is said : —

" 1649, December 20. This most noble pilgrim came to us and remained until February the 14th, affording a remarkable example to all the college from his habit of constant prayer, spiritual conversation, and humility. On leaving us he thought of proceeding to Jerusalem."

Perhaps the most famous of all the visitors of the college were John Milton and Richard Crashaw.

The Palazzo della Cancelleria, built with the columns and marbles of the Barracks of the " Greens " (Factio Prasina).

John Milton had been travelling in Italy since the death of his mother in 1637. He became a guest of the college on October 30, 1638, when he took his first dinner in the refectory, together with the students, Mr. Carey, brother of Lord Falkland, Dr. Holling of Lancashire, and a Mr. Fortescue.

Richard Crashaw, son of William, " preacher in the Temple," born in 1612, Fellow of Peterhouse and Pembroke Hall, Cambridge, was expelled from that celebrated University with four other Fellows on June 11, 1644, because they had refused to sign " the Solemn League and Covenant." He became a Catholic while an exile in France, and Queen Henrietta Maria, then a fugitive in Paris, to whom he had been presented by his friend and fellow poet Cowley, gave him letters of introduction to Italy. The pilgrim-book of the English college contains the following entry : " Richard Crashaw, a pilgrim, arrived November 28, 1646, and remained fifteen days." Other entries show that the poet frequented the hospice for the space of four years. After entering the household of Cardinal Paleotto, he obtained a canonry at Loreto, in which city he died of fever after a few weeks' residence. He was buried in that celebrated sanctuary in 1650.[1]

The reason which prompted English travellers, Protestant as well as Catholic, to seek the hospitality of the college, must be found, first, in their spirit of nationality, superior to religious controversies and questions of creed, and, secondly, in the wretched condition of Roman hostelries, uncomfortable, unclean, and dear.

The oldest and best known inns, known in fact since the institution of Jubilees, were the Albergo dell' Orso, the Albergo del Sole, and the Albergo della Luna.

The Albergo dell' Orso is still extant, and still answering its purpose, although the *clientèle* is decidedly changed. It stands at the corner of the Via di Monte Brianzo and the Via del' Orso, and although whitewashed and slightly altered, its shell and internal arrangements are practically the same. Its guest-book begins with the name of Dante, — at least so the tradition says,[2] — and ends, as far as famous men are concerned, with that of Montaigne, who occupied a room on the street side, for a few days, in 1580.

Another of these venerable establishments, still flourishing in its own way, is the Albergo del Sole, near the Piazza del Paradiso. Its first mention dates from 1469 ; and it has undergone no special change in the course of four hundred and thirty years.

---

[1] Foley, *l. c.* p. xxxiii.; Grosart, *Complete Works of Richard Crashaw;* Fuller's *Worthies' Library*, 1872.

[2] Monti, *Opere*, vol. i. p. 260.

The " Grand Hotel " of the seventeenth century was undoubtedly the Hosteria di Monte Brianzo, in the street of the same name, near the church of S. Lucia della Tinta. In 1628–1629 it gave shelter to three princes of Hesse who were travelling incognito. Burckhard calls it " une hostellerie fameuse au bord du Tibre," and we know from Mancini's " Viaggio " that its façade had been designed

A typical Roman hostelry.

and perhaps painted by no less a master than Baldassare Peruzzi. The inn came to grief about 1669.

The number of hostelries in Rome at the beginning of the seventeenth century (1615) was 360 ; in Jubilee years the number was quadrupled. Giovanni Ruccellai counted 1022 in 1450. Their capacity varied. The Hosteria della Campana accommodated in 1469 thirty-five guests and thirty-eight horses, and in 1489 the Duke Otto of Braunschweig, his suite, and twenty-nine horses. The managers were mostly Germans or North Italians, demanding, as a rule, exorbitant prices.

Ventura, who visited Rome in the Jubilee of 1300, spent forty-four cents a day for his room alone. Matteo Villani says that in the Jubilee of 1350 the stabling of a horse cost ninety cents a day, a loaf of bread twelve cents, a "pintello" of wine five.

The accommodations were not luxurious. The windows had the "impannata," that is, a piece of white linen or canvas instead of glass. The beds were covered by white canopies or "padiglioni." Fireplaces for cooking and heating at the same time were first introduced in 1357 by Francesco da Carrara, Lord of Padua. The innovation is thus described in the "Chronicle" of Galeazzo Gataro.[1] "When Francesco alighted in Rome at the 'Moon' he was surprised to find that there were no chimneys nor fireplaces, the Romans being in the habit of cooking their meals or of warming themselves near a box full of ashes, that is, a hearthstone placed in the middle of the room.[2] Francesco, having brought with him from Padua master masons and artisans of various crafts, caused two chimneys and two flues to be made in the Albergo della Luna, which he decorated with his own coat of arms. Chimneys have since become popular in Rome."

The rooms were marked not by numbers, but by names. That in the Albergo dell' Orso, rented to Giovanni Vicentino in 1570, was called the White Cross (la Croce Bianca.) Gabriel Coyer found in the hotel at Turin in 1763 the rooms of the Madonna, St. Paul, and St. Peter; and Kotzebue mentions four miserable little apartments in the

---

[1] In Muratori, *Rerum Italic. Scriptores*, vol. xvii. col. 46.

[2] The practice is still followed in the huts and farms of the Roman Campagna.

hostelry at Novi, which were named Venice, Rome, Paris, and Naples; and in another place four rooms named from the four parts of the world and a fifth called Russia.

Another curious custom was the hanging of a coat of arms in rooms occupied by a distinguished personage. Montaigne had his own painted in gold and colors at Pisa, at a cost of one and a half scudi. The Marquis Vincenzo Giustiniani gave two guldens to the artist of Aix-la-Chapelle, who painted his armorial bearings over the door of his room.

Lodgings, in the English sense of the word, were also to be had in Rome. When Montaigne left the Albergo dell' Orso in 1580, he took up his quarters in lodgings, Via di Monte Branzo, n. 25, paying twenty scudi a month for three good rooms — salon, dining-room, kitchen — and stables, fuel, and cook. He was charged only for provisions. The same rooms were rented in 1638 to a son of the King of Denmark travelling incognito. The diary of Misson, who journeyed through Italy in 1717, contains the following passage: " En arrivant à Rome nous nous misme dans une Auberge. Mais à notre retour de Naples, nous prisme ce qu'ils appellent un palazzo, et ce qu'il faut nommer en bon François une maison garnie. Nous estions fort honorablement pour vingt piastres par mois." About the same period the daily wages for a valet or laquais were thirty cents, while a good carriage and pair could be hired for thirty dollars a month.[1]

John Evelyn of Wotton says in his diary — edited by William Bray in 1818 — that having reached the gates of the Eternal City on November 4, 1644, wet to the skin, and " being perplexed for a convenient lodging, he wandered up and down on horseback, till at last he was conducted with his

---

[1] Misson, *Voyage en Italie*, vol. iii. p. 229 (La Haye, 1717).

companions to the house of one Monsieur Petit, a Frenchman, near the Piazza di Spagna," probably the " Inn of the
Three Keys," which stood near the entrance to the Via del
Babuino.   This diary of Evelyn, on the subject of which
there is an excellent article by Tesoroni in the " Journal of
the British and American Arch. Society of Rome " (vol. iii.
n. 1, p. 33), is full of useful and pleasant information about
the social and material state of Rome under Pope Pamfili,
Innocent X.   He went once to listen to the sermon which
used to be delivered every week exclusively for the benefit
of the Jews in the Oratorio della Trinità near the Ponte
Sisto.   These compulsory sermons had been established at
the suggestion of a certain Andrea del Monte, a converted
rabbi of the time of Julius II.   The Jews were forced by
the police to listen to the preacher, while a beadle with a
wand woke up the sleepy and chastised the noisy.   Evelyn
adds, with a touch of humor, " A conversion is very rare ; "
yet during his stay in Rome two conversions took place,
one of a Jew, the other of a Turk, Evelyn acting as god-
father to both.   The Turk was a sincere convert, the Jew
an impostor.

In Evelyn's Memoirs we find also a pleasing account of
English society in Rome, for which there were two centres :
one at the English college near the Palazzo Farnese, then
placed under the direction of the Jesuit fathers ; the other
at the Palazzo Barberini, the courteous owner of which, Cardinal Francesco, styled himself the Protector of England.
There were at that time many and distinguished travellers
from beyond the Channel, Lord John Somerset, brother of
the Marquis of Worcester, who had an apartment in the
Palazzo della Cancelleria ; Patrick Carey, a witty person, brother of Lord Falkland ; two physicians, Dr. Bacon and Dr.
Gibbs, attached to the suite of Cardinal Capponi.   Gibbs, a

The English palace in Rome.

Scotchman by birth, educated at Oxford, practised at the hospital of Santo Spirito, and acted occasionally as a guide to Evelyn. "He was an elegant writer of Latin poetry : a small selection of his poems was published at Rome, where he died in 1677 and was buried in the Pantheon." Among the curiosities he saw in the City, Evelyn notes one Mrs. Ward, a devotee, soliciting money for the establishment of an order of female Jesuits!

I will now give an account of the residences of English ambassadors in Rome, two of which have become famous in history, one before, one after the Reformation.

Visitors to Rome are certainly familiar with the Palazzo Giraud-Torlonia in the Piazza di Scossa Cavalli, built by Bramante for Cardinal Adriano di Castelli Corneto at the end of the fifteenth century. The palace is equally inter-esting to the archæologist, to the artist, and to the histo-

rian : to the first because it is built with the stones and marbles of the Basilica Julia and of the temple of Janus; to
the second because of the beauty and purity of its design ;
to the last because it was inhabited by the representatives
of England at the court of Rome before the Reformation.

We know very little about the early career of Cardinal
Adriano, and his end is also shrouded in mystery.[1] It
seems that a great knowledge of Hebrew, Latin, and Greek,
as well as shrewdness in political and ecclesiastical affairs,
won for him the good graces of Pope Innocent VIII., by
whom the young prelate was sent to England with the mission of bringing about peace between the kings of England
and Scotland. Henry VII., in his turn, made him representative of English interests with Innocent VIII. and
Alexander VI., and gave him the see of Hereford, which he
exchanged later on for that of Bath and Wells. Promoted
cardinal on May 30, 1503, under the title of S. Crisogono,
he brought to completion the building of a magnificent
mansion in the Borgo di San Pietro. The street on which
the palace stands had just been opened by Alexander VI.
through the slums of the Borgo, to give a suitable access
to St. Peter's from the bridge of S. Angelo ; and it was
accordingly named the Via Alexandrina. Nothing could
have pleased the Pope more than the readiness of Cardinal
Adriano to raise a costly building on the street which bore
his name. On this score, probably, the cardinal was given
full permission to secure building materials from wherever
he chose, and to lay hands on whichever ruins best suited
his purpose.

The palace was built with money provided by the liber-

[1] Born at Corneto about 1458, he became the most important personage of
the court of Rome under Alexander VI. Disgraced by Leo X. on account of
his share in the conspiracy of Cardinal Petrucci, he fled from Rome. The place
and time of his death are unknown.

ality of King Henry VII., with the help of funds which Cardinal Adriano had been able to lay by in his capacity of collector of apostolic revenues and Peter's pence in England. Behind the palace, in the direction of the Leonine walls,

Alexander VI.

extended a garden,[1] in which one of the most thrilling events in the history of that eventful period took place. On Saturday evening, August 12, Pope Alexander Borgia

[1] More exactly in the direction of the " Via Sixtina prope muros." On the west side it extended as far as the garden of Francesco Soderini, Cardinal of Volterra ; on the east side it touched the garden of Ardicino della Posta, Cardinal of Aleria.

and his son Cæsar, Duke of Valentinois, with Cardinal
Adriano, had partaken of some refreshments in this garden,
the company being restricted to the three personages already mentioned, besides Cardinal Romolino (who had presided over the execution of Fra Girolamo Savonarola) and
another whose name is not mentioned.   Both the Pope and
his son were taken that same evening with fits of vomiting,
followed by a violent fever.   Next day the Pope was bled,
and felt so relieved that he took pleasure in watching some
of his attendants playing at cards.   The fever came back
on the 14th, and disappeared the next day, only to strike
the patient again with increased violence on the 16th.   The
gates of the Vatican palace were closed, Scipio, the head
physician, and his assistant only being allowed free pass.
On Friday, August 18, at eight o'clock in the evening Alexander VI. expired, while his son, thanks to his youth and
robust constitution, was able to leave his bed and seek
refuge, with his followers and his valuables, in the Castle
of S. Angelo.

The rumor .that the Pope had died of poison spread like
wildfire through the City, and we find it received and commented upon in the diplomatic correspondence of Bel-
trando, ambassador of Ferrara, of Giustiniani, ambassador
of Venice, and also of the diarists Sanuto and Burckhard.
The theory of poison was strengthened in the minds of the
members of the court by the frightful appearance of the
corpse : " factus erat sicut pannus nigerrimus . . . os aper-
tum et adeo horribile quod nemo viderit unquam vel esse
tale dixerit," says Burckhard, and Sanuto repeats " mai a
tempo de cristiano fu veduta la più or(r)enda e terribil
cosa."   However, there is no necessity to resort to poison
to explain the fatal consequences of the supper of August
11.   The Vatican district had not improved very much in

salubrity since the days of Tacitus, who calls it " infamis
aëre ! " In fact, the cutting of a deep moat around the Castle
of S. Angelo, the choking up of drains, the transformation
of the once beautiful gardens of Domitia and Agrippina
into a marshy waste had made the Borgo the unhealthiest
district of Rome.[1] The August of 1503 had been particu-
larly malignant ; and half the members of the Pope's household were laid low with fever, many cases having proved

The cenotaph of Alexander VI. in the crypt of St. Peter's.

fatal. Soderini, the ambassador of Florence, could not
keep the Republic informed of the course of events in consequence of an attack of malaria. And yet, if the case was

[1] Cardinal Noris, in a letter dated September 10, 1695, says that seven
hundred persons had already been attacked by fever in the Borgo in the course
of that summer.

as simple as that, how can we explain the fact that Cardinal Adriano's skin fell in strips, a fact which he himself attributed to poisoning? Something terrible must have happened on that memorable evening; but I am afraid that the principal actors must have carried the secret into their graves.

One of the versions, which found its way into the diplomatic correspondence of the time, is that Alexander and Valentino had plotted to poison their host, whose fortune they were eager to confiscate, and that they both drank by mistake the contents of the wrong bottle. Another version, accepted in Venice, speaks of sugar-plums instead of wine as the means selected by the Borgias to deal their blow; and adds that Cardinal Adriano, suspecting the reason which had prompted the Pope to ask for an invitation to supper, had bribed the Pope's butler with a promise of ten thousand ducats if the poisonous candy would be spared to him.

Both versions seem to be wrong, and could eventually be proved so. The student and lover of art has this advantage over the historian and the politician, that he need not embitter his own mind and excite the passions of his readers by discussing the rights and wrongs of the Borgias, to determine whether they were the abominable monsters, the curse of mankind, of whom we have been accustomed to read in cheap books, or if they must be considered as no better and no worse than the average Italian princes of the beginning of the sixteenth century, with whose deeds and politics we have been made familiar by Macchiavelli. I have before me a volume printed in 1887, in which the title of " mostri iniqui e infernali "[1] is attributed, not to the Borgias, but to those who speak of them with disrespect! I have

[1] Infernal and iniquitous monsters.

also before me an unpublished epigram by a contemporary of Alexander VI., a witness of his deeds as a man, as a prince, and as a priest, in which the seven capital sins are distinctly alluded to in connection with his career. To the student and lover of art, however, he appears under a better light as the builder of the Sale Borgia in the Vatican, the most exquisite, the most fascinating production of Italian art at the opening of the Golden Age.

The palace of Cardinal di Corneto, in which this tragic event took place, became English property in March, 1505. By a deed, which is still to be found in the records of the notary Beneinbene, the cardinal granted his property to Henry VII., to his heirs and successors, as a residence for English representatives to the Holy See. It was inhabited by Silvestro Gigli in 1521, and by Christopher Bainbridge, Cardinal of S. Prassede, in 1544. It did not remain long in English hands, for Henry VII. presented it in his turn to his dear friend, Cardinal Lorenzo Campeggi. Afterwards it passed through many hands,[1] until it was sold, March 29, 1820, to Prince Torlonia for the nominal sum of eight thousand dollars.

Rome saw no more ambassadors from the court of St. James until 1686, on April 13 of which year the Earl of Castlemain, the special and, for some time, secret envoy of King James II. to Innocent XI., reached the banks of the Tiber. He was met two miles beyond the Porta del Popolo by Cardinal Thomas Howard and his gentleman in waiting, Paolo Faliconeri, and, leaving his own travelling-

---

[1] Cardinal Tolomeo Galli about 1580 ; Cardinal Scipione Borghese in 1609 ; the Campeggi again in 1635 ; Cardinal Girolamo Colonna in 1650 ; Queen Christina of Sweden in 1669 ; Cardinal Radziekowsky about 1680 ; the hospice for poor priests, called dei Cento Preti, in 1699; Count Pietro Giraud in 1720 ; the Vatican manufacture of mosaics in 1816 ; Giovanni Torlonia in 1820.

The Palazzo Pamphili in the Piazza Navona.

coach, drove with the cardinal to his residence. The ambassador kept his official incognito for ten months; unofficially he was all this time the most talked-of foreign representative in Rome. He had taken up his quarters in the magnificent Palazzo Pamphili in the Piazza Navona, over the gate of which hung two shields, each twenty-two feet in diameter. Whether on account of their extraordinary size, or of the even more extraordinary subjects painted upon them, these two shields became the talk of the town, and a pamphlet was published to explain their meaning to the wondering crowds.[1] One, the shield of the Pope, showed the figure of Britannia paying homage to the Church, assisted and comforted by a venerable old man

[1] *Lettera nella quale si ragguaglia un Prelato . . . delle 2 grand' armi alzate sulla facciata del palazzo Pamfili, etc.* Roma, Ant. Ercole, 1686.

alleged to represent " Christian Zeal," by a female figure
representing Prudence, and by the personification of " Royal
Valor " in the character of Hercules trampling under his
feet the figure of Envy. There was also an altar, with the
Book of the Gospels upon it, resting upon the shoulders
of two Turks, — one in military attire with many horse-
tails, one dressed as a mufti, with a mutilated copy of the
Koran in his hands. The scene was made complete by two
sphinxes, Father Tiber placidly gliding under the Ælian

The Barberini Palace.

Bridge, and branches of laurel symbolizing the victories
of Holy Church.

The other shield, belonging to Great Britain, almost
baffles description. There were the coats of arms of England, France, Ireland, and Scotland, the garter, the lion,
the unicorn, the helmet, the crown, the ermine mantelet,
in a shield supported by two angels. Then came another

Hercules, brandishing the club with one hand and a blue label with the other, with the motto, " Dieu et mon droit," followed by a matron representing Britannia, and by the figure of St. George, clad in armor, with a red English cross on the cuirass. The hydra which he was piercing with a spear had seven heads, representing seven leaders of the Rebellion, among whom was the " impious, infamous, and faithless " Titus Oates. Hercules and Britannia, in the mean time, were trampling under their feet the rebel Colledge (who had a corn thresher in his hands) and Oliver Cromwell, with the characteristic orange feathers on the helmet. Here also the scene was made complete by Father Thames gliding under London Bridge, and by sphinxes, angels, and branches of laurel.

The solemn presentation of credentials to Pope Innocent XI. took place on January 8, 1687, followed by a banquet given by Cardinal Charles Barberini in his great palace on the Quirinal. The table, set in the Sala di Pier da Cortona, was forty-seven feet long, and covered with sugar statuettes representing the " Glories and Deeds of James II. the Invict." The dinner lasted three hours, each of the sixty or seventy courses being announced by a flourish of trumpets. On the adjournment to the next hall, the ambassador was welcomed by all the ladies and gentlemen of the Roman nobility, all in fancy costumes on account of the Carnival, and invited by them to drive in the Corso. He appeared accordingly in the throng of joyous masqueraders, and drove through the historic street in the state coach of the Barberini, accompanied by Cardinals Pamphili, Altieri, and Howard. All these events, by which the population of Rome was so pleased and amused for the time being, are described and illustrated in contemporary pamphlets and prints, the best of all being Michael Writ's " Ragguaglio

POPE INNOCENT XI

della solenne comparsa fatta in Roma gli otto di gennaio MDCLXXXVII dal . . . conte di Castelmaine ambasciatore . . . di Giacomo secondo re d' Inghilterra, Scozia, Francia, et Ibernia . . . in andare publicamente all' udienza di . . . papa Innocenzo undecimo, etc., etc. Roma, Ercole, 1687."

I have found a copy of this rare and curious volume, illustrated with engravings by Arnold van Westerhout, in the library of Sir George Trevelyan at Wallington Hall. It appears that the embassy, which numbered twenty-two members, had embarked at Greenwich on February 15, 1686, on the vessel Henrietta Mary, Captain Fesby, the crossing of the Channel taking over two days and a half. From Dieppe they travelled overland to Avignon, Monaco, Genoa, and Leghorn. At Avignon the papal delegate, Mgr. Cenci, entertained the ambassador at a banquet composed of four courses of fourteen services each, fifty-six plates in all.

On the day appointed for the presentation of the credentials, the Earl of Castlemain drove to the Quirinal in a coach drawn by six bays, a present from the Marchese di Carpi, viceroy of Naples. The coach was escorted by six pages and thirty-two outriders, and followed by three hundred and thirty-five carriages. The procession followed a roundabout way to the Quirinal, by S. Agostino, the Fontanella di Borghese, the Corso, and the Tre Cannelle. On January 14 the ambassador gave his state banquet in the Gallery of the Pamphili palace, painted by Pier da Cortona. On the table, one hundred and thirty palms long, were eighty silver trays supporting lions and unicorns of sugar. One hundred and ninety dishes were served. The public rejoicings were closed by a musical entertainment given by Queen Christina of Sweden in her beautiful (Corsini) palace.

I will bring this chapter to a close by referring briefly to the delightful church of S. Gregorio at Monte Celio, which is, or ought to be, the English national church in Rome.

I have never been able to understand the reason why the Popes of the last three centuries, so generous in the matter of the discovery and safe-keeping of classic remains, should have shown such marked indifference about church antiquities. If we consider that one fifth at least of our city and suburban places of worship date from an age when the level of streets was from twelve to thirty feet lower, and that when their floors were raised to the present level no great injury was done to such parts of the edifice as were doomed to disappear from view, it is easy to understand what an amount of light the rediscovery of the buried portions would throw on the origin and history of each building. The zeal of the Popes seems never to have been roused towards this aim, not even in the case of the houses of Prisca and Pudens, the walls of which, lying under their respective churches, have echoed in all probability with the sound of the voices of the Apostles. The only works of interest in this line, the rediscovery of the Constantinian church of St. Clement, and of the House of John and Paul, were undertaken in 1857 and 1887, respectively, by private lovers of past memories, Father Mullooly and Padre Germano, while the official authorities were planning on their side the ghastly " restorations " of S. Crisogono, SS. Apostoli, S. Angelo in Pescheria, S. Agnese, S. Maria in Trastevere, etc., or the destruction of the Constantinian apse of the Lateran.

No exploration of this kind would have better answered its purpose, and better repaid the expense and time and labor of the explorers than that of St. Gregory's house and oratory, lying at a great depth under the church on the

The church of S. Gregorio.

Cælian. A committee of which I was a member was formed in 1890 for this purpose, under the presidency of Cardinal Manning; a search was made through the cellars of the adjoining monastery, and the fact ascertained that the house of the great pontiff and the monastic establishment from which Augustine started to preach the gospel in Great Britain (see page 294) are in a marvellous state of preservation, and could easily be excavated without impairing in the least the stability of the modern church above. Cardinal Manning had offered two thousand pounds to help the preliminary works, and the city authorities had most willingly given their approval, when the whole scheme collapsed for reasons that it would be out of place to mention here.

The project of sending his apostles to England was conceived by Gregory the Great early in 596, on receiving the news that the Christian aborigines were allowed by the

Anglo-Saxon a certain freedom in practising their faith, and that Æthelbyrht, king of Kent and bretwalda of the heptarchy, had married a Christian princess, Bertha, daughter of Caribert, to whom also full freedom was granted to follow the precepts of Christ.

The apostolic mission, headed by Augustine, started from the House of Gregory in the spring of 596. They followed the course of the Tiber to Porto, set sail for the Gulf of Lyons, and eventually landed at the monastic island of Lerins on the coast of Provence. Here the mission was overtaken by feelings of despondency. The tossing of their ship over the choppy waves of the Mediterranean, the sight of new lands, the sound of unknown tongues, made them regret so profoundly their happy and uneventful life on the Cælian hill that Augustine was sent back to implore from Gregory their release from the perilous undertaking.

St. Augustine leaving Rome for England.

As a token of humble devotion Augustine brought with him a certain quantity of wooden spoons and cups carved by the monks of Lerins for the poor of Rome. Gregory kindly but firmly maintained his former decision : Augustine was sent back with the title of abbot, and with letters of recommendation to Brunehilde, queen of Austrasia and Burgundia, to Clotaire II. of Neustria, and to the Frank or Austrasian prelates. The journey was resumed under better auspices. Of their landing at Tanatos (Thanet), of their settling at Doruvernum (Canterbury), of their reception by Bertha and Æthelbyrht, of their fruitful evangelization of England, I need not speak, as the history of these events has just been written anew and with profound learning by my friend Professor Hartmann Grisar, S. J., the illustrious author of the " Geschichte Roms und der Päpste im Mittelalter." [1]

The same events are commemorated by two long inscriptions in the atrium of S. Gregorio, which contains another monument dear to the English visitor, the tomb of Sir Edward Carne of Glamorganshire. Sir Edward was sent abroad with Cranmer in 1530 to seek the opinion of foreign universities on the divorce of Henry VIII. Later on he became British representative at the court of Rome, and several of his dispatches have been published by Bishop Burnet. On the breaking up of diplomatic relations Paul IV. induced him to remain in Rome, where he died in 1561. Another remarkable tomb of British interest is to be found in the church of S. Cecilia, a church once full of archæological interest and now one of the most impressive specimens of the heinous taste which prevailed in the seventeenth century among Roman artists and their patrons. A discovery, however, has just been made that will lead us to forget the shameful transformation of the church above ground, for the value of what has been found below.[2]

[1] Published by Herder of Freiburg in Breisgau, 1901 (vol. i.).

[2] Compare Crostarosa Pietro, *Bull. arch. cristiana*, vol. vi. 1900, pp. 143 and 265.

The excavations were undertaken in the autumn of the year 1899 by Cardinal Rampolla, titular of S. Cecilia, and his archæological adviser, Mgr. Crostarosa. They found a starting-point in the remains of a bathing-apartment, visible in and around the chapel of the saint at the extremity of the right aisle, and they were able to ascertain at once that these bathrooms formed part of a great and noble palace, the remains of which extend far beyond the area of the present church. The apartments brought to light are divided into two sections by a longitudinal wall without doors or openings of any kind. It seems, therefore, that the church covers the remains not of one but of two distinct houses, the boundary wall of which follows the axis of the nave. The one on the left is the nobler of the two, and contains among other apartments a hall of basilical type, with nave and aisles separated by two rows of clumsy brick pilasters. The house on the right must have belonged to a family of inferior rank, if we accept the conjecture of Professor Maru that the two circular tanks, discovered in the principal room formed part of a tanner's establishment. The conjecture is the more acceptable if we consider that the district in which S. Cecilia is placed was mostly occupied by tanners, the most powerful and the most troublesome of Roman trade guilds. Their headquarters, called "Coriaria Septimiana" from the Emperor Septimius Severus, who rebuilt and enlarged and endowed them at the beginning of the third century, were discovered in 1871 at the corner of the Via de' Salumi, and the Via in Piscinula, not more than two hundred and fifty yards from S. Cecilia. Another indication of the social state of the owner is to be found in the poverty and simplicity of the family shrine, or Lararium. It consists of a recess in one of the walls, shaped like a loophole, with a figurine of Minerva, carved in low relief out of a piece of peperino, at the bottom, while the slanting sides are panelled with a couple of terracotta friezes, representing a vintage scene. This second house is built over and amongst the remains of a much older one, dating from the second century B. C., when the level of the Trastevere was lower by six or seven feet, and when stone was used in domestic architecture instead of bricks. The walls of the nobler house are mostly of the third century after Christ, and its pavements — those, I mean, which have not been destroyed by the gravediggers after the erection of the church — are

The tomb of Cardinal Adam of Hertford.

of mosaic in black and white. Two rather good marble sarcophagi have also been unearthed — one with the Caledonian hunt on its lid, used again for Christian burial at the time of Paschal I., who rebuilt in 821 the old oratory of Urban I. and gave it its present basilican type.

All these interesting relics have been left visible under

the modern pavement, as has already been done with those of St. Clement, of Sts. John and Paul, and as will be done, I hope, at no distant date, with those of the house and monastery of Gregory the Great.

The tomb in S. Cecilia which attracts the attention of the English traveller is that of Cardinal Adam of Hertford, on the right of the main door. (See page 297.) This prelate, a very learned man for the age, administrator of the diocese of London and titular of S. Cecilia, took part in the opposition to Urban VI., and, having been arrested with five other cardinals at Lucera, was carried by that Pope to Genoa. He alone was saved, by the interference of the English crown, the others being put to death in the convent of S. Giovanni di Pre, where their remains were discovered not many years ago.

CHAPTER VIII.

An old tradition relates that Christianity had not long been established over the Roman Empire when one day a youth, weary and footsore, entered one of the gates of the Imperial City. He came from a land in the far north which few had heard of, and he had long travelled " per mare et per terras " in his desire to study the truths of faith by the tombs of the Apostles. How long Ninian remained in Rome is not stated ; however, by command of the Pope, he eventually retraced his steps home, preached the gospel to his fellow-countrymen, and founded the church of Galloway, about two hundred years before St. Augustine landed in England.

Scotland, however, was too far away and the difficulties of travelling too great for many to follow in Ninian's footsteps, and so the clergy was trained, not in Rome, nor on the Continent, but in the local monastic schools, which in Scotland, as elsewhere, were then the homes of learning and the nurseries of science. After the monastic schools came the universities, and St. Andrews and Glasgow and Aberdeen became the great centres of intellectual work. It was only after the religious troubles of the sixteenth century that the project of instituting a Scots college in Rome was formed.

The ancient monastery of St. James at Ratisbon, founded by Marianus Scotus in 1068, had long since fallen into a state of decay, and so had the seminary which Abbot Fleming had instituted in connection with the old abbey. In 1576 another Scotch college was founded at Tournay, not to speak of the one in Paris which owed its existence to Cardinal Beaton.

As far as Rome was concerned, there had been a national church dedicated to St. Andrew, and a hospice for the relief of Scotch pilgrims, long before the Reformation. The modern church of S. Andrea delle Fratte occupies and marks the spot where the devout people from beyond the Tweed found a welcome when they came to visit the holy places at Rome. It was Clement VIII. who, by a bull dated December 5, 1600, gave the Scottish Catholics a national college. Its site, very confined and unsuitable, was in the Via del Tritone, near the church of Our Lady of Constantinople. In 1604 it was transferred to the Via delle Quattro Fontane, opposite to the present Barberini palace, where it has remained ever since.

The history of this institution has been given by Mgr. Robert Fraser, the present rector, in an illustrated article published in the March number of "St. Peter's Magazine" for 1899. It is remarkably uneventful as far as general interests are concerned. More interesting, perhaps, to the reader is another incident in the history of Scottish-Roman relations, concerning the prominent place gained by a Scottish gentleman as an archæological explorer of the Campagna.

The name of Gavin Hamilton was not new in Rome. I have found in the records of the sixteenth century an obligation signed December 3, 1554, by the Reverend Doctor Gavin Hamilton, abbot of Kylwyning and coadjutor to the see of St. Andrews in the kingdom of Scotland, viz., a receipt for the sum of three thousand scudi of gold which he had borrowed from the bank of Andrea Cenami in Paris. For the guarantee of which sum he deposits the papal brief of nomination to the coadjutorship of St. Andrews, and offers the signature of three sponsors, Gavin Matreson, a priest of St. Andrews, D. Bonard, canon of Dingwall, and Andrew Grayme, a priest of Brechin.[1]

His namesake, the painter and explorer of the Campagna, was born at Lanark towards the middle of the eighteenth century, of an ancient and respected family, the Hamiltons of Murdieston. Having displayed from an early age a marked predilection for the fine arts, and not finding opportunities to gratify such a taste in his native land, he moved to Rome, where he soon acquired great renown, and where he passed the rest of his life, revisiting Scotland only at long intervals and for very short periods.[2]

I shall not follow his career as an artist, nor shall I describe his celebrated paintings in the Casino of the Villa Borghese, representing scenes from the Iliad. His partiality as an artist for Homeric subjects is shown not only by the great frescoes just mentioned, but also by smaller pictures, representing such scenes as Achilles standing over the dead body of Patroclus, Achilles dismissing Briseis, and Achilles dragging the body of Hector, which have passed into the collections of the Duke of Hamilton, of Lord Hopetoun, and of the Duke of Bedford.[3] Gavin Hamilton attracts us more as an archæological explorer of the Roman Campagna, as an indefatigable excavator, as a man of enormous activity crowned by extraordinary success. He was not working alone, but as a member of a company, formed, I am sorry to say, more for a lucrative than for a scientific

[1] State Archives, in the Campo Marzio, vol. 6166, p. 475.

[2] See Lord Fitzmaurice's article in the *Academy*, quoted by A. H. Smith, " Catalogue of . . . Marbles at Lansdowne House," p. 7.

[3] These subjects have been engraved by Cunego, Morghen, and others.

purpose. There were three of them, associated from 1769 or 1770 : James Byres, architect; Gavin Hamilton, painter; and Thomas Jenkins, banker. The place of Byres was afterwards taken by Robert Fagan, English consul at Rome. In volume i. of the " Townley Marbles " the Villa of Hadrian is indicated as their principal field of operation; but this is not precisely true. There is no doubt that the discoveries they made in the Pantanello, near the gates of Hadrian's Villa, count among the most successful of the century; but they had the same if not a better chance at Ostia, Porto, Ardea, Marino, Civita Lavinia, Torre Colombara, Campo Jemini, Cornazzano, Monte Cagnolo, Roma Vecchia, Gabii, Subiaco, Arcinazzo, etc. The documents concerning these excavations, unedited for the greater part, will be found in volume iv. of my " Storia degli Scavi di Roma." The second member of the company, James Byres, architect, was the special correspondent and purveyor of Charles Townley, as Hamilton was of William Fitzmaurice, second Earl of Shelburne, first Marquis of Lansdowne, and founder of the Lansdowne Museum of Statuary. Byres, besides working in the interest of the company, carried on a trade of his own, especially in rare books and drawings and in smaller and precious objects, among which were the " Mystic Cista " of Palestrina of the Townley Collection (found 1786), the bronze patera of Antium (found 1782), and the golden fibula of Palestrina, now in the British Museum, etc. Byres returned to his native land in 1790, and died at Tonly, Aberdeenshire, in 1817, at the age of eighty-five.

" Thomas Jenkins first visited Rome as an artist, but having amassed a considerable fortune by favor of Clement XIV. (Ganganelli) became the English banker. He was driven from Rome by the French, who confiscated all they could find of his property. Having escaped their fury, he died at Yarmouth immediately on his landing after a storm at sea, in 1798. For an account of his extensive dealings in antiquities (especially the purchase and dispersion of the Montalto-Negroni collection) see Michaelis, ' Anc. Marbles,' p. 75." [1]

I must say that the dealings of Hamilton and his associates with the government of the land whose hospitality they enjoyed were not always fair and above board. Payne Knight, giving evidence before the Select Committee of the House of Commons, on the Elgin Marbles, in 1793, distinctly affirms that some of the marbles could only be removed from Rome by bribing the Pope's officials, while others were "smuggled" or "clandestinely brought away." In a letter addressed by Hamilton to Lord Shelburne on July 16, 1772, we find the following passage: " In the meanwhile I give your Lordship the agreeable news that the Cincinnatus (discovered at the Pantanello in 1769) is now casing up for Shelburne House, as the Pope has declined the purchase at the price of £500, which I demanded, and has accepted of two other singular figures, . . . which I have given them at their own price, being highly necessary to keep Visconti and his companion the sculptor my friends. Your Lordship may remember I mentioned in a former letter that I had one other curious piece of sculpture which I could not divulge. I must, therefore, beg leave to reserve this secret to be brought to light in another letter, when I hope I shall be able to say it is out of the Pope's dominions. As to the Antinous, I am afraid I shall be obliged to smuggle it, as I can never hope for a license." And in a second letter, dated August 6, he adds : " Since my last I have taken the resolution to

[1] Smith, *A Catalogue*, p. 58 ; Dallaway, *Anecdotes*, p. 365.

send off the head of Antinous in the character of Bacchus without a license. The under-antiquarian alone is in the secret, to whom I have made an additional present, and hope everything will go well."

His luck as a discoverer of antiques was simply marvellous, and many of his reports sound like fairy tales. The year 1769 is the date of the excavations at the Pantanello, the product of which was mostly purchased by Lord Shelburne for the gallery at Lansdowne House. Hamilton himself wrote an account of the proceedings to Townley, a synopsis of which is given by Dallaway ("Anecdotes of the Arts in England," London, 1800, p. 364). The place had already been explored by a local landowner, Signor Lolli. Hamilton and his associates in the antiquarian speculation "employed some laborers to re-investigate this spot. They began at a passage to an old drain cut in the rock, by means of which they could lower the waters of the Pantanello. After having worked some weeks by lamplight, and up to the knees in stinking mud full of toads, serpents, and other vermin, a few objects were found . . . but . . . Lolli had already carried away the more valuable remains. The explorers fortunately met with one of Lolli's workmen, by whom they were directed to a new spot." "It is difficult to account," Hamilton writes to Townley, " for the contents of this place, which consisted of a vast number of trees, cut down and thrown into this hole, probably from despite, as having been part of some sacred grove, intermixed with statues, etc., all of which have shared the same fate. More than fifty-seven pieces of sculpture were discovered in a greater or less degree of preservation." [1]

[1] Catalogue given by Agostino Penna, in his *Viaggio pittorico della Villa Adriana*, Roma, 1833. The exploration of the Pantanello lasted from 1769 to 1772. Piranesi gives another excellent account in the description of his plan of Hadrian's Villa.

A view of Hadrian's Villa excavated by Hamilton.

The search at " Torre Colombara," near the ninth mile-stone of the Appian Way, began in the autumn of 1771. Two spots were chosen about half a mile apart : one supposed to have been a temple of Domitian, the other a villa of Gallienus. Hamilton was struck by the number of duplicate statues found in these excavations, one set being greatly inferior to the other in workmanship and finish, as if there had been an array of originals and one of replicas. The statues lay dispersed all over the place, as if thrown aside from ignorance of their value, or from a religious prejudice. Some were lying only a few inches below the surface of the field, and bore marks of the injuries inflicted upon them by the ploughman. First to come to light was the Marcus Aurelius, larger than life, now at Shelburne House. The Meleager, the jewel of the same collection, and one of the finest statues in England, was next found ; and

also the so-called " Paris Equestris," sold by Jenkins to Smith
Barry, Esq. The same gentleman purchased at a later
period a draped Venus, to which was given the name of
Victrix. In fact, most of the leading European collections
have their share of the finds of Torre Colombara. The
Museo Pio Clementino secured the celebrated Discobolus,
now in the Sala della Biga, n. 615, the colossal bust of Serapis, now in the Rotonda, n. 549, and some smaller objects ; [1]
Mr. Coch, of Moscow, a sitting Faun and an Apollinean
torso of exquisite grace; Dr. Corbett, a Venus ; Lord Lansdowne, an Amazon ; and so forth.

The crowning point of Hamilton's career must be found
in the search he made in the spring of 1792 among the
ruins of Gabii. Ciampini, Fabretti, Bianchini, and other
explorers of Latium had already identified the site of this
antique city, the Oxford of prehistoric times, with that of
Castiglione on the southeast side of the lake of the same
name. Many valuable or curious remains had come acci-
dentally to light in tilling the land, especially in the vicinity of the temple of Juno, which marks the centre of the
Roman municipium, and of the church of S. Primitivo,
which marks the centre of Christian Gabii. These discoveries having become more and more frequent in the time
of Prince Marc' Antonio Borghese the elder, he readily
accepted Hamilton's application to make a regular search.
The work began in March, 1792, and lasted a comparatively short time ; yet the results were such that Prince
Marc' Antonio was obliged to add a new wing to his museum in the Villa Pinciana, to exhibit the Gabine marbles,
the summary description of which by Ennio Quirino Visconti (Rome, Fulgoni, 1797) forms a bulky volume of one
hundred and eighty-one pages and fifty-nine plates. Ham-

[1] Compare Helbig's *Guide*, vol. i. p. 236, n. 331, and p. 217, n. 304.

Gabii.

ilton had laid bare two important edifices : the temple of
Juno, with its sacred enclosure and its hemicycle opening
on the Via Prænestina, and the Forum and the Curia of
the Roman Gabii. Here he found eleven statues or important pieces of statues of mythological subjects ; twenty-
four statues or busts or heads of historical personages,
including Alexander the Great, Germanicus, Cnæus Domitius Corbulo, the greatest Roman general of the time of
Nero, Claudius, Geta, Plautilla, etc. ; seven statues of local
worthies, seven pedestals with eulogistic inscriptions, and
then columns, mosaic pavements, architectural fragments,
coins, pottery, glassware, and bronzes.

The end of the Borghese Museum is well known. The
most valuable marbles, those from Gabii included, were
removed to Paris by the first Napoleon, for which an in-
demnity of fifteen millions of francs was promised to Prince

Borghese. The greater part of this sum remained unpaid at the fall of the French Empire, and is still unpaid.

England, as usual, had her share in the spoils from Gabii. Visconti informs us that a beautiful polychrome mosaic floor, discovered among the ruins of a villa, at a certain

Bust of Cnæus Domitius Corbulo.

distance from the temple of Juno, was purchased by " my Lord Harvey, count of Bristol," and removed to his country seat in Somersetshire.

The year 1717 marks the arrival of the " last of the Stuarts " in the States of the Church. Under the name of the Chevalier de St. Georges, James III., son of James II. and of Mary Beatrice of Modena, sought the hospitality of Pope Clement XI., Albani, in the beautiful ducal castle at Urbino. The Chevalier de St. Georges was not altogether unknown to the Romans. Many among the living remembered the celebration made by Cardinal Howard on the announcement of his birth in 1688, when an ox stuffed with game was roasted in one of the public squares, and served to the populace. A rare engraving by Arnold van Vesterhout represents this event.[1]

The marriage of James III. with Mary Clementina, granddaughter of the great John III., Sobietzky, of Poland, arranged by Clement XI. in 1718, was attended with considerable difficulties. While crossing the Austrian territory, she was detained in one of the Tyrolean castles by order of Charles VI., Emperor of Austria. She succeeded, however, in eluding the vigilance of the keepers, and, disguised in a young man's attire, made good her escape. When she reached Rome in the spring of 1719, the Pope bade her take up her quarters in the monastery of the Ursulines, in the Via Vittoria. This monastery still exists, although transformed into a royal Academy of Music.

The marriage was celebrated in the village of Montefiascone, on the Lake of Bolsena, where the royal couple spent their honeymoon. There is a scarce engraving of the wedding ceremony, by Antonio Frix, from a sketch by Agostino Masucci, bearing the title : " Funzione fatta per lo sposalizio del re Giacomo con la principessa Clem. Sobieski." In Rome they established their residence in the Palazzo Muti-Savorelli, now Balestra, at the north end of the Piazza

---

[1] " Stampa di un bue arrostito intero, ripieno di diversi animali, comestibili in publica piazza, da distribuirsi al volgo, in occassione delle allegrezze celebrate in Roma dal Card. Howard, per la nascita del principe Giacomo." Roma, 1688.

The church of S. Flaviano in the village of Montefiascone.

de' Santi Apostoli, the rent being paid by the Pope. The Pope also offered them an annual subsidy of fifteen thousand dollars, besides a wedding present of a hundred thousand. The old baronial manor of the Savelli at Albano was put at their disposal for a summer residence.[1]

The birth of their first son, which took place December 31, 1720, gave occasion for great manifestations of loyalty. The event was announced by a royal salute from the guns of the Castle of St. Angelo, and by the joyous ringing of

[1] After the death of his parents and brother the Savelli manor passed into the hands of Cardinal York. An English visitor who saw it about 1800 gives the following details : " Cardinal Stuart . . . has a palace in Albano, which was given him by the Pope. He never resides there, but successively lent it to the Spanish ambassador, and to the princesses Adélaide and Victoire, aunts of the unfortunate Lewis XVI. . . . This palace . . . is furnished in the plainest manner, and in one of the principal rooms are maps of London, Rome, and Paris, as also one of Great Britain, on which is traced the flight of the late Pretender." See *Description of Latium*, p. 69, London, 1805.

some two thousand bells. N. 544 of the " Diario di Roma " contains an account of the baptism of the infant prince under the name of Charles Edward. The sponsors were Cardinal Gualtieri for England, Cardinal Imperiali for Ireland, and Cardinal Sacripante for Scotland. Clement XI. said mass in the chapel of the English college, and gave, as presents, a Chinese object valued at four thousand dollars and a cheque amounting to ten thousand.

Their second son, Henry Benedict, Duke of York, was born in 1725 and baptized by Pope Benedict XIII. in the chapel of the Muti palace. Among the presents received on this occasion were the " Fascie benedette." " Fascie " in Italian means a long band of strong white linen, with which newborn infants are tightly swathed during the first months of their life. However ungentle this practice may seem, it is kept up in Italy even in our own days, as the people believe they impart more firmness of limb to their children by swathing them in this manner.

The habit of the papal court of presenting these fascie to the eldest born of a royal house dates as far back as Clement VII., Aldobrandini. This Pope gave them, for the first time, in 1601, to Henry IV. of France, whose second wife, Maria de' Medici, had given birth to the dauphin, the future Louis XIII. The fascie were intrusted to a special ambassador, Maffeo Barberini, who afterwards became Pope Urban VIII.

The presentation of the baby bands to James III. and his Queen Clementina is fully described in no. 1200 of the " Diario di Roma." It took place on April 5, 1725, the prelate selected as envoy extraordinary being Monsignor Merlini Paolucci, Archbishop of Imola. The bands and other articles of a rich layette were enclosed in two boxes, lined with crimson velvet embroidered in solid gold. There were bands also ornamented with gold embroidery, and others of the finest Holland linen trimmed with exquisite lace. The gift to the infant prince was valued at 8000 scudi.

From the same invaluable source, the "Diario di Roma" (n. 2729), we gather many particulars about the death of Queen Clementina, which took place on January 18, 1735, and about her interment in St. Peter's. The theatres were closed, much to the annoyance of the managers and the public, as it was carnival time; also the illuminations and fireworks prepared in honor of the newly elected Cardinal Spinelli, Archbishop of Naples, were given up. The funeral ceremonies began in the parish church of SS. Apostoli, where the body of the Queen was exposed on a catafalque, of which we have an etching by Baldassarre Gabuggiani. The funeral cavalcade from the parish church to the Vatican, of which there is a print by Rocco Pozzi, was attended by the college of cardinals in their violet or mourning robes. On the preceding day the governor of the city, Monsignor Corio, had issued the following proclamation : —

" On the occasion of the transferment of the mortal remains of Her Majesty Clementina Britannic Queen, which will take place to-morrow with due and customary solemnity, and with the view of removing all obstacles which might interfere with the orderly progress of the pageant from the church of SS. Apostoli to St. Peter's, we, Marcellino Corio, Governor of Rome and its district . . . order, command, and bring to notice to all concerned, of whatever sex or condition of life, not to trespass or intrude over the line of the procession with their coaches, carriages, or wagons, under the penalty of the loss of the horses besides other punishments for the owners of the said coaches, carriages, and wagons, while the coachmen or drivers shall be stretched three times on the rack then and there without trial or appeal.

Given in Rome from our residence this day, January 21, 1735." (Signed) Marcellino Corio, Governor ; Bartolomeo Zannettini, Notary.

The college of the Propaganda commemorated the event

The catafalque raised in the church of SS. Apostoli for the funeral of James III.

by holding an assembly in which the virtues of Mary Clementina were celebrated and sung in twenty different languages, including the Malabaric, the Chaldæan, the Tartaric, and the Georgian. Two monuments were raised to her :

one in SS. Apostoli, one in St. Peter's. The first consists of an urn of "verde antico," and a tablet of "rosso," containing the celebrated epigram : —

> Hic Clementinæ remanent præcordia : nam Cor
> cælestis fecit, ne superesset, amor.

I have a suspicion that the distich was written by Giulio Cesare Cordara, S. J., a great admirer of the late princess. The same learned man wrote a pastoral drama, called " La Morte di Nice " (Nike's Death), printed at Genoa, 1755, and translated into Latin by Giuseppe Vairani. The body was laid to rest in St. Peter's, in a recess above the door leading to the dome (Porta della Cupola). The tomb, designed

The Sacre Grotte Vaticane.

by Filippo Barigioni, cut in marble by Pietro Bracci, with a mosaic medallion by Cristofori, was unveiled on December 8, 1742.[1] It cost 18,000 scudi, taken from the treasury of the chapter of St. Peter's.

[1] Literature : *Vita di Maria Clem.*, etc., Bologna, 1744 ; *Parentalia Mariæ Clem. Magnæ Brittanniæ reginæ*, Romæ, 1735 ; *Solenni esequie di Maria Clem.*, etc., *celebrate in Fano*, Fano, 1735 ; Casabianca Francesco, *Epicedium pro immaturo funere Mariæ Clem.*, Romæ, 1738 ; *Il Cracas*, n. 3960, 3322, 2990 ; Pistolesi, *Il Vaticano descritto*, vol. i. p. 257.

It seems that the happiness of Queen Clementina's domestic life was occasionally affected by passing clouds. After her death the king took even more interest in Roman patrician society. In a book of records of Pier Leone Ghezzi, now belonging to the department of antiquities of the British Museum, I have found the account of a visit paid by the king to Cardinal Passionei in his summer residence at Camaldoli near Frascati, on October 19, 1741. "The King of England," Ghezzi says, "was accompanied by the Princess Borghese and the Princess Pallavicini, alone, without any escort of ' demoiselles d'honneur.' "

Many interesting particulars about the life of the pair in Rome, related by contemporary daily papers, are now almost forgotten. They were very fond, for instance, of enjoying the popular gathering called the Lago di Piazza Navona.[1] This noble piazza, still retaining the shape of the old Stadium of Domitian and Severus Alexander, over the ruins of which it is built, used to be inundated four or six times a year, during the hot summer months, by stopping the outlet of the great fountain of Bernini, called the Fontana dei Quattro Fiumi. Stands and balconies were erected around the edge of the lake; windows were decked with tapestries and flags; bands of music played, while the coaches of the nobility would drive around where the water was shallow. It was customary with the owners of the palaces bordering on the piazza to send invitations to their friends, and treat them with refreshments and suppers.

The first mention I find of the presence of James and Maria Clementina at this curious gathering dates from Sunday, August 11, 1720. They were the guests of Cardinal Trojano Acquaviva, who had built a stand in front

---

[1] See Francesco Cecconi, *Roma antica e moderna*, 1725, p. 669.

of his church of S. Giacomo degli Spagnuoli, hung with red damask trimmed with bands of gold. Refreshments were served, and the royal guests took such a pleasure in the spectacle that twice again they appeared at that same balcony before the season was over, on August 25 and September 1.

The young Prince Charles was allowed to see the Lago for the first time in 1727, August 4. The following year, taking advantage of the absence of his mother, Charles amused himself by throwing half-pennies [1] into the water and watching the struggles of the young beggars to secure a share of the meagre bounty, "cosa di poca decenza per un figlio di Re." [2] I find the last mention of their presence in 1731, in the balcony of Cardinal Corsini, whose pastry-cooks and butlers had been at work for three days and nights in preparing the supper-tables.

The Lago is thus described by de la Lande in his "Voyage en Italie dans les Années 1765 et 1766," v. p. 111 : "La grande quantité d'eau, que donnent ces trois fontaines [of the Piazza Navona] procurent en été un spectacle fort singulier, et fort divertissant. Tous les dimanches du mois d'août, après les vêpres, on ferme les issues des bassins. L'eau se répand dans la place, qui est un peu concave, en forme de coquille. Dans l'espace de deux heures elle est inondée sur presque toute sa longueur, et il y a vers le milieu deux ou trois pieds d'eau. On vient alors se promener en carrosse tout autour de la place. Les chevaux marchent dans l'eau ; et la fraîcheur s'en communique à ceux même, qui sont dans la voiture. Les fenêtres de la place sont couvertes de spectateurs. On croirait voir une naumachie

---

[1] The "mezzi bajocchi" were coined for the first time in 1611, by Pope Paul V., Borghese.

[2] The criticism is by Valesio.

THE LAGO DI PIAZZA NAVONA

antique. J'ai vu le palais du Cardinal Santobono Caraccioli rempli ces jours là de la plus belle compagnie de Rome. Il faisoit lui-même les honneurs de ses balcons par ses manières nobles, et engageantes, auxquelles il joignoit les refraîchissemens les plus fins. Autrefois on passoit la nuit à la place Navone. On y soupoit, on y faisoit des concerts. Mais Clément XIII. a proscrit tous les plaisirs. Dès l'Ave Maria on commence à désécher la place. Il arrive quelque fois des accidens à cette espèce de spectacle. Des chevaux s'abattent, et si l'on n'est pas très-prompt à les dégager, ils se noyent. C'est ce que j'ai vu arriver aux chevaux du prince Barberini en 1765. Mais quand on suit la file avec modération, l'on n'est guères exposé à cet inconvénient. L'eau ne vient pas au delà des moyeux de petites roues dans l'endroit où les carrosses se promènent."

In Sir Alexander Dick's "Travels in Italy" (1736), printed in "Curiosities from a Scots Charta Chest," by the Hon. Mrs. Atholl Forbes, there are many jottings about the Duke of York as a boy of eleven : "The little young duke . . . was very grave and behaved like a little philosopher. I could not help thinking he had some resemblance to his great-grandfather Charles the First." . . . "The Duke of York . . . danced very genteelly," etc.

Charles Edward, after the death of his father, lived in retirement under the name of Count of Albany,[1] and, following the advice of France, married the Princess Louise of Stolberg, his junior by thirty-two years. After they had spent some time together in Tuscany, as guests of the Grand Duke Leopold, the countess left the conjugal roof and established herself in Rome under the guardianship of her brother-in-law, Cardinal York. We shall deal no

[1] Compare *L'Ascanius moderne, ou l'illustre aventurier, histoire de tout ce qui est arrivé de plus mémorable et secret au prince Charles*, etc., Edinbourg, 1763.

longer than is necessary with this lady; she died in Florence in 1824, after many adventures, with which any one who has read the life of Alfieri, the great Italian tragedian, must necessarily be acquainted. Charles Edward died in Florence on January 31, 1788. His body was removed to Frascati, the episcopal see of his brother, and a " recognitio cadaveris " was performed before the entombment in St. Peter's. The body was found clad in a royal robe, with the crown, sceptre, sword, and royal signet-ring; there were also the insignia of the knighthoods of which the sovereign of Great Britain is the grand master *de jure*. The cardinal did his best to obtain a state funeral in Rome; but the Pope refused, on the ground that Charles Edward had never been recognized as a king by the Holy See.

The Duke of York, younger son of James III., was elected cardinal on July 3, 1747, while in his twenty-second year.[1] Officially he was called the Cardinal Duke of York; but after the death of the elder brother he proclaimed himself the legitimate sovereign of Great Britain and Ireland, under the name of Henry IX. Within the walls of the Muti palace, or of the episcopal residence at Frascati, he claimed the title of Majesty, but among his colleagues of the sacred college he was simply styled, " His Serene Highness Henry Benedict Mary Clement, Cardinal Duke of York." Such a profusion of names was not calculated to please his colleagues, who more than once found a way of showing their disapproval.

[1] Compare *Life of Henry Benedict Stuart, Cardinal Duke of York*, by Bernhard W. Kelly, London, Washbourne, 1899: " A good little work, which might have been much better had its author gone to such accessible sources as von Reumont's *Gräfin v. Albany*, Mr. Lang's *Pickle the Spy*, and above all James Browne's *History of the Highlands*. The last, a great but neglected storehouse of Jacobite lore, contains more than a score of letters by, to, or about the cardinal " (Athenæum).

The episcopal church of Cardinal York, Frascati.

The friendship between Pope Benedict XIV. and the young prince of the church became rather strained in 1752. It seems that the latter had taken an extraordinary fancy for a certain Mgr. Lercari, his own "maestro di camera," while his father could not tolerate his presence. Lercari's dismissal was asked and obtained; but the two friends continued to meet almost daily, or else to communicate by letters. Annoyed at this state of things, James III. applied to the Pope for advice and help, with the result that young Lercari was banished from Rome on the night of July 19. The cardinal resented the measure as a personal offence, and on the following night he left the paternal home for Nocera. Benedict XIV. wrote several letters pointing out how such an estrangement between father and son, between Pope and cardinal, would give satisfaction to

their common foes on the other side of the Channel. After
five months of brooding the duke gave up his resentment,
and accepted Mgr. Millo as " maestro di camera." The
reconciliation, which took place on December 16, pleased
the court and the people beyond measure, because father
and son, king and cardinal, had won the good graces of
all classes of citizens by their charities and affable manners,
so different from the dignified gloom characteristic of the
Anglo-Saxon race abroad.

His nomination to the bishopric of Frascati, July 13,
1761, is the next important event we have to chronicle, as
it was the indirect cause of the destruction of one of the
noblest monuments of the old Latin civilization. In the
mean time there are some curious particulars to be called
to mind in connection with his residence at Frascati, the
diocese of which he governed for forty-three years. He
loved this residence so dearly that whenever he was called
to Rome to attend a consistory or a " Cappella Pontificia,"
more than once he killed his carriage-horses in his haste
to get back to Frascati. His banqueting hall was always
open to guests, and very often messengers were dispatched
to Rome on the fastest ponies to secure the delicacies of the
season. The members of his household were all handsome and imposing, their liveries superb. The library
of the local seminary contains still a valuable set of English standard works, and the cathedral many precious vessels, the gift of this generous man. It is a pity that we
should be compelled to bring home to him an act of wanton
destruction, for which I can find no apology.[1]

---

[1] There is a fine portrait of the Cardinal by Pompeo Batoni in the National
Portrait Gallery. *Sins of the Drunkard*, a temperance tract by him, is read to
the present day, I believe in every church of the diocese of Liverpool, twice
a year.

Visitors to the Eternal City and students of its history know how the beautiful Campagna is bounded towards the south by the Alban Hills, the graceful outline of which culminates in a peak 3130 feet high, which the ancients called Mons Albanus, and moderns call Monte Cavo. On this peak, visible from Latium, Etruria, Sabina, and Campania,

The Villa Conti at Frascati, for some time the residence of Cardinal York.

stood the venerable temple of Jupiter Latialis, erected by Tarquinius Superbus as the meeting-place of the forty-seven cities which formed the Latin confederation. The temple was reached by a paved road which branched off from the Via Appia at Ariccia, and crossing the great forest between the lakes of Nemi and Albano, reached the foot of the peak in the vicinity of Rocca di Papa. The pavement of this Via Triumphalis, trodden by the feet of Q. Minutius Rufus, the conqueror of Liguria, of M. Claudius Marcellus, the conqueror of Syracuse, of Julius Cæsar, as dictator, etc., is in marvellous state of preservation; not so the temple of

Jupiter Optimus Maximus, which stood at the summit of the road.

From a rare drawing of about 1650 in the Barberini library we learn that the federal sanctuary stood, facing

The Via Triumphalis leading to the temple of Jupiter on the Mons Albanus.

the south, in the middle of a platform enclosed and supported by a substructure of great blocks of tufa. Columns of white marble, or of giallo antico, and marble blocks from the cella of the god, inscribed with the "Fasti Feriarum Latinarum," lay scattered over the sacred area, in the neighborhood of which statues, bas-reliefs, and votive offerings in bronze and terracotta were occasionally found. These remains were mercilessly destroyed in 1783 by Cardinal York, to make use of the materials for the rebuilding of the utterly uninteresting church and convent of the Passionist

monks which he dedicated to the Holy Trinity on October
1 of the same year. This act of vandalism of the last of
the Stuarts was justly denounced by the Roman antiquaries,
and we wonder why so great an admirer of ancient art as
Pius VI. did not interfere to prevent it.

The temple was one of the national monuments of Italy,
and no profaning hand should have been allowed to remove
a single one of its stones. It was not necessary to be a student or a philosopher to appreciate the importance of the

A view of the Monte Cavo.

place. " On the summit of Monte Cavo," writes an English visitor contemporary with these events, " it is impossible not to experience sensations at once awful and delightful ; the recollection of the important events which led the
masters of the world to offer up at this place their homage
to the Deity is assisted by the great quantity of laurel still
growing here." The same visitor saw in the garden of the

A view of the Roman wall.

convent "fragments of cornices of good sculpture; and when we were on the hill the masons were employed in making a shell for holy water out of part of an antique altar."

How often have I sat on one of the few blocks of stone left on the historic peak to tell the tale of its past fortunes and glory, wondering at the strange chain of events which prompted a scion of the savage Picts to lay hands on the very temple in which thanks had been offered to the Deity for Roman victories and Roman conquests in the British Isles! When the Romans were raising their mighty ramparts to confine the Caledonian tribes within prescribed boundaries, and cut them off, as it were, from the rest of mankind; when Agricola was building his nineteen forts, A. D. 81, between the Forth and the Clyde; when Lollius Urbicus completed this line of defence, A. D. 144, by the addition of a rampart and ditch between old Kirkpatrick and Borrowstoness; when Hadrian raised his wall and his embankment, A. D. 120, between the Tyne and the Solway, subsequently repaired by Septimius Severus, did they dream that the day would come when one of the Picts yonder would follow in their footsteps along the Via Triumphalis, and wipe off from the face of the earth the temple of the god to whom the conquering heroes had paid respect, and presented votive offerings from the islands beyond the Channel?

There is another and more glaring instance of this striking irony of fate to be found in Rome itself. The palace

The gate of the Villa Mills on the Palatine, with the emblem of the Thistle.

of Augustus on the Palatine Hill, where the emperor lived for forty years, kept in repair as a place of pilgrimage down to the fall of the Empire, this most august of Roman historical relics, after having been plundered in 1775 of its contents by the Frenchman Rancoureuil, fell in 1820 into the hands of Charles Mills, Esq. This Scotch gentleman caused the Casino (built and painted by Raffaellino dal Colle near and above the house of Augustus) to be recon-

structed in the Tudor style with Gothic battlements, and
raised two Chinese pagodas, painted in crimson, over the
exquisite bathrooms used by the founder of the Empire.
And for the branches of laurel and the " corona civica,"
which in accordance with a decree of the Senate ornamented the gates of the palace, Charles Mills substituted
the emblem of the Thistle.

The death of Cardinal York, which took place at ten P. M.
of July 13, 1807, was mourned by the population of the
diocese of Frascati as an irreparable loss.   He had been
their good and generous pastor for half a century, he had
been cardinal for sixty years, he had been archpriest of
St. Peter's for fifty-six ; in his long career he had won the
good graces of every one, and made no enemies.   The body
was removed to Rome and exposed in the main hall of the
Palazzo della Cancelleria.   The funeral was celebrated on
the following Thursday, July 16, in the parish church of
S. Andrea della Valle, in the presence of Pius VII. and
the Sacred College.   The same evening the coffin was removed to St. Peter's, and placed in the crypts, near those of
his father and brother.   The three last representatives of a
valiant and noble race, whose faults had been atoned by
long misfortunes, were thus reunited and laid to rest under
the mighty dome of the greatest temple ever raised for the
worship of the true God.

I need not dwell on the cenotaph raised to their memory
opposite that of Maria Clementina, nor on the well known
dedication REGIÆ STIRPIS STVARDIÆ POSTREMIS !   The
Duke of Sussex, sixth son of George III. and brother of
George IV. and William IV., who contributed fifty guineas
towards the erection of the memorial, was a special admirer
of the old cardinal, having been his neighbor for one whole

CENOTAPH OF THE STUARTS — THE MOURNING ANGEL

summer on the hills of Tusculum and Albano.[1] Kelly says in connection with his visits : " It is said on good authority that one of the brothers of George IV. took a journey to Frascati, to receive in orthodox fashion from the hands of Henry IX. the healing touch which had been denied to the rulers of his own dynasty," and that knowing the cardinal's pretence to a royal title, he, the son of George III., had not hesitated to comply with his wish.

English describers of Rome are in the habit of quoting with relish the well-known passage of Lord Mahon : " Beneath the unrivalled dome of St. Peter's lie mouldering the remains of what was once a brave and gallant heart ; and a stately monument from the chisel of Canova, and at the charge, I believe, of the house of Hanover,[2] has since risen to the memory of James III., Charles III., and Henry IX., kings of England, names which an Englishman can scarcely read without a smile or a sigh." Lord Mahon could have saved both his smiles and his sighs if he had simply read with care the epitaph engraved on the monument, which says : " To James III., son of James II., King of Great Britain, to Charles Edward, and Henry, Dean of

[1] The Alban and Tusculan hills have always been in favor with the English visitors to Rome since the eighteenth century, and there is no villa in that district which might not be associated with an historical name. The Duke and Duchess of Gloucester lived some months in the Villa Albani at Castel Gandolfo, and the Duke of Sussex passed a whole summer at Grottaferrata, within the diocese of the last of the Stuarts. Pius VI. gave a dinner to the duke in the farmhouse of la Cecchignola, on the Via Ardeatina, where the venerable old Pontiff used to go in the month of October, to amuse himself with the *Paretajo*. The Paretajo consists of a set of very fine nets spread vertically from tree to tree in a circular grove, in the centre of which flutter the decoy birds. At the time of the great flights of migratory birds the catching of one or two hundred of them in a single day is not a rare occurrence, if the Paretajo is skillfully put up.

[2] The monument was really erected at the expense of Pius VII.

the Sacred College, Sons of James III., the last of the Royal House of Stuart." Let us join, however, with Lord Mahon in the prayer which is heard so often in Roman funeral services : Peace be with them ! REQUIESCANT IN PACE !

INDEX.